VOLUME I

Reminiscences

of

Hanson Weightman BALDWIN

U. S. Navy (retired)

U.S. Naval Institute
Annapolis, Maryland
1976

PREFACE

Eight tape-recorded interviews were held with Hanson Weightman BALDWIN at his home in Roxbury, Connecticut, in 1975. The first of the series came on February 24 and the final one on December 8. They were all conducted by John T. Mason, Jr., as part of the Oral History program of the U. S. Naval Institute. The interviews cover the career of Mr. Baldwin from the time he was a midshipman at the U. S. Naval Academy in Annapolis (class of 1924) to the present, when he is recognized the world over as a military analyst and journalist of the first rank. Baldwin's inflexible adherence to the belief that a journalist stands accountable for what he writes is in some measure responsible for his remarkable success.

The researcher will find in these two volumes of recollections a wealth of material on many subjects. Care has been taken in the preparation of a subject index which is at the back of each volume.

Mr. Baldwin has read the transcript and made minor corrections...but, in keeping with his appreciation for the fact that the spoken word is a lively conveyer of fresh and vigorous impressions he resisted any temptation to alter his sentences to a more polished state. The interviewer is aware that this could have been a temptation for a writer such as Mr. Baldwin, who commands a very lucid style and one that is concise and forceful as well.

A small number of miscellaneous documents and papers are included as appendices at the end of the second volume.

                                                  John T. Mason, Jr.
                                                  Director of Oral History
                                                  U. S. Naval Institute

                                                  April 30, 1976

Biographical Sketch
of Career
of
Hanson Weightman Baldwin
(As taken from 1970-71 Edition of
WHO'S WHO IN AMERICA)

Military editor; born Baltimore, Maryland, Mar 22, 1903; son of Oliver Perry and Caroline (Sutton); preparatory education, Boys' Latin School, Baltimore; graduate of U.S. Naval Academy, 1924; married Helen Bruce, June 8, 1931; children - Barbara Bruce, Elizabeth. Commd. ensign U.S. Navy 1924, and advanced to lt (j.g.); served aboard battleships and a destroyer on East Coast, Caribbean and in European Squadron; resigned, 1927; police reporter Baltimore SUN, later general assignment reporter, 1928-29; with New York Times since 1929, as military and naval correspondent, 1937-42, as military editor since 1942. Author: MEN AND SHIPS OF STEEL (with W.F. Palmer), 1935; THE CAISSONS ROLL-A MILITARY SURVEY OF EUROPE, 1938; THE ADMIRAL DEATH, 1939; WHAT THE CITIZEN SHOULD KNOW ABOUT THE NAVY, 1941; . UNITED WE STAND! 1941; STRATEGY FOR VICTORY , 1942; THE PRICE OF POWER, 1948; GREAT MISTAKES OF THE WAR, 1950; SEA FIGHTS AND SHIPWRECKS, 1955; THE GREAT ARMS RACE, 1958; WORLD WAR I, AN OUTLINE HISTORY, 1962; BATTLES LOST AND WON GREAT CAMPAIGNS OF WORLD WAR II, 1966. Editor: We Saw It Happen (with Shepard Stone), 1938. Contributor to New York Times magazine, U.S. Naval Institute Proceedings, Harpers, Atlantic Monthly, Saturday Evening Post, Office: New York Times, New York City, 36.

DECLARATION OF TRUST

The undersigned does hereby appoint and designate as his (her) Trustee herein, the Secretary-Treasurer and Publisher of the United States Naval Institute to perform and discharge the following duties, powers, and privileges in connection with the possession and use of a certain taped interview between the undersigned and the Oral History Department of the United States Naval Institute.

1. Classification of Transcript.

(✓)a. If classified OPEN, the transcript(s) may be read or the recording(s) audited by the qualified personnel upon presentation of proper credentials, as determined by the Secretary-Treasurer of the U. S. Naval Institute. — Open

( )b. If classified PERMISSION REQUIRED TO CITE OR QUOTE, the user will be required to obtain permission in writing from the interviewee prior to quoting or citing from either the transcript(s) or the recording(s).

( )c. If classified PERMISSION REQUIRED, permission must be obtained in writing from the interviewee before the transcribed interview(s) can be examined or the tape recording(s) audited.

( )d. If classified CLOSED, the transcribed interview(s) and the tape recording(s) will be sealed until a time specified by the interviewee. This may be until the death of the interviewee or for any specified number of years.

2. It is expressly understood that in giving this authorization, I am in no way precluded from placing such restrictions as I may desire upon use of the interview at any time during my lifetime, nor does this authorization in any way affect my rights to the copyright of my literary expressions that may be contained in the interview.

Witness my hand and seal this 8th day of January 1976.

Hanson W. Baldwin

I hereby accept and consent to the foregoing Declaration of Trust and the powers therein conferred upon me as Trustee:

Baldwin #1 - 1

Interview No. 1 with Mr. Hanson W. Baldwin

Place: His residence in Roxbury, Connecticut

Date: Monday morning, 24 February 1975

Subject: Biography

By: John T. Mason, Jr.

Q: Well, Mr. Baldwin, this is a series I certainly have looked forward to with interest. It's quite different in nature from the naval interviews I've done, but it should be a highlight. I'm delighted that you consented to talk about your very illustrious career, both in the Navy and out of the Navy.

Would you begin, Sir, in the proper way by telling me the date and place of your birth and something about your family, something about your background?

Mr. B.: I was born in Baltimore on March 22nd 1903, which will make me 72 next month. I'll be able to get social security then!

As indicated in that letter from Ed Hooper, there was a kind of a naval tradition in my family although I was only dimly aware of it as a boy. My great-grandfather, who was a young man at the time of the War of 1812, either served with - and this I've never tracked down - or was a great admirer of, probably the latter, Oliver Hazard Perry. So he in turn named his son Oliver Hazard Perry, and my father was named Oliver Hazard Perry, Jr.

My great-grandfather was in the Navy for a brief time, until he disappeared with a sloop of war, the Epervier. He left a widow and two young children, my grandfather and his sister - the sister was born after her father disappeared - and without much means. The family moved subsequently to Virginia but, in the interval, my grandfather became a midshipman in the U.S. Navy and served briefly aboard the sloop of war Falmouth. That's the journal which I sent to the Office of Naval History. He was apparently a midshipman for only a few months. Then later he became interested in journalism and he moved to the Valley of Virginia, variously Staunton and Lexington. He did nearly all the jobs that a small town country editor in those days did.

He married a Sheffey from Staunton, Virginia, whose father was a Judge Sheffey and was rather well known in the South at that time. Ultimately he became editor of the Richmond Dispatch and various other Richmond papers, and he was in Richmond during the Civil War.

My father was ten years old when Richmond burned and I remember his telling me about that, walking over the railroad ties with another boy to see the town. He remembered the cavalry skirmishes that occurred in the little town of Ashland, where they lived, outside of Richmond. Incidentally, a lot of my father's and grandfather's papers are in the possession of the Virginia Historical Society, and they also have family papers that I hadn't known about.

Q: Have you looked them up?

Mr. B.: No. I sent them last December, some of my father's letters and my grandfather's letters, as I sent to Ed Hooper the two things pertaining to the Navy. But I haven't seen those that deal with the Sheffey family and I haven't seen those - given to the Society by others - that dealt with my grandfather. My grandfather became quite well known because he was a considerable orator and he apparently orated on many occasions of consequence in the Richmond of those days. His name is on the record. I don't know whether you know V. Dabney or not - Virginius Dabney - who's a delightful person. V. Dabney first referred me to a number of Virginia newspaper books which contain my grandfather's name.

Q: He must have been a candidate for Congress or something, if he was an orator?

Mr. B.: Well, in any case, my grandfather, after the Civil War was over, found the family fortunes ruined and he moved his family to Baltimore, hoping to recoup those fortunes.

My father went to the University of Virginia and graduated about 1872 in law. Then he briefly practiced law in Baltimore and was a member of the Maryland legislature for a very short time.

Then he, like my grandfather, joined the staff of the Baltimore Sun. My grandfather wrote for any paper that would take his contributions in an effort really to keep bread in the mouths of his children. My father had a great many sisters. Nearly all of them died, one after the other, of TB. They lived in considerable - I wouldn't call it poverty, but certainly straitened circumstances, and the letters are full of the problems of economics. My father wrote to my grandfather from the University to ask for a few cents for buttons for his clothes. This letter illustrates the problems that confronted the defeated after the Civil War. But both my father and my grandfather remained unreconstructed rebels to the end of their lives, I think.

Q: Yes.

Mr. B.: Dad served on the Sun for almost fifty years. He was married twice. I was the son of a second marriage. He had had two previous sons, one by his first wife and one by his second, who died in infancy. He had named them Oliver

Perry Baldwin, and he had a superstition about this after they died, so he named me for a family connection, Hanson Weightman. The Hansons and the Weightmans were from Maryland and Virginia.

Q: The Weightmans from Virginia?

Mr. B.: Yes. So I took on this ungainly name, which caused me a lot of grief when I was very young, especially because the girls would always translate it from Hanson to Handsome just to see my blush! I was extremely sensitive and shy as a young boy. Later I think it was an asset because people remembered the first name when I was writing.

Q: I think you're very right.

Mr. B.: In any case, Dad was variously managing editor and editorial writer on the Sun - he was an editorial writer in the part of my life that I remember best. He was managing editor up until about 1916, or something like that, and then he was an editorial writer and he wrote articles or columns which he signed "By An Old-Fashioned Fellow," and they were usually quite outspoken and aroused a lot of comment.

Q: Was his identity known?

Mr. B.: In Baltimore, not elsewhere. Then he also would go

occasionally to New York to review primarily the new Shakespearean actors. He loved the theatre. He had a classical education and all that went with it, something we often don't get nowadays, so he had a long view of history and he had very decided ideas about how Shakespeare should be played. He would go to New York intermittently when there was a new Shakespearean actor. He had seen all of them since the days of Julia Marlowe. In fact, in his possessions I found an old photograph of Julia Marlowe signed to him. He had seen the Booths.

He would often take my younger sister, who died about two years ago, with him, and he would take great delight sometimes in her contrary opinion. She was then in her teens and maybe she thought this actor she saw was great and Dad would compare him with Booth or somebody else and say, "it's awful." But he took great delight in the fact that his younger daughter had independent opinions. I remember once, I think, he ran one of her criticisms in the paper alongside his!

Q: Did his love for Shakespeare brush off on you?

Mr. B.: Yes, although I was never a Shakespeare scholar — nor was I a scholar of what were then considered the classics in the days he went to the University of Virginia. Macaulay, for instance, he loved Macaulay of all the historians. I never had the classical education that Dad did, although I did go to what was called the Boys' Latin School. It was originally called Dunham's, in Baltimore, for the name of the principal. He called it a Latin school. Then later, when he died, it was called the Boys' Latin School.

Q: What constitutes a Latin school?

Mr. B.: I suppose the original one was the Boston Latin School, and in all Latin schools there was great emphasis on the teaching of languages ancient and modern - Latin and some Greek, but not much Greek in the days I was there. We had a professor named White who achieved quite a reputation in his time, not only as an eccentric but as a novelist. Strangely enough, he didn't write many novels about ancient Rome, although he taught Latin and spoke it perfectly, but he wrote chiefly about South America. He used to keep the boys awake in class by fashioning catapults and, if he saw someone drowsing, he would let them have a piece of chalk behind the ear with the catapult!

He told all sorts of funny stories, and he was a professor you could never forget. However, I never liked Latin very much and I never absorbed very much of it. I was looking over some of my marks and I found - at Boys'

Latin School - that I hadn't gotten too high marks, although I had about six or seven years of Latin. They emphasized, too, other languages. I had about five years of German, English literature, and mathematics, of course, and physical education. They had what was rare in those days, their own gymnasium and a small swimming pool. We had one of these old German turnverein professors who ran the thing, and he had the same kind of physical tests and measurements that I found later - (he may have copied it from the Naval Academy) the Naval Academy had in its physical education process. They'd measure your biceps, measure your weight every year to see how you were developing. That used to be a part of the Naval Academy physical education program. In order to correct deficiences, weak backs or lack of adequate back muscles or something like that, they would see each year how you were developing, and if necessary, give you corrective exercises.

Q: I suppose it arouses a competitive spirit, too, doesn't it?

Mr. B.: If you're talking about the midshipmen rather than my classmates at the Boy's Latin School, I think many of the midshipmen thought it was a pain in the neck because they'd then have to do some extra work to remedy weak muscles.

For instance, if your grip was deficient - they actually had these things you had to grip so often to get your hands stronger. At the Boys' Latin School this instructor - Bauerlein was his name - this physical education instructor, was, however, a real inspiration to the kids and he was famous in his field. He used to be asked down to the Naval Academy, and that's one reason I took an interest in it, to judge the gymnastic meets. He was usually one of the judges at these meets. He was an expert in his field and he stressed gymnastics. Each year at the Boys' Latin School we used to have these gymnastic exhibitions which he would supervise.

I went there from I guess about 1912 or 1911 till 1920, when I graduated.

Q: Was the discipline rather severe in a school like that?

Mr. B.: No, it wasn't. It wasn't terribly severe at all. Mr. Bauerlein, the physical education instructor, insisted on discipline in his classes and he always insisted that a boy finish whatever he started. If he tried to do some sort of gymnastic exercise on the parallel bars or the horizontal bars or what not and failed, he must try again. I remember once I tried to jump through the bars and I caught my toe in the bar and started to fall down, he caught me. It scared me to death but he insisted I go out and do it again, and right away, which is the only thing to do, of course. He was that kind of a man. He taught me to swim. He taught all his boys to swim in this little pool which we would consider a bath tub now.

I think he provided inspiration, just as the original founder of the school, Mr. Dunham, did. He died while I was there and the school passed on to a man named Dr. Shipley, who was a little of a fuss-budget and who didn't have as much respect from the boys as Mr. Dunham had had.

The school was on Brevard Street, which is now a bad section. It was right across from the Baltimore and Ohio Mount Royal railroad depot, diagonally across from what was then Bryn Mawr School, where my older sister went, and the Bryn Mawr girls used to sometimes pass by the school on their way to class. I remember very vividly one of the first girls I ever had went to Bryn Mawr and I'd watch her pass by at the window. The other boys knew that I had taken her out once, saved my money, and they teased me unmercifully. I was very susceptible to teasing, especially by girls at that time. I was very shy and bashful.

Q: You blushed!

Mr. B.: Yes.

I was very interested in athletics. I wasn't very good

at anything, but I tried football and I played on a very bad team, which lost most of its games.

Q: How about lacrosse?

Mr. B.: We didn't have lacrosse at Dunham's at that time. They did have it later and they became quite good at it. Gilman was our great rival and we usually lost to Gilman. We played Donaldson, where Joe Worthington went, occasionally.

We had track, of course, and I competed in high jump and running. I won one meet because I was tall. I was about 6 feet 2 when I was about sixteen - or 6 feet 1 - I grew up very fast and was very thin. I tried gymnastics and swimming and so on.

I think I became interested in the Naval Academy, first, because of its proximity, then I heard from my father about this naval tradition in the family and he said he was the only one who had skipped it. He hadn't been in the Navy. I don't think this was a conscious influence at all, but it was probably a subconscious one, because I knew very little about it then.

Q: Did he encourage the idea?

Mr. B.: He didn't encourage or discourage it. We were far from a wealthy family and it would have been a very severe problem for them to finance my education at college, but I could have gone to Hopkins and lived at home, which would have been far less expensive in those days. My older sister, for instance, went to Goucher College. Many of my classmates and friends from Boys' Latin School went to Hopkins.

In any case, I sort of set my sights for Annapolis several years before I graduated from Boys' Latin - perhaps two years. Those were the years of World War I and we got all worked up about that, many of us, and, although in 1918, when the war ended, I would have been just fifteen, on my way to sixteen, I and another boy were talking about running away from home and entering the Marine Corps when we were sixteen! We didn't do it, of course.

I read, along with many of my contemporaries, a lot of books that were popular at the time. I've never forgotten one series, called Dave Darin at Annapolis. You've probably heard of those?

Q: I have heard of them.

Mr. B.: And they influenced me.

Q: Maybe we need a modern series on that pattern!

Mr. B.: I went down to Annapolis, and I'm trying to remember the year. I guess it was either 1918 or 1919 - the fall of '19. The Naval Academy had produced undefeated football teams coached by Gil Dobie, who had been at Cornell and had a couple of all-Americans on the team. The Great Lakes Naval Training Station had corralled a lot of football stars during World War I, as often happened in service football teams in those days. This was a sort of postseason championship game and the Naval Academy was to play Great Lakes. Great Lakes brought down a whole lot of gobs - we used to call them gobs, sailors. The midshipmen were on one side of the field and the sailors on the other, not in this present stadium, which didn't exist, I guess they called it Farragut Field.

Q: On the grounds there, wasn't it?

Mr. B.: Yes, which is now a track (near the present Field House) and it had stands on either side.

I went down to that game. It was really a terrific game. There was no doubt the Naval Academy had the better team. They were leading 6 to 0 and the game was almost over. I think it was the days of Ingram, among others who were playing.

Q: This is Jonas Ingram?

Mr. B.: Yes. Ingram and someone else were down almost on the Great Lakes goal line. They'd taken the ball and actually went over the goal line but somebody knocked the ball out of his arms and a Great Lakes player picked it up and started down the field. At that time, football rules were different. The penalties for twelve men on the field of play were half the distance to the goal line. There was a substitute end warming up on the sidelines, a man named Sanders, who was I think the class of '22, and Dobie - nobody knew this until later - but Dobie told Sanders to get the hell in there and tackle this guy. Nobody else was near him. He was well clear and he would have made a touchdown and Great Lakes could have won by one point if they'd kicked a goal. So Sanders went in and tackled him.

I thought there was going to be a riot! The sailors swarmed out of the stands and the midshipmen came out of their stands. The referees had a great consultation, and the Navy finally conceded Great Lakes the goal to prevent, I guess, bloodshed and mayhem! They kicked the goal and Great Lakes won 7 to 6. Time ran out. In the next couple of days Sanders got a terrible roasting from the press very unfairly, I think. In fact, I think it really affected the poor guy's career. He subsequently died of TB, but he was very much affected by this, as I understood it, but it was really Dobie's fault. Dobie was a dirty player and he had at that time some unfortunate coaches, very good coaches, but all they wanted to do was win.

Well, that scene influenced me. Then, I had a classmate at the Boys' Latin School. He left the last year and went to Hopkins for one year, but he was set on going to West Point. He was a neighbor of mine and we'd grown up more or less together. He went to West Point and I went to Annapolis.

Q: You had no difficulty getting an appointment, I assume?

Mr. B.: I did. I got a second alternate's appointment from Senator France. My father wrote . . .

Q: Senator Joseph I. France, was it?

Mr. B.: I think so. My memory on this is a little vague, but I'm sure it was Senator France. I don't think this was a man - Senator France - who ever took much interest in appointees. I don't think I ever got a letter from him or met him in my life.

In any case, I took one month off from the Boys' Latin School in the spring of 1920 and went to Severn School to prep for the Naval Academy examinations which were not, as you remember, universally required and I can't remember why

I took it. I don't know whether or not the Boys' Latin School was a fully "accredited school", but this business of fully accredited schools in those days was, as I found later at the Naval Academy, extremely loose in interpretation and a very inadequate system because graduates from some schools which had high accreditation just couldn't make the grade later at the Academy. They were hopeless misfits and should never have entered. Others with no accreditation at all did very well. In my case, I went to Severn for a month and that was in the days of Mr. Teel, who founded Severn School. I did nothing but study and grind and took the exams in Baltimore and passed all right. We didn't have much fun at Severn, except one escapade I remember which might have been dangerous and was awfully stupid on the part of the boys. The Washington, Baltimore, and Annapolis - I've forgotten what they called it, the Wobble, Bumble, and something . . .

Q: That was a railroad, I gather, or a streetcar?

Mr. B.: Yes, our electric railroad. That was the only thing that ran then, the only way you could get to Annapolis unless you had a private automobile and, in those days, most people didn't. The W.B. & A. would come in and stop at Severna Park on its way to Annapolis. Just before we finished preping, we had the idea we ought to go out and soap the rails of this railroad so that the engineer would be puzzled and couldn't stop. We did that one morning and the engineer applied the brakes and he went on past the station for some distance. There was nothing in the way, fortunately. He tried to back up and he had a little difficulty doing that. We were hidden in the underbrush, laughing, then finally we decided we'd better get back to our quarters. That's about the only thing I remember of note about Severn.

Q: The grind also, you remember that part?

Mr. B.: A terrible grind, yes, because we really studied, and Teel was really an excellent principal. He made that school and it was a fine school. It turned out some fine people. It was then purely a prep school really for the Naval Academy. Later it broadened. It had a great wrestling team and there was a young chap who was later on the Naval Academy wrestling team who, I think died or was killed - I think he died - in an airplane accident, Fitz Rhea, and there were a good many others, but I didn't get to know any of them very well because there just wasn't time. It was chiefly study.

I don't remember much else about Baltimore or the past. I could fill in some gaps if you don't think that's enough.

Q: That gives a fairly good picture, I think. You passed as an alternate?

Mr. B.: Yes, as an alternate. I'm not sure just how this came about. All I know is that I was notified that I had the appointment, but I was told, as I remember it, that the principal had either declined the appointment or failed the mental examinations. The first alternate had failed the physical. There were then three alternates, you know. I had the second alternate appointment. So I was next in line and I passed mental, then went to Annapolis to take the physical. I grew up so fast and was so thin, that my doctor had told me I had a slight heart murmur. The doctors in Baltimore had said, "you'll outgrow this, this is common in boys your age." They said to take it a little easy on athletics. Well, I took it easy after a fashion, but I was still running and jumping and playing football.

I went to Annapolis, and the doctors detected this heart murmur. I was just seventeen when I entered. The entrance age then was sixteen to twenty, so they had a lot of very young kids who'd never been away from home before, just as I hadn't. They scared me to death because when they detected this heart murmur, they said, "Well, we don't think you can enter, but we don't know. You'll have to come back for some more tests later on," and they gave me a date to come back in about three days.

I really wanted to get into the Navy then. I was really set on getting into the Naval Academy, and I remember going out to St. Anne's Church. I was brought up an Episcopalian, I'm afraid I'm a little bit of a backslider now because I was taken to church so much when I was a boy, but I remember going out to St. Anne's Church and praying earnestly that I would pass the physical. I came back some days later and they passed me provisionally. They said, "We'll let you in but on your annual physicals hereafter if there's anything wrong you may have to be dismissed." It was never mentioned again. That was the end of that.

Q: It was one doctor's opinion, I suppose?

Mr. B.: I did crew and water polo. The only thing I made varsity was water polo. I went out for plebe football and so forth, so it couldn't have been serious. It hasn't been all my life.

Q: How did your mother feel about your entering the Naval Academy?

Mr. B.: I don't know. I think in a way she was proud of it but I think she would have preferred my doing something else. Dad wanted me to do anything I wanted to do. I think they were both intensely patriotic - my father, as an old-fashioned fellow, was one of those Americans who believed in his country and who believed that men in the service had a high moral tone and that they were performing a duty which was worth doing.

Q: It certainly was a prevailing attitude in their time, too, wasn't it?

Mr. B.: I think there's no doubt about it, although people didn't know the Navy at all, they didn't know the services. It was very small. Remember, in those days the Navy was less than 90,000 men. There were only 6,000 or 7,000 officers. You could get to know most of those of your contemporaries rather quickly.

I remember my indignation when I was home on leave once at a Baltimore railroad station being mistaken for a railroad conductor or something by somebody.

Q: That was a comedown!

Mr. B.: My first impressions of Annapolis after these high ideals were quite disillusioning because plebe summers in those years weren't supervised by any upper classmen at all. The upper classmen were all away at sea on summer cruises. Nobody was there except the fourth class and the duty officers, and things were not well organized. These green kids came in from all over the country, many, as I say, from high schools which should never have been accredited.

Q: They straggled in, did they?

Mr. B.: No, they all came in at aboue the same time. There were a few late arrivals but, generally speaking, most of them were there by the end of June. I've forgotten the date I came in, but it was sometime in June, probably by the 15th of the 20th. The upper class had left. Bancroft Hall was deserted.

Literally, a few of my classmates - we had about 875 entering, I think - had almost literally never worn shoes before. There were one or two from the hills of Kentucky who were really primitive types, many of them with absolutely no table manners. Plebe summer, as I quickly discovered, if you were going to survive you had to grab at the table because, if you didn't, there wouldn't be anything left to eat. It was at first chaos, and many of us - in fact, the great majority, I think - thought this was pretty terrible. It gradually settled down, but not completely until the upper classmen returned, when we came to with a jolt.

Q: I can see, Sir, why the emphasis was put upon training a midshipman to be a gentleman!

Mr. B.: It was very essential. Actually, the entering midshipmen are a cross section of the country and I must say the Naval Academy did a shaping job which was impressive over the years. That's one of the things to be said for a tough plebe year, and we had a tough plebe year. It got rid of the weak and winnowed out some of these people who should never have come to the Academy; it made others shape up, and so on.

Upper class midshipmen in those days went on about three-month summer cruises right after graduation in June. There would be a midshipmen's squadron which would take the upper classmen, all three upper classes -

Q: And you went on battleships?

Mr. B.: On battleship, on long cruises, lots of time at sea, and they would not get back till about the 1st of September and then would go for a month's leave - the end of August or first of September. Then they would start the academic year at the end of September or first of October. The football team would come back earlier for practice, of course. That was our first exposure to the upper class, but then the real tough time started when all of them came back and started to make the plebes shape up.

There was real hazing in those days. It was heavy and physical, and some of it brutal.

Q: Can you give me some examples?

Mr. B.: Oh, yes, I was about to. As a matter of fact, one of my classmates did commit suicide and at least one other was hurt and hospitalized. As a result of the suicide, Congress ordered a congressional investigation. While this was starting, the Navy took all the plebes and put them in one wing of Bancroft Hall, put armed guards around the wing, allowed no upper classmen to come into that area. The class of 1924 were the segregated plebes. We didn't like this at all.

Q: Was that to . . .

Mr. B.: To prevent any more hazing. The hazing included a lot of silly stunts and physical exercises like push-ups and asymptotes, as they called it, where you put your nose on a chalk line, curved, chalked on a wall or locker and try to erase with your nose while, in effect, doing knee-bends. And there was "cuckoo." They had big tables - study tables - in the center of each room in Bancroft Hall, they were usually two-men rooms in those days. In the old rooms, the ones that now in the front of Bancroft Hall, the old wings were three-man and very occasionally, but not usually, four men rooms. The present new wings weren't built in those days.

The cuckoo game was to put a plebe under the table in the center of the room and he would try to stick his head out from under the table and say "cuckoo" before the upper classmen on top of the table could swat him with a folded magazine. Sometimes these swats were pretty hard.

The worst of the hazing that was really physical was what they called "assume the position," which meant bend over. Then the upper classmen would get a broom and paddle you with a broom as hard as he could.

Q: Was there any offense involved in this, on the part of the plebe? Was there anything to really provoke it?

Mr. B.: Sometimes. It depended on the man. Of course, there are always some pure sadists. There were one or two in the first class there who came to be known as sadists. I'll tell you about that in a minute because one very interesting incident came about because of that. But there were others who were simply trying to bring the plebes up right, and they usually were the ones who never did any really serious physical hazing. They would make you do push-ups or say "Sir." Plebes always double-timed in the corridors, cut square corners, and they came in and stood at attention in an upper classman's room, all that sort of thing, and they would have to memorize and repeat all sorts of things. Usually, at the mess hall they had to sit on the edge of the chair and cut square corners with their fork and things like that, and always keep the upper classmen supplied with food and help themselves last of all. The meals were very uncomfortable experiences because you were constantly being questioned and harassed and hazed.

Then you always had a particular upper classman to whom you had to report every morning and night in his room. It depended on him whether or not he administered some physical punishment.

Q: You reported your wrongdoings during the day?

Mr. B.: No, you simply reported to him for any orders, any sort of admonition he wanted to give. You were just supposed to report to him. Sometimes you made up his bed for him, sometimes you did other things like this.

Now, you had an alternative in the worst cases. The alternative - at least, this was the tradition - was that any plebe if he felt these things were an infringement on his dignity or if he refused to accept it, could fight the upper classman concerned. He could actually put on boxing gloves and take him to the gymnasium. This was not done very often. Usually because, I think - my recollection on this point is hazy and ought to be checked, because I think it was not always the man you challenged who fought you. It might often be an upper classman who was an expert boxer or who was a member of the boxing team. I'm not sure of that. I don't remember. It never occurred in my case.

Q: Who acted as referee in a case like that?

Mr. B.: The midshipmen themselves.

The harassment was so continuous. It wasn't often really severe. In my own case, I think I only got paddled two or three times in the whole year, one time just before the first class graduated in June, and it wasn't the most brutal kind of paddling. Some people could really do damage to a boy because the upper classman would stand on top of a table and swing the broom from one corner of the room to the other. There was one particular nemesis - or several, particular first class nemeses - I'd better not mention their names, I guess, in the Spanish Battalions. You see, they separated the people by the two languages taught, the French and Spanish, and the French battalions were in two wings and the Spanish battalions in two wings. The Spanish battalions were traditionally in those old wings fronting on Bancroft Hall, which were a maze of corridors and small rooms. The plebes used to think it was worth their life to go walking down there; they would be beckoned into one of these rooms by an upper classman and then the torture would start!

And there were a couple of brothers who were particularly ingenious about devising new kinds of plebe things to do.

Q: I could almost guess the names!

Mr. B.: I'm sure you could. But, as I say, I don't remember when this segregation started. It must have been about the middle of the year, or sometime during the first term. It must have been just before Christmas, I guess.

Q: For how long a period did it last?

Mr. B.: Again I don't remember that but it continued until almost the end of the year. That's on the records, I'm sure. I just don't remember. This period was very uncomfortable, first, because the upper classmen made it clear they blamed the Plebes for segregation whenever we fell in - we did everything then, in formation, we marched to classes, to meals, and every thing else. The upper classmen made it very clear that they despised us, that the segregation was terrible, and they were also very much afraid of the hazing investigation that had started and they didn't want any of the plebes to tell anybody that they'd been hazed.

The Navy undertook the first part of the investigation. I don't know what Congress did about it ultimately. I think they took the Navy's investigation as part of their own. The superintendent, who was then Admiral Scales I think, before Admiral Henry B. Wilson came in - Admiral Scales had two beautiful red-head daughters, I remember - he had a board set up to investigate it. A captain was the head of the board, and they called in various plebes to try to see whether or not they'd been hazed and if they could pinpoint who did it. I was one of the plebe witnesses; other classmates - Ed Rawlins and various others - were also called in. I was very young and very naive, very scared, and very impressed. The captain was of an exalted rank, I couldn't have dreamed of in those days and the idea of talking to a captain about this was astounding! He started to ask me various questions. The first question I remember he asked was, "Did you know Johnny Vest?" and I said, "Yes, I know Johnny Vest. He spooned on me." Well, that ended that. You know what "spooned on" means?

Q: Yes.

Mr. B.: Johnny Vest was from Maryland and so was I, but they were obviously after Johnny Vest for something. Then they started to ask other questions. They asked me had I ever been hazed and I said yes. Then the captain started to ask me about specific people and I was then faced with the problem of whether I give him specific names or whether or not I just refused to tell him. So I didn't say anything. I stood there mute, trembling really. I don't believe in the criminal code of not telling - I never have believed in this - but, on the other hand, I didn't think this was a crime and I'd never really been hurt by any of the hazing I'd gotten. In some ways it had helped me because I was a very naive boy. It did toughen a lot of boys and it did weed out a lot of boys who shouldn't have been there. There's no doubt about that. And so I stayed mute.

The captain got very angry. He said, "I order you to answer this question." I still didn't answer and he got extremely exasperated and said, "I shall recommend you to the superintendent for the highest punishment he can give." Oh, my God, I went out of there trembling and I expected to be dismissed. I was scared to death, really literally, for days.

Q: What an ordeal to put a young lad through!

Mr. B.: Well, I thought the way it was done was pretty terrible, really. It was quite in contrast with the next superintendent, too. I was about to say Admiral Wilson had the universal admiration of the midshipmen. In any case, I waited for quite a few weeks, and this is why I think segregation must have been over sometime in the spring, but I'm not sure - sometime along about the best season of the year I heard my name read out. They used to read out the demerit lists.

Q: Was this in the mess hall?

Mr. B.: No, at noon formation, standing in front of Bancroft Hall. You could get all the midshipmen down there. There weren't so many, you see. They would be within range of the voice of the battalion adjutant or the regimental adjutant. It was a regiment of midshipmen then. They would read out all of what they called the pap sheet - that was the slang for the demerit list, "Baldwin, H. W., 4th Class, 4th Battalion, deliberate disobedience of orders, 100 demerits." I thought it was a terrible sock, 100 demerits would lower you a good deal in class rating and in those days you had to walk off demerits by various means. When we first entered the Academy the duty officer on Saturday afternoons would take you on long hikes to "walk off" demerits, and each duty officer would try to exceed the distance the other one had set with this group of straggling midshipmen behind him.

Q: Across country?

Mr. B.: No, we'd walk up the highway towards Baltimore and various other places, wherever the duty officer selected, at high speed, as far and as fast as you could go, and we'd do this for three or four hours. Later, for that, were substituted two other things - walking back and forth on the terrace with a rifle on your shoulder for hour after hour, the same thing they do at West Point, or sometimes in very bad weather, a study period in which you were very closely supervised, not in your room but in a specific room which you would have to remain in. And then you were deprived of all privileges, whatever privileges you had. You had very few privileges plebe year, anyway, because you weren't even allowed to go out in the town of Annapolis - at least for a long period. I don't think I got into the town of Annapolis plebe summer at all. We had no leave except one day, I think, at Christmas, and we never were allowed to go to dances. Plebes didn't have dances until the end of the year. We were never allowed to do any of those things, so there were very few privileges except that I think in the latter part of the year you could go out into Annapolis for two or three hours on a Saturday afternoon.

Saturday afternoon was generally free. At least you could go to athletic events on the grounds and you could do what you wanted. That's one reason, incidentally, why so many midshipmen joined church parties in town, just to get outside of the walls on Sunday morning. I belonged to the Episcopal Church parties in town, just to get outside of the walls on Sunday morning. I belonged to the Episcopal Church party and used to go to St. Anne's.

Q: But you had to go in formation, didn't you?

Mr. B.: Oh, yes, you marched. You marched everywhere. Of course, there were usually only a few to a dozen or so midshipmen in the town church parties and the marching was very informal.

So I spent the rest of plebe year walking off these demerits. I was so greatly relieved when I found I wasn't going to be dismissed that my heart leaped up. I remember standing in formation with these first classmen beside me, who were really scared to death that I was going to pinpoint them, you see - they knew all the plebes who had been called up - and one of them sort of whispered to me when these demerits were read out, "Good show," or something like that. I don't remember his exact words.

Q: Words of encouragement!

Mr. B.: Yes, which wasn't very much help later on when I was marching. Essentially, though, these people in the squad and area where I was, most of them were perfectly decent people. They were not sadists, those that I came in contact with. There were one or two that I didn't know as well in different parts who were. I was going to come to that.

There was one chap who was very much hated. He had all during plebe year really been brutal. There was a tradition at the Academy in those days - I don't know whether it exists or not now - but after June Week, just before the first class graduated and just before the plebes became youngsters, you could retaliate for one night by going to upper classmen's rooms - first classmen's rooms - and putting them under the shower. For instance, one of the things a lot of upper classmen used to delight in doing with both Joe Worthington and me - Joe, however, was not my roommate plebe year, he was all the rest of the time but they did it to him as they did it to me - was to put us under the shower and they made me stand on my head and try to sing "Anchors Aweigh," and I can't carry a tune. So that was the reason they enjoyed that.

Q: Did they let you strip before they made you do that?

Mr. B.: Oh, yes, but they thought the way I sang was the funniest thing they'd ever heard! They would call in spectators, you know, to share this. And they were quite right. I have a grandson like me. He can't carry a tune either.

In any case, usually it was the night before graduation, or two nights before graduation, when you could go around to upper classmen's rooms and they would take orders - the tradition was that they would take orders then from the plebes.

Q: You didn't have to use physical force on them?

Mr. B.: Well, that was the tradition, that you didn't have to use physical force, and the decent ones would always obey. Then you would all shake hands and say "good chap" and so forth and all the past was forgotten. But this one guy had been particularly mean and nasty and he barricaded himself in his room.

The rooms had glass windows in the doors on the outside in this wing and he moved his cruise box or something up against the door. The plebes got out fire hoses and broke the glass, squirted the room full of water, and he started throwing pieces of jagged glass at them. Somebody could have really gotten hurt. It was disgraceful. We swarmed in on him. The DOs were nowhere around while this was going on and, while the plebes didn't beat him up, he knew he had been in quite a rough house. I don't think he ever forgot that. I think the rest of us never forgot it anyway.

Q: Incidentally, did he turn out to be a good naval officer?

Mr. B.: No. No, he didn't. To the best of my knowledge and belief, I don't think he lasted too long in the Navy. He was like a classmate of mine that I can come to later.

What I've recollected were the highlights of plebe year, plus a terrific amount of study.

Q: It sounds like an inferno!

Mr. B.: It was tough. It was designed to be tough, and for most boys like me who had led a rather sheltered life, who'd never been away from home before, were very young, aged sixteen to twenty, it had in some ways a lot to commend it. In other ways, not too much. Of course, the British Navy always took midshipmen much younger than that, as you know, and sent them to Dartmouth when they were twelve or thirteen, which I think is much too young. But the kids of sixteen really got indoctrinated in the tradition. Unfortunately, they got indoctrinated in some other things that were not so good.

In addition to this, of course, you were under intense academic pressure because plebe year was the hardest year there. You had to learn to concentrate or you just didn't survive. You had 100 or 150 pages a day in which you had to be prepared in anything, no matter what the subject was, navigation or anything else. For people who were green or had never really come from a well-based high school, were in real trouble.

Q: You had an advantage, however, did you not?

Mr. B.: I had a certain advantage, except that I never was particularly good at mathematics and it was an engineering course. I could get by, but I didn't like it. I never liked mathematics or the physical sciences as much as I liked language.

Q: You chose Spanish, did you?

Mr. B.: I chose French because I'd had a little French and I thought that would help. Actually, languages were badly taught then. Indeed, most subjects were. The curriculum was not nearly as good as it is now. Of course, it's so much broader now there's no comparison. Then it was rigid, it was fixed, it was the same curriculum for everybody. The only exception was French or Spanish, whether you were in the Spanish "Bat" or French "Bat". The curriculum was thrown at you and the instructors were generally said to be referees between you and the book, and that's about what they were. There were a few exceptions to this.

Q: You recited by rote, did you?

Mr. B.: Very often. You had to have the correct answer. The idea was every midshipman be called upon every day to recite, to get a mark nearly every day. The only outstanding exception that I remember - and I think my whole class would agree - was the head of the Department of English, a man named C.Alphonso Smith, who had come to the Academy from the University of Virginia. He was an inspirational professor who really captured us. He died while we were still midshipmen. As I remember it, he must have died sometime just after plebe year. I'm not sure, maybe during plebe year. He loved the midshipmen and the midshipmen loved him. He would get up and lecture to the class and you could feel yourself uplifted. He was wonderful. A few others were shining exceptions to the rote business. Of course, Smith's subject was not emphasized then, English, and what should have been highly emphasized, naval history, was the worst course you can imagine. It was really terrible.

They were very strong on seamanship and navigation and ordnance and gunnery and engineering. On all of those things I got by all right. I got quite good marks in seamanship, I guess, but it was still a struggle to keep up academically, for anybody who was going to try to get through the course. A great many of them didn't, they failed along the way. Another classmate of mine who was really a mamma's boy and who was from Baltimore lasted about three days after the upper classmen came back. He sent in his resignation. He just couldn't take any of this. Curiously enough, this man followed a civilian career and tried to get back into the Navy in World War II and the Navy wouldn't take him because they didn't think he'd shown officer-like qualities. The Navy was a little wrong in this. They could have used him because he had been in France and he had an almost bilingual French ability. In any case, he has now turned out to be one of the most ardent rooters for the Navy and the Naval Academy, although he was the most miserable man I've ever seen in my life while he was waiting for his resignation to take effect.

There's only one other incident, which I'm very foggy about in my mind, but I know it occurred. I don't know the name of the man, but I remember the occasion made a terrific impression on me. I think it must have been very early in plebe year, soon after the upper classmen got back from their September leave, because we were all assembled in regimental formation on the terrace. A midshipman was brought up between two "Jimmy Legs", as we called them, two Naval Academy police guards, on either side and stood in front of the regimental staff. The adjutant then proceeded to read out the sentence given to this midshipmen for theft from his shipmates' lockers, apparently on the cruise, and for selling Spanish fly to his shipmates. He was utterly disgraced. I've never seen a ceremony like that. It was like the old Foreign Legion custom, I believe. The "Jimmy Legs", when the adjutant was finished, tore the stripes off the culprits uniform, (they'd been loosened beforehand), and pulled off the buttons. He was then marched under their control to the gate and told never to set foot in the yard again. It was really a brutal thing but, for young chaps, a terrifically dramatic occurrence. I don't know the name of the man, I don't think I knew it then, but it made a terrific impression on me. He was a bum, there's no doubt about it, but they deliberately chose this method of dramatizing the reward of evil.

Q: They didn't do it in every instance, though?

Mr. B.: That's the only instance I ever saw or heard of. It must have occurred before because this had obviously been -

Q: A procedure?

Mr. B.: Yes, but it didn't happen again while I was at the Academy, and I don't think it ever happened after that. That must have been about the last time because the Academy gradually liberalized and changed.

Q: I take it the press wasn't very vigilant about such things in those days?

Mr. B.: The press wasn't there, no. No, it was much more closed than it is now, much more, both to keep the midshipmen in and, I guess, to keep the public out.

Q: What are your comments, in retrospect, on the value of marching to class and doing all those things and the very rigid rules which prevented you from going in town?

Mr. B.: I think they were probably too rigid, in retrospect. On the other hand, I think I learned in plebe year two assets which have been invaluable to me throughout my life. First of all, I learned concentration, which I'd never really learned. I could learn to deliberately focus on a book and study and try to get the subject matter into my mind as fast as possible. If I hadn't been able to learn concentration I couldn't have survived. And second, I learned discipline. It was discipline imposed from without, but I also learned -

and I started, I think, to learn this in Baltimore - some discipline imposed from within.

The marching to class and that sort of thing was a part of it. I don't think it was an essential part. It would be impossible to do with the present curriculum. When you had a rigid, fixed curriculum and everybody went to the same class it was easy to do it. Then there was a certain pride in marching, which probably doesn't exist today to the same extent. Although you scorned it, or said you scorned it, you were actually sort of proud that you could march as a body.

Q: And do it with precision.

Mr. B.: Yes. I'm just trying to recall anything else in connection with plebe year. I think the great relief at the end of the year when we used to run on Lover's Lane calling, "T'aint no more plebes", was the outstanding feeling of all of us.

Q: I would imagine that all this pressure upon a group of young boys drew them very close together?

Mr. B.: Well, it did, except the class was too big. I was coming to this in a minute. This perhaps is looking ahead a little, but I had one very strong conclusion about the Academy of those days, and that was that class spirit was emphasized too much at the expense of not only Naval Academy but Navy spirit and our clear goal or higher duty to the Navy. If you were a classmate you expected your other classmates to favor you. These were the days, you remember, of Green Bowlers, they were just ending. I subsequently much later, after World War II, wrote some pieces for the *Times*. In fact, I had a whole list of Green Bowlers which I'd gotten from Captain Crommelin who had made a great fight about this, as you recall. I was never a Green Bowler and I haven't known anyone who was, but I then tried to compare the list I got from him - this was much later in life, when I was working for the *Times* in 1948 or so - with the list of those who were promoted and honestly I tried to see whether a man was unduly favored for promotion because he was a Green Bowler. I don't think that was so, but there were lesser things when you were a classmate. Other classmates expected sometimes that their lateness to formation or their absence from formation would be overlooked by whoever was in charge that day. I'm anticipating a little here, because this incident didn't occur until first-class cruise, my last cruise at the Naval Academy, but I remember I was what was called division commander - they had divisions aboard ship and they had the midshipmen divided into these too. One of my classmates, a very bright chap who subsequently became a vice admiral, "Wally" Beakeley, used to want to sleep in every morning. He was habitually late and sometimes didn't show up. I warned him a couple of times. I said, "I'm not going to take the rap for you. If you are not at formation I'm going to report you the next time." He paid no attention, I reported him, and he wouldn't speak to me for about seven years. We subsequently became very good friends.

But it was this deeply ingrained, this idea of class spirit. Maybe this terrible strain of plebe year helped to create that. There was no honor code then, for instance, and the higher concept of higher loyalty didn't seem to me to be emphasized nearly enough, although there was emphasis on tradition in the Navy, duties to the country, and so forth - I felt that too often the class got the benefit of the doubt in the Navy which they shouldn't have got.

Q: What was the role of the chapel?

Mr. B.: Well, you had to go to church, either in the chapel or in a town church. As I say, I went to the chapel frequently. I liked the chapel, but I didn't go regularly because I was in the out-of-town church party to St. Anne's Church throughout most of my years. You signed up when you entered as a midshipman as to your affiliation, whether you wanted to go to the chapel, whether you wanted to go to town in a church party. I'd been brought up in Baltimore in the Episcopal Church and had a great affection for the rector there, who was a very fine man.

Q: Where? Emmanuel?

Mr. B.: No, this was on Bolton Street. Page Dame was his name. His father was Page Dame, Sr., and looked like a white-bearded saint. He'd been a drummer boy in the Civil War, on the Confederate side, needless to say - and that undoubtedly influenced me.

In any case, you signed up when you entered Annapolis as to your affiliation and whether you wanted to go to out-of-town church parties or not. I signed up for St. Anne's, partly because some of the midshipmen I knew went there. I came to know the Worthingtons pretty soon; they lived there in Annapolis, and Joe went to St. Anne's and also because of my background in Baltimore. Then later, I think because it was just a relief to get out and march out into town.

Is there anything else about plebe year?

Q: Yes, there's another incident.

Mr. B.: Yes, just an amusing incident. I went out for plebe football. They did now allow plebes to play on the varsity in those years. The Navy had produced really some top-notch teams both in football and, as you remember, they won the Olympics in crew in I think 1920 and these people were famous athletes at the time. Eddie Ewing was the captain of the football team in 1920 when I entered as a plebe. I was really much too light for football. I weighed only about 154 pounds, which is just about what I weigh now. I gained some later, as I grew up, and I lost it again later on.

Anyway, the coach, I think that year probably was a man named Bob Folwell. I'm not sure of this name but we had a man from the University of Pennsylvania who was one of the most foul-mouthed coaches I've ever heard, who was the varsity coach. The Varsity had played a game or two and Folwell hadn't liked their basic tackling and blocking and so forth, so he had set up a tackling and blocking drill for that particular afternoon when they were practicing. The plebes were practicing over on that area which has been filled in near the Severn. The varsity was practicing on what was then the varsity field, Farragut Field, I guess it is - that field right next to the Field House which is now used as a track was the football field. They were over there, running through tackling drills, and Folwell, as I recall, yelled over to the plebe coach and said, "Send me over the lightest guys you've got." He picked these plebes and I was one of them - there were four or five of us sent over.

Q: You were always vulnerable, weren't you!

Mr. B.: Vulnerable as hell. Folwell gave the first man the ball. I was third in line. And he said, "I want you to run straight, no dodging, no darting," and he had the varsity lined up, these big hulks. The men were to come out and tackle us and learn how to tackle properly, you see. This, of course, didn't fill us with much enthusiasm because these people weighed up to 250 and we were skinny and little.

The first man ran down the field with the ball and he wasn't knocked out but he was tackled so hard that he was obviously groggy. He barely got up. The second one ended with a broken arm, and I was the third. Eddie Ewing was the man who was to tackle me. He was an All-American end. Oh, gosh! I lost my nerve. I dodged and he missed me! He got hell and I didn't, so I felt much relieved at that. I didn't have to run a second time. Subsequently, I became great friends with Eddie Ewing. I remember seeing him off Korea later on when he was on his flagship out there, but he filled me with a lot of perturbation then, when he was a first classman and the captain of the team, an All-American!

Q: Tell me that incident involving the company officer and some idea of how they functioned.

Mr. B.: The duty officers were assigned as both company officers and battalion officers. In those days there was a regiment of midshipmen, not a brigade of midshipmen, it was much smaller, and during the segregation period of our plebe year, these officers seemed to feel that the plebes were primarily to blame for segregation and frequently they took it out on us, just as the upper classmen did. They let us know by various means that they didn't like us or like our attitude. Segregation applied to the mess hall, as it was then called, as well as to sleeping quarters. The plebes ate in one section of the mess hall and the upper classmen in another section.

One meal, I think it was a night meal, supper, someone became a little rambunctious and, as I recall it, probably threw a piece of bread or something at another plebe. The company officer saw this but didn't see who had thrown the bread, and he got very indignant. He marched us out of the mess hall before we'd finished our meal and stood us at attention just outside the mess hall on the basement floor and raged up and down in front of us and said we were going to stand there all night if necessary at attention until we told him who had done it. I think he was the one that we called "Outside Calipers" - there were two of them, one "Outside Calipers", one "Inside Calipers", so-called by the midshipmen because they were bow-legged, their legs bowed out or in. We stood there for a long time. As I recall, it must have been the better part of an hour, but he was getting tired, as we were too, and finally he dismissed us, still raging.

The duty officers of those days and the company officers were not really close to the midshipmen, except in very few instances. Sometimes they were not well selected at all. They had been to sea, they thought they were salty, and this was sort of a school for kids. I can't say that they won the confidence of the midshipmen or that they were any great help in solving their problems.

Q: Especially when they employed tactics like that.

Mr. B.: Yes, specially when they employed tactics like that. There seemed to be a resentment on the part of many of them because they felt they were on the spot in this segregation business and congressional investigation, just as we were. They thought we had put them on the spot. They were being called to book because they were responsible for what was going on in Bancroft Hall, and, here, hazing had been going on, some of it brutal enough to cause a classmate to commit suicide, and they hadn't done anything about it. So they were on the spot.

Q: That's what I wanted to ask. Didn't the administration at the Academy feel some responsibility for what had taken place?

Mr. B.: I think obviously it did, because that was the

attitude of the captain who interrogated me, you know. I think they all felt that Congress had put the Academy on the spot, but instead of accepting that responsibility really and looking into their own faults, and there were faults, they sort of passed the buck.

Q: It was an example of a failure of moral courage, wasn't it?

Mr. B.: Yes. I think it was a failure in leadership, too. There were a lot of sundowners in the Navy in those days, veterans of World War I and the long years before World War II, and some of them were really good, tough, hard people, many of them with moral courage. I'm sure Admiral King had great moral courage, even though he was a sundowner. But others were simply people who had been promoted by the numbers and really were authoritarian, completely authoritarian, and didn't really have the qualities of leadership, least of all for young boys like that. They didn't inspire the young boys as they should have done. There were exceptions to this. Don't misunderstand me.

I don't have any very vivid recollections of my own company or battalion officers. They didn't make any impression on me, one way or another. I never was close to them. That may not have been true of some of my classmates, especially those in other companies or other battalions.

Similarly, there were only one or two professors who made much of an impression. I've mentioned one and there was another one, I think called Cyclops, because he had one eye. I think, but I'm not sure, that he was a mathematics teacher and I think he deviated a little from this routine of a recitation every day and the fixed sort of rigid curriculum.

There were some others who were famous in our class. I didn't personally have the experience of being taught by them so I couldn't speak firsthand about them, but there were at least two or three others, and I think in every case except one, they were all civilians who won a warm place of affection in the hearts of those who did study under them. I personally didn't have them so I don't know. You see, you were on such a rigid course of studies and my class was so large, that you didn't experience all these professors. You couldn't choose your professor. You went where you were assigned by section.

Q: And you didn't keep one for a whole term, did you?

Mr. B.: Not necessarily. It depended. No, you didn't, you were assigned by sections and the sections went to one professor for a time and then to another. If he was sick or something went wrong, somebody might take his place, but you would go there for, I don't know how long, a limited period. There wasn't a cross-pollinization and there wasn't a great deal of exchange of ideas between sections or between professors. A few of the older professors who had been there for a long time, who had learned the establishment and the ropes dared to deviate from this rigid curriculum.

Q: They felt more secure?

Mr. B.: Yes, and they brought humor into it and some inspiration.

Smith was unusual. I don't know who brought him there. Somebody must have brought him there from the University of Virginia, where he was quite a famous professor and highly thought of. I guess maybe he retired from the University and came to the Academy later, but they must have felt the lack of any kind of leadership in the English course because he gave it life for that period while he was there, real life. But, of course, he was the head of the department, although he did teach some classes. It was usually at larger lectures that we were exposed to him. These large lectures sometimes included all or a majority of the class, and Smith would talk on Shakespeare or whatnot, and I believe the whole class felt that he just sort of lifted them up. There were not too many like him. There were a few others. I don't want to leave the impression that they were all rigid.

Particularly in plebe year, there was a lot of what they

called "P work," or practical work in the curriculum. It was the bane of most midshipmen. You had to go, for instance, to engineering and start with the basics. You would be given a steel block and you would be taught how to shape this into a perfect rectangle and then to bevel its edges so it was absolutely perfect. You would be given the tools to do it. Well, some kids had that natural ability for work with their hands and their blocks would come out shining and beautiful. Mine were always a botch. I couldn't possibly get this thing straight, nor could I with any chisel or any tool, really produce anything. I'd never done anything like this before in my life, and you didn't get much instruction, maybe one period. The rest of it was P work and you'd spend at least an hour and a half, perhaps two hours a day, on P work. Not necessarily just on that, but on other things of the kind which were supposed to give you the basics in working in engineering or in seamanship. For instance, in seamanship, we would go out and toil over the oars in these old cutters they had housed then in a boat shed near the gymnasium. A former chief petty officer of the Navy in charge, would try to show you a little bit about coming alongside, tossing oars, rowing in time, how you came smartly alongside a gangway as they used to do in the old rowing boats. It was of absolutely no use in the modern Navy, but it was very interesting.

We had one old boy who'd been there for many years,

a retired Navy quartermaster, chief quartermaster. He must have been in his seventies. He was not on active duty but he was employed by the Academy, and he was almost illiterate but he knew his seamanship. He would take us out and give us the devil and show us how to anchor the cutter. Once I remember, on one particular occasion he said, "Throw over the anchor," and the midshipman in the bow said, "There's no line on it, Sir." He said, "Throw it over, anyway, it might do some good!"

We used to toil over that P work and the rowing drill and that sort of thing. On the other hand, sailing, which is now well developed in Annapolis, was rather neglected in my period there. It was just an interim between the era when they had emphasized sailing, a lot of sailing . . .

Q: Prior to that?

Mr. B.: Prior to that - and later on when they started to emphasize it again, really not until after World War II.

Q: Why the variations? Why did they not do it?

Mr. B.: They had it, but we didn't have any very good craft. We had the old America, which was rotting, presented by the America Cup people, and we never sailed in big craft. We had what they called half-raters - a half-rater was simply a mainsail and jib. The other type - called a cat-boat, had simply a large and cumbersome mainsail which was very hard to handle. These were small boats and we used to go out sailing in those occasionally. We never got too much instruction in it. I got more because first-class year, in the spring, I decided I was going to cut out everything else. I'd been toiling at crew and other things and I was going to have some fun before I graduated, so I went out sailing about every day and learned something about sailing, but only with the available means there which were not great.

The other thing that I remember which really tormented me during the first phase of the Academy, was mechanical drawing, and that was emphasized strongly in plebe year. You had a special little box with all the drawing tools in it. You had to carry it to class. You had calipers, inside and outside, and a compass rose and parallel rulers, the special ink that you had to use, and all the rest of it. You spent countless hours on this P work, on just trying to draw a side view, overhead views, cross sections, and everything else, whatever they gave you. I think the thing in which I came closest to failing was mechanical drawing. The final examination defeated me completely.

I believe it was plebe or youngster year when the exam required that you imagine a glass turned on its side with an ice cube in it half-melted in the water. You were asked to sketch that side view and overhead views. I was absolutely stymied. I didn't have any idea. I could not envisage things in that graphic way. I couldn't even draw a line. You know, Winston Churchill once said, after the war when he was visiting here in the U.S. (he was speaking of politics), "England never draws a line but she smudges it." Well, that was me exactly. I smudged everything!

So, my memory of plebe year is one of considerable horrors, both academically and discipline-wise in some ways.

Q: I wonder that you had the fortitude to continue on.

Mr. B.: I managed to get through. I was greatly relieved when plebe year was over, but I did have periods of great enjoyment. I was out for sports. I tried out for the plebe crew. I went out for plebe football. I guess I took to the general atmosphere. At least, my interest in the Navy was still great enough to keep me going. I never thought of resigning.

Q: At the end of the plebe year, of course, you were due for a cruise?

Mr. B.: That's right, and in those days what they used to do was to issue cruise boxes, as they call them. They were great wooden chests, and they would be outside each room in Bancroft Hall, and you would pack all the belongings you weren't going to use on the cruise but would need next year, such as books and other things.

Q: Were they stored in the summer time?

Mr. B.: Yes. Your name would be stenciled on the boxes and they would be kept in one part of Bancroft Hall.

Incidentally, the first thing you get when you entered the Naval Academy as a midshipmen, was a stencil of your name, with lots of stenciling ink.

I don't know how they were moved around because I wasn't there during the summer. Then you would pack up the things you were going to take on the cruise. There would be no interval between the end of June Week and graduation and going on the cruise. In fact, you would embark on the cruise ships the next day after graduation, except the graduating class. The graduating class, of course, then ensigns, would go for a month's leave and then report to their ships.

The other three classes would usually go down to the sea wall and there would be a lot of motor launches and cutters and other things to take them out to the cruise ships which were anchored right out in Chesapeake Bay. They were invariably these old, old ships but were still useful. The ones I cruised in were the old _Delaware_ on one cruise, and the _Florida_, and the _Michigan_. They were all ancient.

Q: Coal-burning ships?

Mr. B.: Oh, yes, all coal-burning. In fact, my first battleship after I was an ensign was coal-burning.

They had cage masts, they had large secondary batteries which were useless or really almost useless, because they were not in the kind of barbettes we have today in destroyers, but they were in casemates along the side, like the guns at the Battle of Manila Bay. Big steel shutters opened up, and when you opened those in any sort of sea the sea simply came in. You would often get an awful lot of spray in there in any kind of sea anyway. They were too low.

In addition to that you'd often get a terrific blast from the main battery which would communicate itself through these open shutters to the guns down below, particularly if the main-battery guns were bearing in a certain direction. I remember on one midshipman cruise, I think it was the first time we'd ever fired these casemate guns, they were 5-inch, and we were doing some night firing, I think. None of us had ever seen a 5-inch gun fired before, and we were assigned as midshipmen after a certain captive drill on the loading machine. They had a loading machine aboard ship to practice with dummy shells and powder. There was no fixed ammunition in those days. You put the powder in behind the shell, it was pretty heavy and you had to be well drilled. You had, of course, the gun captain and you had the man who opened and closed the breech. There were seven or eight people on a 5-inch gun, as I remember, some passing ammunition.

I remember this one night in particular when they fired the 5-inch gun because the thing made a hell of a noise and a terrific flare - at night it made a tremendous flash, as you can imagine. And it seemed to come right back into our compartment. It scared the hell out of us. One man just got up, jumped up, and ran out of the compartment - a midshipmen. That just about cooked him because you see, the rest of us all flinched and were really frightened, but he was the only one who ran.

Q: He was showing qualities not fitting for an officer!

Mr. B.: That's right. As a result, I don't think he ever became an officer or really finished more than that one year.

Q: How did you know where your target was when you fired at night?

Mr. B.: You had the gun-pointer and the gun-trainer who were presumably looking through the telescopes and the target was supposed to be illuminated either by star shell or by searchlight. This was short-range battle practice. The target was right up close against us, only a couple of thousand yards away.

The cruises in those days were long cruises. They lasted three months, usually, almost all of June, all of July, and virtually all of August. They rarely got back to Annapolis before the end of August or the first of September.

Q: That's all right, you avoided the heat!

Mr. B.: They took us to many interesting places. We went to Europe, I think, the first year. It took us about twenty days to cross the ocean in these old coal-burning ships. We went up around the north of Scotland and finally ended up in Christiania or Oslo. I remember we were frightfully impressed by a crew of Viking girls, all beautiful blondes, coming rowing out to meet us, and for hungry sailors fresh from the sea for twenty days, this was a great impression! We've all liked Oslo ever since.

Then we went on down, I guess stopping at various ports. I don't remember but I could check it, I think. I know we stopped in Lisbon. I have one letter here which is an amusing letter from the skipper of my ship in response to one my father wrote him. I think my father was spurred on by my mother because I know I was disgusted when I heard about it.

Q: That was interfering in your affairs, wasn't it?

Mr. B.: I thought it was.

Q: Yet to an outsider it would be a very natural thing for a parent to do.

Mr. B.: Oh, yes, it was. Dad was very interested in the Academy and wrote a lot of editorials while I was there about the Academy and the Navy. I've retained some of them. Apparently the superintendents wrote him some letters - this one's from Henry B. Wilson - about one or two of them in which he asked for reprints or the right to reprint.

Q: This is gratifying. The Navy in those days was concerned about its press.

Mr. B.: Yes. Well, there was a closer relationship. There wasn't all this fuss about it. There were no such things as public relations officers. They didn't have them in the Navy. You see, the captain of a ship - and this is what we were talking about a moment ago - and the superintendent were responsible for their young gentlemen. Henry B. Wilson always called us "young gentlemen" and he expected us to live up to it. The real leaders felt this sense of responsibility and they didn't need an artificial prop. They didn't need a specially trained public relations office. I've always thought that the Navy emphasized too much the machanics of public relations and not enough of the basics. I still feel that about most of the Navy's public relations officers. I must say I think that they're a necessary evil today because the whole thing has gotten so big, but only a few of them were really good. Long ago - and you know Count Austin, I guess?

Q: Yes.

Mr. B.: He was a classmate and I admire him greatly and Count was public affairs officer in the Navy Department. He knew not a damned thing about it when he took it over, but I've always said I'd much rather have a good naval officer who can learn than a man who's come from a public relations medium and is not a good naval officer. I think the good naval officer will end up being the better public relations officer. I certainly think this was true in the case of Count and another classmate who was a public relations officer, Admiral Smith, who had the Atlantic Fleet. He didn't know anything about it either, but he turned out to be quite good.

I have felt very strongly that people who come up from this specialized background of journalism schools and so on just don't inspire the same respect that they know their stuff, that they can answer the questions themselves. That's my feeling, my personal feeling.

Q: Do you mind if I read this into the tape?

Mr. B.: No, not at all.

Q: It being an illustration of the point I attempted to make that the Navy was concerned about its image and what you said in your discourse.

Mr. B.: Yes.

Q: This is from Admiral Henry B. Wilson, who was superintendent. It's dated the 26th of August 1922 and is addressed to your father?

Mr. B.: Yes.

Q: "My Dear Sir,

I have just observed with much gratification the able editorial appearing in the Baltimore <u>Sun</u> this morning regarding the debt problem which has prevailed among the midshipmen at the Naval Academy during recent years. It is a source of pleasure to see such a contribution in such a paper as the

Baltimore Sun and I assure you it is appreciated and will result in estimable value to the midshipmen of the Naval Academy.

May I ask your permission to make a reprint of this editorial for distribution to the parents of all midshipmen, giving full credit to the Baltimore Sun, as shown on the attached clipping. Kindly return this clipping to me.

Thank you in advance for this courtesy,

        Very sincerely yours,

        Henry B. Wilson"

Well, Sir, you had to work very hard on the battleship going on this cruise because you had to coal her, did you not?

Mr. B.: The routine on these cruises was usually that you spent half your time in the deck gang and half the time in the black gang, but that changed depending upon what class you were in. The youngsters, of course, got all the dirty work. They were the captains of the head and they did the coal-heaving.

Q: You were the gobs, were you not?

Mr. B.: Yes. They took some of the crews off the ships and

replace d them, but not entirely, by midshipmen. You couldn't leave everything to inexperienced midshipmen. For instance, you had to keep the boilers in top condition, so you always had sailors down there, who took advantage of the midshipmen whenever it became awful hot! Later on, when you were more senior, you spent more time in such things as junior-officer-of-the-deck duties and navigation and things of that sort. Most of youngster year, your first cruise, you kept a journal of whatever you were doing. When you were in the deck gang they tried to alternate you between some of the divisions - you might be in a turret, you might be in a casemate gun, you might then be in the fire-control division. You always were responsible for keeping the decks clean and the brass-work polished, that's one of your greatest jobs. Every morning, the old memory of the trousers rolled up, in bare feet, and the holystoning of the deck, the salt water hose and squeegeeing it. When my grandsons ask what a squeegee is, I say, "I can tell you!" And, of course, using sand and canvas.

Those early ships, the Michigan, Delaware, Florida class, the Michigan was the most modern, I guess, but all of them were very deficient in refrigeration and deficient in storage space for fresh provisions. The food was terrible. They were crowded. We slept in hammocks. There was no place for bunks, except a very few places. Hammocks were slung close together. Of course, you made your seven hitches around the hammock in the daytime and put it in the hammock netting. In the old days, the hammock nettings were supposed, as you know, to provide some protection against splinters from round shot in wooden hulls, That's why they put them outboard. Hammock nettings on those old battleships were outboard. They were down an alleyway. They called it the "hammock passage" or "alley." You'd have to pick your hammock out at night and sling it.

The meals, particularly if you'd been at sea for a long time, were quite bad. Sometimes the meat was spoiled and the potatoes were spoiled and things of that sort. So you didn't eat well until you got into port, when things improved considerably. Some of the young midshipmen and, of course, some of the sailors didn't know how to keep themselves clean, and they used to have a very definite remedy for that and it was applied. It was always efficacious. If one midshipman or sailor was just so bad at taking baths, and, remember, there was no plentiful supply of fresh water - it wasn't easy to keep clean because you didn't have showers like you have now, or if you did, you had to turn it on, get wet, turn it off, soap up, turn it on for a fraction of a second, and that's all. There were very few of those. You often bathed out of a bucket, and when you came up from the fireroom, grimy as hell, it was very hard to get yourself clean.

In any case, a midshipman who didn't keep himself clean or a sailor who really became offensive in these close compartments were warned, after repeated offenses they would get what was called a "sand and canvas," which you've heard of undoubtedly. They'd strip them down, their classmates or their fellow sailors, right on the deck, turn the salt-water fire hose on them and get literally canvas and sand as if you were holystoning the deck. They'd scrub the offender with sand and canvas. His skin wouldn't be rubbed raw, it wasn't torture, but he would know he'd been through a tough bath and unless he shaped up he'd get it again. Once was enough usually for all these people. I've only seen that done once, and I don't think it happened often because most sailors have instincts to keep clean. But it was tough to keep clean in those ships because your normal allowance was a bucket or, maybe two buckets of fresh water a day in which you had to wash and bathe yourself and scrub all your clothes. So you usually did the routine of washing yourself first, then you would wash your clothes in the same water, then try to rinse them in fresher water and whatnot.

The old hands who knew how to use what they called salt-water soap - you could get plenty of salt water from the hoses and what not, a very rough and abrasive soap -

Q: A lye soap, wasn't it?

Mr. B.: Yes, it was, but it produced a very little amount of lather in salt water, not much, but a little. Those who knew how to use this, and most of them were former enlisted men, were always the ones who were impeccably white and their uniforms shone at captain's inspection. I remember the envy we used to feel for them. The rest of us couldn't do it.

So, the early cruises would have been considered rugged, particularly sometimes when you got into the firerooms. A lot of people don't like to go to sea for twenty days at a time and we would literally be at sea - I think the first cruise to Oslo took us just about twenty days from Annapolis. We didn't stop. We went very slowly and also we did a lot of tactical evolutions and a little bit of gunnery practice, very little live firing because we were more or less in the shipping lanes and we simply trained people how to fire. We did the live firing later.

Q: Did you have instructors on board also from the Naval Academy?

Mr. B.: There was supposedly one representative from the Naval Academy I think on each ship, but no instructors per se. They didn't do any instructing. They were just responsible really for the administrative end of the thing, that's about all it was. The rest of it was left up to the ship's officers, particularly the petty officers and enlisted men. That's my memory. I think my memory serves me right, but I mistrust it. I never remember seeing a Naval Academy representative on board any of the ships, but I'm sure there was one on each ship.

Q: There was some value, however, in so many of the midshipmen going on a single ship, was there not?

Mr. B.: Yes, I think there was value but I think the value depended almost entirely on the captain of the ship, how he organized the training, and how his officers and enlisted men administered it. There was not nearly as much responsibility put on the first class, (but there was some) for training the underclassmen as there is today. The first classmen again used sort of the authoritarian system they used in plebe year at the Naval Academy. There was no hazing during the cruises, but they would expect the youngsters to do all the dirty work, get the heads clean and all this sort of thing. But no great amount of instruction in anything was given them from the first class. What instruction there was came from the ship's officers, and I think there was advantage in having the midshipmen together, in person, in spirit and in morale, but it varied widely from ship to ship.

Q: I was thinking in constrast to the present method of dispersing them throughout the fleet?

Mr. B.: I really think our cruises were better from the point of view of getting to know the sea, seamanship, of knitting together the regiment of midshipmen, because, mark you, after plebe year you knew no one really except your own plebe class. Here, on the cruise, you got mixed with other classes and did get to know them, and you did often form friendships which were lasting. Also, you met members of your own class you'd never met before because usually these things were done alphabetically - Baldwin would be in the Bs and so on right down the line, and you would be assigned to a ship or a division by those initials. So you would haphazardly meet classmates you'd never even seen - they may have been in the Spanish battalions at the Academy.

The two other features of the cruises that I think were of great interest, and I'm talking generally now, not just about the youngster cruise, were one, they were all coal-burning ships and, as I said, poor refrigeration ships. In addition to bad food, you had the challenge of keeping steam up. Keeping steam up was not easy, particularly in the tropics, particularly with a following wind, and most of all with Welsh coal. Welsh coal has a notorious habit of clinkering if you've never handled it, so when we stopped at British ports like Gibraltar and coaled ship from our own colliers with British coal we'd be faced with the task of coming back across the Atlantic with this Welsh coal, often with a following trade wind behind us. Hence, the ventilators - there was no forced draft in those days, of course. We just had these great wind flaps at the top to pull air down, air scoops, down into the fireroom. In effect, however, with a following wind, the ship was practically at a dead stop and no air would flow in the firerooms and the temperature would get up to 150° or more. You would have to fight to try to keep the steam up because this Welsh coal was such poor-burning stuff. The challenges were two, coaling ship, and second, keeping the steam up. Coaling ship was an all-day operation, all-hands operation.

Q: How frequently did that occur?

Mr. B.: It would depend, of course, on how far you had cruised. You usually have at least two to three "coaling ships" during a summer cruise, no matter how far you went. Sometimes more than that. The bunkers on these ships were fairly big and we went usually at quite slow speeds, so we conserved a certain amount of fuel. But certainly after we crossed the Atlantic the first time we coaled ship not too long after that, I think. I know we coaled ship in Gibraltar, we coaled ship in Guantanamo many times, and we coaled ship in Halifax, and so forth. This was, as I say, an all-hands job. Nobody was supposed to be excused. The people who had it best were the ship's band. They would sit on top of the after turret usually and they'd play tunes supposedly to inspire you to greater effort all day. The efficiency of the coaling and the rapidity with which it was done depended to a great degree on the collier or whether you had to do it from barges alongside. Sometimes they brought coal barges alongside and you had to flip out these heavy, 200-pound canvas bags down into the coal barges, shovel the coal into the bags, and whip them up again, and dump the coal on the deck and people with wheelbarrows and shovels would push the stuff down into the scuttles and chutes and down into the bunkers, way down at the bottom of the ship. The whole ship was filthy when this was done and, needless to say, everybody with it. Then there would be the business of cleaning it up afterwards.

It was not infrequent that you would start, say, at four in the morning. I remember one coaling which was particularly long and stretched out, partly due to the collier, the inefficiency of the collier, and partly due to the quality of the coal. I think that was at Gibraltar and I believe that went on continuously till about 2 a.m. the following morning. Then the next day was field day for all hands. You got about three or four hours' sleep then got up and started cleaning up all over again.

Q: This must have had a culling effect on the midshipmen, those who wanted to continue their careers?

Mr. B.: I think it did. The summer cruise got rid of some more of them. Plebe year got rid of most of those who were either faint-hearted or just said, "this is not for me," or just couldn't stand it. The summer cruise got rid of some more, particularly those who were prone to chronic seasickness, and there are such people. Those old tubs used to roll heavily. They didn't pitch so much, although they could pitch, but they rolled quite heavily and a lot of people couldn't stand this.

Q: It must have been hell on board ship for somebody who was seasick and the coaling process, too!

Mr. B.: Well, when you're coaling you're at anchor, you see, in port.

I remember the cruise back - I'm not sure whether it was later on in the first-class year or whether it was on the _Michigan_, I think it must have been the _Michigan_ and the youngster-year cruise because I don't believe I would have been shoveling coal as much as a second classman. We had this Welsh coal aboard and we were going back to Guantanamo from Gibraltar, having visited Lisbon and various other ports - Lisbon was then, by the way, the dirtiest, filthiest place on earth - and again we got a great deal of disillusionment in Lisbon, many of us. Remember, this was the era of prohibition and nobody knew how to drink or could drink, and when American sailors got into a foreign port they were really the most disgusting people and so were many of the midshipmen. Lisbon was a foul city then. It was full of prostitutes of the most terrible kind. People met you on the dock and tried to sell anything from their sisters to anything else. I remember vividly the scenes in the evening - I don't think there was any overnight liberty - when they were coming back to the ship and you would literally pour these people into these motor sailers, sailors and midshipmen, too - they'd be drunk and sick and disreputable and dirty. Part of this was due to a let-down after World War I. Remember, this was 1921. You had kept in the enlisted ranks some of the people who couldn't make it in civilian life on the ebb side, and also, for the midshipmen, it was the first time they had been exposed to foreign ports, the first time, probably, that they had tasted any amount of liquor.

That was the worst occasion. I don't think it ever was that bad again as I saw it, but that visit to Lisbon sticks out in my memory.

Anyway, coming back across the Atlantic from Gibraltar to Guantanamo was a long haul, shorter, I think, than the first trip across, but is was something like fourteen or fifteen days. We were in the trade winds following us most of the way. I know I was down in the fireroom in this terrific heat and no real ventilation and very little fresh water. The evaporators always broke down. They didn't work, so we were down to a very limited supply of fresh water. When you try to get coal dust off with salt water, you're really in trouble. We would have a lot of people pass out in the firerooms. Sometimes, the sailors would pretend to have passed out so they could pass the work on to the midshipmen.

The dirtiest job was getting way back into the bunkers, particularly when the coal got low, back into what they called the wing or the side bunkers, which meant you had to shovel the coal from near the hull of the ship - the outside hull of the ship, through one hatch or doorway over the raised sill into the inside bunkers, then you had to shovel it from there out on to the floor plates of the fireroom. You had to keep a pile of coal in the middle of the fireroom ready for the firemen. You were the coal passer when you went in the bunker, and I remember being in that bunker, absolutely airless and full of coal dust, a little bulb hanging over you. You had to be in that bunker and get the stuff out and keep up with this insatiable demand of the boiler for more and more coal. The firemen, who were usually second classmen, would shovel the coal in and use the sluice bar to break up the clinkers and rake out the ashes. The first classmen were usually the watertenders. But, of course, they were all under the supervision of regular personnel because you can't fool with a steam boiler, as you know. If you let the water get low, the old saying was "Haul fires or haul ass," one of the two, because they'd blow up without water. So we were always watching the water, regardless.

But there were a lot of people who really fainted and some who had to be taken to sick bay. Perhaps because I was long and lean and because I always perspired profusely, unlike some other people, I never passed out. But it was a very rigorous passage and they had to relieve people much more frequently. In fact, they brought some additional second and first classmen down to the fireroom, which was unheard of, to fill out personnel that had to be replaced.

We used to get in the firerooms, what were called "steaming rations," which really meant a meal in the middle of the night for those who had the mid watch. This used to be corned willy and bread, whole loaves of bread. Someone would go up to the galley and draw it. And then coffee, which you would make yourself, and we had a routine of making this over the fires of the furnace. We'd wash a shovel off with salt water and put the corned beef on the shovel and get the corned willy heated up and the bread toasted and the coffee heated, and we'd enjoy it more than any food we ever had!

At least, on this first cruise, the youngster cruise, we ended up at Guantanamo and did our firing down there, as they still do today in many cases. Then we'd come back to Annapolis and get our September leave. It used to be the routine for those who'd spent the last part of their cruise in the fireroom to promptly head ashore after they had started their September leave and get into a Turkish bath, to get all the grit out of them. Actually, I did that in New York one Saturday night.

Q: It would just ooze out?

Mr. B.: Well, you were absolutely ingrained with this stuff and you didn't have enough fresh water aboard ship to get rid of it. It was impossible. I'd get a haircut, everything, a manicure, my nails would be full of it. You couldn't get rid of it with the fresh water available. You could get rid of the worst of it, of course. So you always luxuriated if you could in something like that. They didn't have saunas in those days.

But I think these cruises did us good and they were interesting. We learned things that were completely new to us about foreign nations and foreign customs.

Q: And there was a certain implementation of what you'd learned from textbooks, wasn't there?

Mr. B.: Oh, yes. As a matter of fact, in youngster year in the cruise journals you had to keep, you would go through the old business, you learned about Babcock and Wilcox boilers, you'd learned that at the Naval Academy and you'd sketched and described them - that used to be a favorite question in Steam, as we called it, Steam Engineering - sketch and describe the B & W boiler, and boy, you went through that again and again. B & W then provided nearly all the boilers the Navy had. Then you learned actually in the fireroom just how these things worked and how careful you had to be about the water gauge. And you learned about the ash-ejector system. That was another thing that really gave us the willies, the ash ejectors. When you got all the ashes out of the fire, there had to be some place to put them, and there was this gadget which you've probably seen or heard of. It was a big steel hopper over to one side of the fireroom, and this hopper was actuated by hydraulic pressure, sea water, and it fed in a long chute up above the waterline and supposedly ejected the ashes out into the sea by water pressure. Sometimes, if you didn't get the thing operating properly, it spat back in your face.

You would fill the hopper up with ashes and close the lid tight and then shoot it out. Then, again, another bad habit it had, if you were ejecting ashes to windward, and you were always supposed to ask permission from the bridge before you did your ashes' ejection or clean tubes because you got soot from the tubes . . .

Q: The bridge didn't want that in their face!

Mr. B.: No, and you cleaned the tubes with a steam lance. To be fair, they always tried to do it at sea, when possible, so you wouldn't contaminate a port, but sometimes you made mistakes and these things went off to windward and then you got ashes and soot all over the decks.

Those were some of the problems you had, but they were interesting problems, challenging ones, in a sense. There was a challenge, to me at least, both in coaling ship and in keeping steam up, and seeing if you could do it and still keep up with the rest of these people. I think many midshipmen felt that challenge.

The firing was sort of a dramatic highlight, the actual firing of the guns. As I recall it, and I'm not sure of this, we never fired the main-battery guns. I think it was all 5-inch in short-range battle practice. I may be wrong about that. I certainly have no recollection of ever being in a turret while it was being fired.

Q: Would this have been for the sake of economy?

Mr. B.: I think partially that. This could be checked very easily. I'm just quoting from memory - partially also because they felt it would be putting too much on the midshipmen in the short summer, that they could learn this gradually later. They took them through the turrets, they trained them in how to operate them, and maybe in the last cruise we did fire the main battery, but I don't have any recollection of it.

My last cruise, however, was shortened anyway for reasons I can expand on later, so it may have occurred then.

I think the cruises on the whole were beneficial. They certainly taught you much more about the sea than I think they tend to get today. Today they're far more technical, far broader. The Navy today is so much more technical, of course, than it was. We navigated by guess and by God, and by sun and star sights; you had no radar, we frequently went through fog in formation and we had no Loran or radio crossfire. I remember on the midshipmen's cruise we steamed through fog with the old towing spars towed astern. The ship astern kept the spar in sight all the time to show you were the proper distance behind the others.

Q: Then, too, the purpose of a cruise like this was a learning cruise, wasn't it, whereas today the boys are put on operating units of the Navy and the purpose isn't entirely learning?

Mr. B.: No. I don't know which is better, whether by osmosis they learn more today than we did by doing. I don't know. It depends again, I guess, on the ship and the skipper and the officers, whether or not they allow these young midshipmen today the responsibilities.

Q: Well, Sir, tell me about your second year at the Academy?

Mr. B.: It was a much more pleasurable year. The first class who had experienced the brunt of segregation because they were the senior class at the time had graduated and gone on out into the service. Segregation was forgotten and we were all back together again, all four classes mixed up.

Some of my classmates, as youngsters, were inclined to feel that we should take out on the plebe class what we had suffered ourselves, but most of us I think took the opposite tack. In fact, the great majority of them felt that a tough plebe year was very important and vital, but brutality no, and there wasn't any trouble that I remember of any serious nature.

Q: Was the administration now more vigilant about such things?

Mr. B.: Well, yes. There was a different superintendent for one thing. Henry B. Wilson from sometime in the summer, and he was universally respected and admired by the midshipmen. Scales was a very nice man, I guess, but he was never really close to the midshipmen and they didn't know him, as far as I know. The classes before mine may say something that's contrary to that, but certainly we as plebes never did. We felt that Henry B. Wilson was our superintendent and our class has always regarded him as that and always had a high admiration for him. It was this same man when we were talking of moral courage who, you remember, took responsibility for the false armistice in World War I. He was Commander, U.S. Naval Forces, Europe, and I think he was in Brest and Roy Howard came in to see him. You remember that story. Roy Howard sent through the U.P. the report of the false armistice, which Wilson gave him in complete integrity because he had received this high-level message from Paris, which was sent out by mistake. Someone had jumped the game by a week. But Wilson believed the war was over and he told Howard that, and Howard put it on the wires. Then Howard was under terrific fire, and Wilson said, "Well, I told him."

Very few people would have done that, you know.

He had that same kind of integrity. I remember we had a terrible tragedy - at least terrible from the point of view of young midshipmen. I guess it was when we baptized our rings. The idea was that you put on your first-class rings, as you know, at the end of second-class year and in those days that used to mean dunking in the Severn. One of the reasons they are doing the modern "Ring Dance" business now is because of the tragedy that occurred in 1923.

We went over the sea wall usually to dunk the rings, right there by Dewey Basin. That used to be where all these half-raters and cat boats were anchored. They would move some of those aside, but not many, and leave a little open space. In this particular case, someone was pitched off and then the horseplay started. Everyone was piled into the drink at once, they fell in on top of each other and one kid was under the mess and he was drowned. Henry B. Wilson was watching this from the sides. I was in but I was a good swimmer, I'd played water polo, and I was in and out again and up on the bank. Then we suddenly discovered that somebody was down there. We got him out and worked on him and worked on him. Wilson was superb through this. He was deeply, deeply concerned, as he should have been. That ended that business of going over the sea wall which had been a tradition up until that time.

In both stress and at other times Wilson was the type of leader who had consummate dignity. He looked like an admiral, a seafaring man. He always had his cap slightly cocked on the side like Beatty, and he had a great sense of justice and fairness. He had this World War I record behind him, which was all to the good, in the eyes of the midshipmen who were growing up with tradition.

I'm skipping around a lot now. I've gone from my third-class year up to the second class.

As I remember my Academy service, I remember getting more accustomed to the routine I suppose and I managed to do somewhat better on academics than I had plebe year. All those things that I couldn't do like mechanical drawing and P works were more or less behind me, or came behind me as I became a third and then a second classman.

I got, I guess, my highest marks in seamanship and I found life more enjoyable. I was always involved in athletics, never in the Log or never in the Lucky Bag, although I had a lot of classmates who were. I had edited my school paper in Baltimore, but I didn't have much interest in that in Annapolis. I started out for football in the fall, was too light for it, and never got anywhere. After plebe year I concentrated on class track and then on water polo, which was a rough game in those days. They've changed the style completely, in fact, they don't play it any more at Annapolis. And then crew in the spring. Again, I was too light for crew but I plugged along for three years, was on the training table, and . . .

Q: Did you play tennis?

Mr. B.: I didn't play tennis at all. Joe did all the time. Oh, I played a little, of course, but not actively.

Q: Wrestling was high on the sports list at that time?

Mr. B.: Wrestling and boxing. Spike Webb was the great boxing coach. And so was crew, of course. They had this world championship crew from the Olympics. They also had all-Americans on the football team. After the rise of professional sports, it made all the difference, it made it impossible for the Navy or the Army to compete. They've been arguing this in the Alumni Association for all these last seven or eight years. I think the schedule they play is absurd. We should go back to the Ivy League where we belong.

Anyway, I found a lot of pleasure in athletics. I guess I'm the sort who enjoyed the kind of methodical life that we had to lead there. I had no particular girl while I was at Annapolis. There were a number that I knew from Baltimore.

Q: You brought them down for the hops, did you?

Mr. B.: Some. I wasn't what they called then a Red Mike. A Red Mike was a woman-hater, but the other type - I've forgotten what they called it in midshipman's slang, I wasn't really as interested in the hops as some. We had one function which was unusual. We had what they called a gymkhana, which is now completely forgotten. This actually occurred in my plebe year I think, but it continued, the gymkhana, for another year or two before it ended.

During Lent, instead of having hops, midshipmen dances, they used to have roller-skating parties in old Dahlgren Hall, where the ice rink now is. There used to be a smooth floor in place ideal for this sort of thing. Your roller skates would be rented and available to any who wanted to come. Girls could come, and they would have little stands around the sides where you could get soft drinks. The plebes were supposed to act as waiters on roller skates. They would carry the trays. They couldn't bring any girls. I remember vividly going to the gymkhana and carrying a tray and running into an upper classman and dropping the tray and drinks all over him and me, too. I thought I was going to get hazed unmercifully for that but fortunately he overlooked it. It was his fault really.

That gymkhana thing, I guess, was a sort of derivation of the same thing that they had at West Point. It was dropped some time after that. They used to have another thing that they called the Hundredth Night, which they still have at West Point. I believe that's 100 nights before graduation, I'm not sure, and they had all sorts of songs - derivation of the same sort of thing they had on board ship in the fleet in those days, which they called "happy hours." Do you remember that term?

Q: I know it on a different kind of occasion!

Mr. B.: Well, these were shipboard entertainments, either afloat or in port. All the amateurs sing, play instruments, boxing matches sometimes for fleet championships; tremendous interest centered in those days on fleet athletics and midshipmen took part in these things on the summer cruises. For instance, we always had midshipmen race boat crews during the summer. I rowed on the <u>Texas</u> crew - not the <u>Texas</u>, the <u>Michigan</u> crew - and I think one or two others. We'd race usually down around Guantanamo in the Caribbean at the end of the season. There'd be terrific betting on these races, particularly when midshipmen weren't aboard and the whole fleet was there. The fleet would have race boats and these races in those days were fabulous events and would end up with hundreds of dollars being wagered by the sailors amid terrific shouts and encouragements.

Happy Hours were the shipboard entertainment which really, outside of some very bad and inadequate movies, were the only recreational things you had to do aboard ship. They would come periodically if you were on a long cruise, sometimes as often as once a week. You'd dredge up whatever talent you had on board and if you were at anchor you might have inter-ship boxing matches and things of that sort.

That was the same idea as the gymkhana.

I think the only other event that occurred to me personally of any great significance was at the end of my - not of as great significance as I feared at the time - at the end of my second-class year, sometime in May, just before we took the final examinations. We, a lot of my classmates, were over on the rifle range across the Severn, where we had to go periodically, not only for rifle practice but for practical work in learning how to disassemble and assemble a Springfield rifle and machine guns. There were Marines who were our instructors in this.

On this particular occasion we were being taught how to disassemble a machine gun. A Marine corporal was the instructor and there was a group of classmates crowded around this wooden table with steel supports in a shed. The Marine had a machine gun on the table and was showing us how it was disassembled. He was using a live cartridge to press in on springs and then take it apart. The machine gun was mostly disassembled. In fact, the breech bolt was out and this classmate of mine who had better remain unnamed because he did some other awful dumb things later on, put the cartridge in the breech and somehow it went off. The Marine was sitting on the side of the table with one buttock on the table. The bullet slithered through the wood and went right in through his buttock. It was a nasty wound, carrying a lot of splinters into it. It went down through the wood into the steel support and ended up in my Achilles tendon in my leg and stayed there.

Well, we were both taken to the Naval Academy Hospital. It was Monday, I remember, and this Marine was really vocal. The Marine knew all the lurid vocabulary of the world and he taught all the words to me on our way to the hospital. He was lying on his stomach. I thought by that time, after three years at the Naval Academy, that I was sophisticated, but I wasn't. Fortunately, neither one of us was too seriously hurt. He had a nastier wound by far. They had to extricate the splinters and clean it up. As Marines do, this crazy guy went out of the hospital and went swimming in the Severn and got it infected before it was healed, but he came out of it all right. My wound became infected. I was very fortunate because they had a surgeon at the hospital named Clifton who had been with the Marine Brigade in France all during World War I and he knew how to treat bullet wounds. He was a top-notch surgeon and a very good doctor.

Of course, the bullet had been sort of crushed and broken apart in the process of hitting the steel support and all this entered. They had to split my tendon in order to take it out and they were afraid for a while that I might be lame. Then again, it had gone through all this guck and there was some infection. My mother and father became quite concerned, unknown to me. Here's where Joe Worthington comes into the picture because he was my roommate for three years and I have a great and ardent admiration for Joe. I told him not to tell my father and mother under any circumstances when I was going to the hospital. He defied me, as he had to do, I guess. He told them and they became concerned when the infection set in. They got a Hopkins specialist to come down. Dr. Clifton was just as fine as he could be. They'd put drains in my leg and got it disinfected. But, to make a long story short, this took a while and the Naval Hospital in those days was a very pleasant, quiet place with relatively few patients and some very nice nurses and good doctors. I guess I was in there about a month or something like that.

I missed some of my exams. I'd taken some, as I remember, but I missed some of them, and the cruise had already started. I was given convalescent leave and told to finish getting the wound healed up. It was virtually healed when I left the hospital. As a result I was late in getting to my first-class cruise. I did take the exams I'd missed before I went on the cruise and then I went to join the fleet. Again, the midshipmen cruise was at Lisbon, the second time I'd been there. They were at Lisbon by the time I was able to join them sometime in July.

Q: How did you go over there?

Mr. B.: I went aboard the old USS <u>Richmond</u>, which was a light cruiser of the 7,050-ton class, which, you remember we built in that interim period in the twenties. She was new and I really welcomed the chance to go on her. I was assigned as a sort of supercargo and, although I got a little instruction on the way, most of it was a free ride. She went at fairly high speed.

So I joined the midshipmen's cruise squadron in Lisbon and then spent the rest of the summer with them. I probably missed one month of the cruise anyway.

This same classmate - he always managed to do dumb things later on - I'm jumping ahead but I might as well bring it in here.

Q: Surely, yes.

Mr. B.: This is after we were graduated and were on that round robin after graduation. Certain ships to which you might be assigned were assigned the midshipmen's cruise squadron and the recent graduates, who had a months leave after graduation, therefore did not join their ships until the midshipmen's cruise was over, in September. Therefore, in July and August they employed a lot of these young ensigns who were assigned to ships of the midshipmen's cruise squadron in what they called the Washington-Dahlgren-Indian Head round robin. We would go to the Washington Navy Yard gun factory, presumably for instruction, and to the optical shop there, and then to Indian Head to see how powder was made, and how it was used, and then to Dahlgren, Virginia, where the guns were proved.

At Indian Head - I can come back to this later, but this one incident concerns the same classmate who put the bullet in the breech of the gun and shot two of us at once, something that had never been done before!

Anyway, he was along at Indian Head. They took us into one of the magazines to show us the various forms of powder, and they had every type of powder in glass jars, really for exhibition purposes. Not much of it but enough - there were hundreds of glass jars - in each to make a very nice bang. The instructor was taking these off the shelves, handling them carefully - it was his fault really - and sometimes he passed one to a midshipman so he could see what the grain of the powder was like and how it was formed. You could see these powder grains. He took a jar of fulminate of mercury and said, "This is the most delicate powder we have," and he handed it to this classmate. The guy started to drop it. Fortunately, he caught it before it hit the floor, but a lot of us were turning white!

Then, not content with that, this same guy, having been warned that that powder was simply a fast-burning material in the open - it was when it was compressed that it exploded - he decided to take a grain of this black powder which he found and put it under his hat and got it lit somehow. His hat exploded and disappeared altogether. He was always doing silly things like that!

Q: It might have gone the other way!

Mr. B.: Well, he was a strange man. I think he settled down much more later on. He changed his name from what his midshipman name was, I think to one that was considerably more euphonic and more distinguished-sounding than his midshipman name. But he did rise to the rank of captain in the Navy and apparently had very creditable service as far as I know, especially in World War II. But for a time, partially because of these things, his classmates were down on him for a while.

I don't know whether there's anything else about Annapolis or not.

Q: Tell me about the progressive privileges you began to enjoy as you stayed at the Academy, the leave in town and that sort of thing.

Mr. B.: Well, I'm sure the present generation wouldn't think they were privileges at all, but we looked forward to them. I don't remember the details. They could be very easily checked. But I do know that as you went up the ladder from youngster to first class more privileges, liberty in town, later liberty was extended to you. But everyone, including the first class, had to check in at a certain hour. You were allowed usually if you had a hop at the Naval Academy and then took your girl home to where she was staying in

Annapolis, you would be allowed usually, forty-five minutes to go there and back again. I think that was the first-class rate, as I recollect. I believe it was only thirty minutes for second-class men.

Q: Barely time to kiss her goodnight!

Mr. B.: Sometimes she lived some distance away and you invariably walked because you were not allowed to go in automobiles or taxis, so you walked. The brick sidewalks of Annapolis are very rough and uneven and the poor girl with her high heels usually was having a tough time to try to keep up as you were racing to get back in time. You often had barely enough time to get back, and you were checked in. You had to report in at the rotunda in Bancroft Hall. There would be two midshipmen sitting there, and the duty officer in the office nearby, and you'd have to check your name off the hop list. If you were late, you got demerits or a reprimand, unless there was some unforeseen cause for it.

Leave became a little more liberal as you got more senior. That is, leave to go outside of Annapolis, but it was still very much circumscribed compared to what it is today. You usually had one night on the town after an Army-Navy game and that was generally played in New York at that time. That was always looked forward to.

Q: That was a night on the town in New York City?

Mr. B.: Yes. I'm trying to think when we had to report back. We got back on the train to come back to Annapolis and if I'm not mistaken it was at some very early hour in the morning.

Q: No doubt!

Mr. B.: For many midshipmen, of course, it would have been the first visit to New York, which was a very exciting thing. The old Polo Grounds was invariably the scene of the football game. The midshipmen would parade in and West Point would parade in. It was the big game of the year, not only for the Army and Navy but also for college football. I remember at that time, I think Joe Worthington was with me, Texas Guinan and Will Rogers were great entertainers and they were playing in some night club in New York, and Joe and I with others went to see them. Of course, they played up to the midshipmen. They knew there were a lot of midshipmen there. Will Rogers was twirling his lariat and cracking jokes about the Army, and Texas Guinan was doing her usual stuff. We felt we were very much men about town!

Q: It was worth waiting all those years for!

Mr. B.: It was indeed. Annapolis itself, of course, has

changed fundamentally. It was a small village then and had none of what is now the yacht basin or the Hilton Inn. It was nothing but an undeveloped harbor. In fact, that sea wall that the Naval Academy has built to extend its land was much farther inboard than it is now. There were no high-rise buildings of any sort or modern apartment buildings. Carvel Hall was still existing, with its old retainer who used to wear the admiral's stripes on his sleeves. That old darkie who had been there for so many years and knew all the admirals by name - by first name.

The town itself was a quiet, sleepy little old town. The sidewalks were just about the same as they are now, but there were no modern shops. There were a few of the shops that catered to midshipmen like, Bailey, Banks, and Biddle, which is still in Philadelphia and in existence there I think - class rings and clothing. One or two others. This is what Admiral Wilson was writing about in his letter to my father. In those days when you graduated from the Naval Academy you were required to have a full set of uniforms, including all these dress uniforms, a boat cape, which I still have, made of broadcloth, a big velvet collar. I tried to give it to my wife for an opera cloak but it was much too heavy. She couldn't wear it. Also a tail coat, the old frock coat, you had to have a fore and after hat, a dress sword and belt, evening dress, two suits of blues and the white uniforms and all the rest.

You couldn't wear a midshipman's uniform because they

were the tight, high-collar things in those days, which officers had abandoned and had gone to the other. The result was that midshipmen would contract for these uniforms before they graduated and they would go into debt to get them, many of them, because they cost quite a lot. When you added it all up it was a very major element in cost, especially the gold braid. You took great pride in the gold braid if you got the French gold braid. That didn't tarnish so easily. So you spent a lot of money on these things and that was one of the reasons, I think, that they abolished a lot of these dress uniforms and quite rightly. They were old fashioned. I only wore them on two or three occasions in my whole life.

The town itself had very little to offer in the way of entertainment. There were a few restaurants there on King George Street. There's an inn next to the Paca House and we used to call it in those days the Blue Lantern. It's changed hands any number of times. It's always failed, I think, but in my days it used to be a nice place to take a girl for a quiet supper by candlelight.

Q: Yes, it was very dark in there!

Mr. B.: Now, it's turned into a hippie joint and various other things, I think. There were one or two other places that you could go, but no particularly distinguished eating place. Carvel Hall was the sort of center of the social life of the midshipmen. There were no inns, no motels outside of town or around town. The Maryland Inn was still there, of course. The only other things I recollect now were trips up the Severn occasionally and this usually was reserved for people who went out for crew. I wouldn't say it was necessarily a deliberate reservation but they managed to wangle it. We rowed way up the Severn. Training practices for crews frequently took us twelve miles a day or longer. We'd go up to Round Bay, off the head of the Severn, and then row back and race part of the way, often against the varsity. There were one or two canoes down at the boathouse. It wasn't the present boathouse, it was on the other side of Spa Creek. The old boathouse was on the Academy side of Spa Creek and was a much more ramshackle affair, but at least it produced under Glendon this world champion crew and some other good crews.

There were a couple of canoes down there. I don't know who they belonged to, but occasionally when we had an afternoon off we'd try to paddle those up the Severn. I remember on one occasion when a man named Frank Andrews, who has since died, I think he resigned from the Academy or from the Navy and had a successful civilian career in Chicago, a very nice guy, and I decided to try to paddle way up the Severn to see a girl that I knew, called Margaret Henry - the Henry family are pretty well known about Annapolis. I'd known her in Baltimore and we thought we'd be able to get up there and back in time. We found quickly, before we got half-way, we'd never make it so we turned around and started back and just about under the railroad bridge we turned over. It got choppy, you see, and the canoe filled with water and we clung to it for a while but we turned it over. Then a motor boat came along and helped us and we got back, both of us dripping wet. I remember jogging back through the yard, dripping wet trying to avoid duty officers and others, into my room to get changed in time for formation.

I think that was first-class year. I wouldn't have dared do that at any other time.

Those are about the things that I recall now.

Baldwin #2 - 98

Interview No. 2 with Mr. Hanson W. Baldwin

Place: His home in Roxbury, Connecticut

Date: St. Patrick's Day, March 17, 1975

Subject: Biography

By: John T. Mason, Jr.

Q: Sir, it's very nice indeed to see you on this pre-spring morning.

I think you have more recollections of your days at the Academy during the period of 1920 to 1924, more recollections that you'd like to add at this time?

Mr. B.: Yes, I thought of a number of points which it seemed to me in the interests of history ought to be brought up.

First, a minor point, I do not remember whether or not in the previous interview when I was talking about C. Alfonso Smith, the head of the Department of English at the Naval Academy I used the quote that he is reported to have sent in his final message to the midshipmen when he was dying. I do not remember the exact year he died, but my recollection is that it was sometime toward the end of plebe year or during youngster year. He was an inspirational teacher, as I said, and very much beloved by the midshipmen. He was one of the few who were inspirational teachers, and he is supposed to have sent a final message to the midshipmen from his deathbed and said in a rather dramatic way, which really affected all of us, especially those who were younger:

"I greet the unknown with a cheer."

That was quite a dramatic saying which we all remembered. I think the Class of '24 still remembers that.

Q: I would think so!

Mr. B.: As to the Naval Academy itself in those days it seems to me that I left out two or three or four important points.

There was no honor system, as it's now known. The Academy was deficient in that respect. West Point had an honor system, the same old traditional one. The Naval Academy had none, not even a semblance of one. That wasn't started until long after we graduated. However, I was never aware of any cheating. There may have been some, but I was never aware of it.

Other vices of midshipmen: Liquor - remember, this was the prohibition era, and I've already mentioned the excesses that occurred during our summer cruises, particularly to Lisbon. There may have been a lot of liquor-drinking but I think most of it was probably outside the Academy walls. Again I wasn't too aware of it, partially because I didn't drink, neither did Joe, my roommate for three years. Undoubtedly there was some liquor drunk inside the Academy and undoubtedly there was some intoxication, but it wasn't very obvious.

Again undoubtedly there were some pretty obnoxious places in Annapolis but due to the restrictions and the fact that you didn't have anywhere near as much liberty as you have nowadays, I doubt if the midshipmen indulged in them too much. There was a rather juvenile, typical adolescent approach to sex. You will notice in some Lucky Bags underneath some pictures the cognomen "Pink N," and you're probably aware that it's supposed to have meant that the midshipmen had sexual relations inside the walls of the Academy, which usually was a boast and not a fact. That was the kind of thing that they indulged in.

Q: More wishful thinking than anything else?

Mr. B.: I would think so. There were more opportunities for this on the summer cruises, of course, and when they got to foreign ports I guess a good many of them probably did visit houses of ill repute and so on.

There was a byproduct of this, which was one of the unpleasant aspects of plebe year. In hazing, at a table in the mess hall and elsewhere, upper classmen would ask plebes all kinds of questions, most of them, unlike the present day, having nothing to do with professional advancement. Some of the questions were professionally apt. You'd have to know all the actual ropes aboard ship, not lines, but ropes, and you'd have to know the number of masts and the names of the masts in a seven-masted schooner. But many of them would be, "How many days to the Army and Navy game?" "How many days, hours and minutes to Christmas?" and so on.

Q: Tedious little details.

Mr. B.: One of the questions that would often be asked was, "tell me about your first experience," and by that they meant your first sexual experience. This used to rile some people who had a perfect right to refuse to answer and some people did, or you said you'd never had any and that made them laugh at you, something like that.

I suppose the most obvious, I was going to say "vice," (it wasn't a vice but habit, maybe, at the Naval Academy while I was there) was smoking. Smoking was prohibited and no one was supposed to smoke in Bancroft Hall. So the upperclassmen who smoked or wanted to smoke or wanted to just because it was forbidden were always trying to find what they called a "tendency." A tendency was a draft that would take the smoke out of the window and out of the room so that the duty officer coming into the room wouldn't detect it. Certain rooms had better "tendencies" than others. They would open the window a crack at the top and at the bottom so there wouldn't be too much obvious smoke coming out, and a group of them would congregate there and smoke. Finding a tendency was one of the preoccupations of these bad boys who were smoking!

Baldwin #2 - 102

Q: Did Smoke Park exist as such?

Mr. B.: No, there was no Smoke Park and there was no place in Bancroft Hall where you could smoke. It was just against the regulations.

There are two other things that I think should be mentioned. There were no Negroes in the Naval Academy in that day whatever, and I think if any had come he would have met a rather violent reception. There was a myth that one had attended before my class entered the Naval Academy and that he had ended up on a can buoy in the Severn in the middle of the winter. This was a myth, I'm sure, but it was a myth that was widely believed by the midshipmen.

Mr. B.: None whatsoever. There had been none so far as I know, except perhaps in the Civil War; there had been no colored officers in the Navy. This is my own recollection, but not checked by any records. There had been colored enlisted men. On the summer cruises we would encounter down in the firerooms some good old petty officers, Negro petty officers, who had enlisted and reenlisted and been in for years, and they were highly respected. There were not many. That was the key to their ability to get along. If there were anywhere near as many as there are aboard an aircraft carrier today, for instance, they wouldn't have gotten along. There were few; they knew their business, they were professionally competent, and they were respected by their white shipmates. There was no trouble that I was ever aware of.

There was a definite anti-Negro bias. There was also an anti-Semitic bias.

Q: Were there Jewish lads there?

Mr. B.: I was coming to that. There were some. Of course, that was in the days of Rickover. Rickover was there but I didn't know him, and I was never aware that Rickover was in the Naval Academy until long after he graduated. Strangely enough, when he was a captain he invoked the anti-Semitic bias, as you know, to get promoted. He started this business about anti-Semitism in a speech to a Jewish club in Pittsburgh, at least so I am told. Rickover is a lot like J. Edgar Hoover. He has been able to strike all the notes of public relations and he cozies up to the congressmen and the press. He never misses a trick.

Whenever a new nuclear submarine did anything -- cruised under Arctic ice, went to the North Pole, circumnavigated the world, or just simply went on its first trials or shakedowns -- a whole flood of cachets, or special envelopes, postmarked "Aboard So-and-So, North Pole (or what not), would be mailed, each with a small message from Rickover. Recipients were all Congressmen, many members of the Press, officials in government and anyone else to whom Rickover wished to send a message. Rickover was not above bluster and bluff; he sometimes

Baldwin #2 - 104

tried to frighten green reporters with threats (as old as journalism) that he would complain to their publishers, if their stories were not favorable. He even tried to have the last word -- or an important say -- in selecting the commanding officer of the first British nuclear-powered submarine. He was a consumate political propagandist, a kind of J. Edgar Hoover type in uniform -- but at the same time he was a good bit more than that. He was a good engineer; he knew how to pick, on the whole, good men to work for him; he knew the Washington bureaucracy and how to use power, and he had that rare sense, that gift, of being able to translate a technological fact into a naval operational advantage. He was not, in the full technical sense of the term, "the father of the nuclear submarine", but he deserves great credit for understanding its potentialities and for pushing it through to successful conclusion.

Q: He bears a Christian label now, does he not? He claims to be an Episcopalian.

Mr. B.: I guess he does. One of the most disgusting and disgraceful anti-Semitic things occurred while I was at the Academy, though it had nothing to to with Rickover. I don't know whether you've ever seen this, but this is a Jew who graduated in the class of 1922, Leonard Kaplan - and this is the Lucky Bag for that year and you'll note there's a perforated page. Instead of having his roommate's photo opposite him, as was customary, they have this, a disgusting caricature and biography. That created quite a sensation. I might point out, and should point out, that the editor of the Lucky Bag that year was a man named Olmstead, who graduated Number One in his class. Kaplan graduated Number Two, and there was a great rivalry between Olmstead and Kaplan. Olmstead had a brother at West Point at the same time who later went on to a fairly successful career.

Apparently without the knowledge of the officer-in-charge of the Lucky Bag or of anyone else - apparently, I say, because I didn't have anything to do with the Lucky Bag, Olmstead had this perforated page inserted in the 1922 Lucky Bag. Nothing was ever done as far as I know to Olmstead, but he died the next year, after he graduated from the Naval Academy. It ruined his reputation among the midshipmen. Most midshipmen didn't particularly care about Kaplan or know him; I didn't know him, and many midshipmen weren't particularly fond of Jews, but, on the other hand, they weren't violently anti-Semitic and they thought this was just poor, awful, damned dirty pool.

Q: It was certainly an affront, wasn't it?

Mr. B.: It was a real affront, and I'll give Kaplan credit. He stayed on in the Navy and rose to the rank of Captain. He went into the Construction Corps, I think, and retired after World War II. I saw him over at the Brooklyn Navy

Yard years later when he was on duty there. I didn't know him when he was a midshipman. I just thought of this and if you really read this sketch, it is one of the most disgraceful things that ever occurred. It was largely done by that one man, Olmstead, I believe (although I have no proof of this), and as far as I know the Academy authorities didn't catch up with this until after it was done.

I wanted to mention those two things that were part of the Naval Academy at that time. I think that covers the points I missed about the Naval Academy.

Q: All right, Sir. That's a really rounded picture of the Academy you've given me in that period. It will be immensely valuable to the archivist at the Naval Academy when they come to write the history.

Mr. B.: He's undoubtedly aware of that Lucky Bag 1922. The name of the man is Leonard Kaplan and the editor was Olmstead. The curious tragedy of it, as I say, is that Olmstead died, I think from natural causes, about a year after graduation, but his brother at West Point went on in an Army career. I don't know how long he stayed in but I think he had the rank of brigadier general when he retired.

Q: There's one other thing I wanted to ask about and that is the existence of the Reina Mercedes and the punishments.

Mr. B.: Well, the Reina Mercedes had been there for a large number of years before I arrived. I don't know how long. She was moored permanently in the Severn, along with the guard ship for the mess attendants in Bancroft Hall. The Reina Mercedes was used for extraordinary punishment for very bad midshipmen. They were transferred there from Bancroft Hall when they had really infringed very seriously. This didn't happen to me when I got my 100 demerits. It had to be for something I guess a little bit more heinous. I don't know why, but some of my classmates were subsequently assigned to the Reina Mercedes, and this may have been because of drinking or perhaps going over the wall, "frenching," as it was called. The Reina Mercedes was a topic of conversation among the midshipmen and was always viewed as a kind of jail for the young gentlemen. It was also a sort of a joke in a way. I don't know what the routine in the Reina was. I think they were required to attend classes but they had a very spartan life and didn't get very good food. It was a part of the Naval Academy scene, and that's about all I remember about it. I never had the misfortune to be assigned to it and I don't think I ever set foot on its decks.

Q: I did. I went there to visit one time. That's why I recall it so vividly.

Mr. B.: A couple of final points about the old Naval Academy before we leave it to the past.

The curriculum, as I have said, was rigid and required; there were no electives (except Spanish or French). Mathematics was the basis of the entire course, and 2½ years of mathematics, from relatively simple college freshmen "Math" to differential equations and the higher forms of mathematics, was an immutable part of academic life. "Math" loomed so large in our lives that when the 2½ years were over, the middle of second class year, there was a traditional ceremony, called "The Burial of Math." The authorities permitted it; it had long been a tradition when I was there. At the time of the last Math recitation, the second classmen would get dressed up in fantastic costumes of any sort. West Point blouses, or dress hats, won from cadets by midshipmen in bets over the Army-Navy game, were mixed with uniform blues, or white works or what-not. All of the Math books we had studied, or as many as we could carry, plus slide rules and what not, would be piled high, and we would solemnly go to class, dressed like Cox's army. We recited and got marked, but not quite as usual, I guess. That was about all there was to it, except somehow we got rid of the Math books, or most of them afterwards, either by sale, or we threw them away. It was just a way of letting off steam, of expressing joy in "Crabtown", over the end of the most strenuous course in the curriculum.

A word or two about the hops, or dances. They were far more structured and formal than they are now; the orchestras were nothing to boast about, mostly they played Fox Trots and Waltzes. There was a very small stag line; usually very little cutting-in. There were formal Hop-Cards, often elaborately decorated with signal flags, etc., and these were given to the girls and the names of every man she was to dance with were printed opposite the number of the dance. The signal flag on the Hop Card, next to the number, indicated where she was to meet her partner, the flags used to be hung from the railing of the balcony around Dahlgren Hall.

A few Crabtown girls used to come to most of the hops; some were older than the midshipmen who escorted them, and some supposedly had a reputation of having tried but failed to snare midshipmen from many past classes. Once, a classmate of mine, far more sophisticated and daring than I, was - escorted one of these experienced ladies, and I had a dance with her. I was then very shy and, at least as far as women were concerned, totally unsophisticated; I was pretrified. I was even more so when I discovered she was wearing a necklace made up of class pins, dating back for quite a few years.

Incidentally, we used to wear at all the formal evening hops, not, of course, at the occasional and few "Tea Fights" in the afternoon, the old "Monkey Jacket" or dress uniform, bound with leather, tight-fitting, two rows of brass buttons down the front, which the girls used to complain about. They hurt, they said, but, nevertheless, many of them tried to snip a button or two off as souvenirs.

The Army-Navy games were tremendous occasions, particularly because they were then played in New York, and the regiment would march out to the Washington, Baltimore and Annapolis Railroad station near State Circle, near where the State Office Building now is, at about 4 or 5 a.m.; before dawn, to board B and O or Pennsylvania trains for New York. We marched informally, singing and every other step shouting "Beat Army!" It used to be the fashion for die-hard Navy rooters to get out of their beds, put on bathrobes, and sometimes light flares and put out placards as the midshipmen marched by. I remember vividly that Professor Cusacks, I think he taught French at the Academy -- and his two beautiful daughters, who then lived in what is now Alumni House, were always on hand on their front lawn, cheering the midshipmen on. We used to take box luncheons on the train, and invariably when we passed through Baltimore, the custom was to pull the shades down, much to my disgust, since I was from Baltimore. This custom started, I think, because Navy had once lost by some huge score to Army in Baltimore.

The Army-Navy game nearly always evoked bets between misdhipmen and cadets, sometimes, as in my case, between two friends who had gone to the same high schools before entering the service academies. It used to be particularly smart to bet articles of uniform; particularly desirable was the West Point bathrobe. I never won one of those but I did get from my friend, Randall Sollenberger, a West

Point dress hat, for which I had no earthly use, and, I think, something else. In my time at the Academy, we hauled in a good bit; for my class experienced two victories over Army, one defeat, and one tie.

Incidentally, I forgot to mention that part of the course of instruction in those days was dancing. We were exposed to it, I think, in Plebe Year, and I believe in Memorial Hall, or the space just under it. The "professor" was much ridiculed, and I think, found it difficult to keep order; we danced with each other; most of us were quite deficient in the ballroom dancing of those days. The instructor had a piano player, and he would beat out time by hand and voice, saying, "One, two, three, cut; Boom, drip, drip; Boom, drip drip . . . "

Finally, I think I should stress, that despite all the criticisms I have expressed of the old Academy; its narrowness and its limitations, I believe it did, on the whole, a superb job, in some ways superior to the job being done today. It did shape character; it did teach concentration and self-control; it helped to teach leadership, and above all it inculcated tradition, spirit, morale, patriotism, call it what you will, and created a band of brothers, with a common dedication. I owe much, indeed, to my Academy training.

Q: Now, tell me about your graduation and the first summer.

Mr. B.: My memories of graduation are rather vague, except for throwing our caps in the air and then getting the ensign's stripes pinned on by my mother, I guess, and probably my sister. I do know I took about three girls to the Naval Academy June Week. I thought there was safety in numbers, and Joe used to kid me about that, largely because I thought I was keeping secret from each of the girls the fact that I was asking another one to come at another time. They were all old friends in Baltimore where I lived and they all exchanged data beforehand! So when one of them would leave, she'd say, "Have a good time with so and so," much to my consternation.

Q: Incidentally, was Kay on the scene then?

Mr. B.: Oh, no. Joe didn't even meet Kay as far as I know until about the time his brother was married. That was much later on and then, although Joe met her very early in his career, they didn't decide to get married till during World War II, when Joe was up at Newport. Joe used to drag one sister and I dragged another (but this was another pair of sisters - from Baltimore) at one time. Neither one of us was - I've forgotten the midshipman expression for it, meaning women-lovers. We didn't have time for it. I prided myself on being what I called a "red mike," which is a woman-hater, but actually I wasn't!

In any case, after graduation and a month's leave, we were assigned first to the Washington Navy Yard, which was then called the Washington Gun Factory. Also at the Washington Navy Yard, in addition to the gun factory, there was the optical shop and the range-finder shop. They had a round-robin course of instruction there which showed you how guns were made and at the same time exposed you to range-finders, stadimeters, and all the optical instruments then in use. It was supposed to teach you their principles.

After a certain amount of time there, you were then transferred to Indian Head, Maryland, where the guns were proven - I mean to Dahlgren, Maryland, where the guns were proven, and then to Indian Head, where the powder was made.

Q: This was an ordnance summer, then, wasn't it?

Mr. B.: It was an ordnance summer, and it was only for those new ensigns whose ships were not available. There were not too many of us, only those of us assigned to the Texas, and perhaps one or two other ships on the midshipmen's cruise. Others who were assigned to the West Coast reported to their ships immediately.

It was an interesting summer but you didn't have to work very hard.

Q: Did it prove to be valuable?

Mr. B.: Professionally? Of very limited value, I would think. It exposed us to some things that we hadn't seen before, but it was a very brief sort of survey course and it didn't require very much work, practically none. You were told things, lectured to. My memories of it are going to Washington, I commuted from Baltimore, because I lived in Baltimore, and going to Washington on the train and then getting on a streetcar to get down near the Washington Navy Yard, and then walking. I remember getting off the streetcar in all my white glory on a hot Washington day and a car came along; the driver didn't stop in time, and knocked me off my feet and got me all dirty! I was very disgusted but my dignity was hurt much more than my person.

We used the model basin in the Washington Navy Yard off hours for a swimming pool, and it was delightful because . . .

Q: That later became the Taylor Model Basin?

Mr. B.: No, the Taylor Model Basin was moved out to

Cardarock, Maryland. The one in the Navy Yard, as far as I know, was used after the development at Carderock only for minor experimental purposes. It was the only model basin the Navy had in those days. It wasn't nearly big enough for the modern ships then about to be built, or the new sophisticated tests that would have to be made, but it was about 18 feet deep and it was long and it was in a cool, shadowy place, and Washington was infernally hot in the summer and there was no air-conditioning in those days.

Q: You use the past tense!

Mr. B.: Yes. However, you can get out of the heat now with air-conditioning. You couldn't then. So when we got permission to use the model basin pool after working hours, when they had finished with it, to take a swim, this was one of the delights of the Washington summer.

At Dahlgren we discovered, I guess all of us, for the first time how parochial and small a sort of shut-in naval station can be. My chief recollections of it are that I met a beautiful young lady who was an in-law of one of the officers there, one whom you probably knew, Ballentine, who later became a vice admiral.

Q: Oh, Bally I knew very well, yes.

Mr. B.: Well, Bally married a Shield from Yorktown, and Letty Shield, her sister, was visiting them. Bally was then a lieutenant commander, I think. A very nice guy, and Letty was a lovely and delightful girl and I became enamored of her. We used to go swimming. I remember Letty claiming she could swim so well and we started to swim out to some buoy. It developed she couldn't swim so well. She got to the buoy but she couldn't get back. I was in a box because I couldn't tow her. We finally got a boat or something. I thought I was going to get unshirted hell for that but fortunately Bally and Letty's sister gave her the hell!

Anyway, I discovered that when I made a date with Letty the telephone operator would listen in and my classmates would say, "I hear you've got a date tonight." They knew it before I knew it.

Q: That's living in the country!

Mr. B.: Yes. At the Naval Proving Ground we had an observation party. We would observe the firings. Lieutenant Sauer was the officer in charge. The mess statement for meals ashore was $2.75 for Hanson Baldwin and the meals on the sub-chaser 192 were 35 cents. My total charge for meals for an observation party for one day was $3.10. Those days are gone forever!

We went through Indian Head from Dahlgren. There, I think I've already mentioned the escapade of my classmate, the same one who shot me on the rifle range at Annapolis, Indian Head again was a sort of a visual experience, which means you had very little work and I don't think most of us learned very much from it. We found out how powder was made and some of the properties of it and so on.

Sometime in September - and the exact date I don't remember - I reported to the Texas, which had just returned to the Chesapeake Bay area from a midshipmen's cruise in Europe. We were ordered to report at Annapolis, but as I remember she had left Annapolis. The midshipmen had disembarked and she had gone back down to Hampton Roads, and so we had to report down there. I recall that we remembered strictly the protocol of reporting aboard ship for the first time.

We came aboard - she was out at one of the piers at the naval base. In those days there were very few piers and the naval base was very small. We saw that there were barges of coal alongside and we didn't like that sign. In any case, we went aboard and were assigned to temporary staterooms and we got dressed up in our white uniforms and put on our swords and gloves and reported to the executive officer. I think we reported first to the gunnery officer, who was acting as exec, Miles P. Refo. He was only acting for that day. He was a very sardonic but a very nice guy. He took one look at us and said:

"What in the goddam hell have you got all that silly stuff on for? Take it off and get over the side into the coal barges and help coal ship."

We came in and saluted and said we'd like to report to the captain and that was our greeting!

So we got into dungarees –

Q: You never did get to the captain!

Mr. B.: Not then, no. We got over the side and my chief recollection of that was getting knocked down by a coal bag. It could have been serious because these things weighed about 200 or 300 pounds when they were filled with coal and they could really knock a man out. They'd hitch them on the end of these long whips and hoist them from the barge. You had to fill the bags with shovels and you had a bunch of people in the barge doing that. I was the ensign in one barge that was helping to fill the bags.

We weathered that, got scrubbed down and cleaned up,

and I think we went over to the Navy yard in Portsmouth for a while. I have an old roster of officers aboard the Texas at that time, and the captain was a really sort of Prussian type who was very dour-looking and tough. His name was I. C. Wettegel. I don't think he ever got beyond captain, and I don't think he should have, but he was effective enough. The commander was Michael. I always remember Miles P. Refo particularly well because he was the head of the Gunnery Department and I was really thrilled and excited that when I went aboard ship I was assigned to the F Division, the fire-control division, which was supposed to be a high compliment. My class standing wouldn't have indicated that I should have been. They usually picked the brightest people for that and I certainly wasn't one of the brightest. I was only barely in the first half of the class. I had as division officer, in charge of the F Division, Ted Wirth, who was one of the finest officers I've ever met. He never unfortunately got beyond captain, but should have.

Ted immediately smoothed the path for everyone who was assigned to him, and I was fortunate, too, in having as one of my fellow officers in the F Division - Bill Sebald. Do you know Bill Sebald?

Q: No, but I know about him.

Mr. B.: Incidentally, sometime you ought to try to talk to him, if you can, because he has had a remarkable career. He was in ONI during World War II. I just had a letter from him. I told him I'd talked to you.

Q: He lives in Florida, doesn't he?

Mr. B.: He lives in Naples. He has already taped a great deal for a study of the State Department. He was MacArthur's first ambassador and then went on to be ambassador to Burma and Australia. He said he had done a lot of taping for the State Department, oral interviews, I think for Princeton, but I'm not sure.

Q: He was with the Dulles regime?

Mr. B.: That's right, but he has or should have a lot of knowledge of the Navy because he ended up, after being transferred out of ONI into running the intelligence section for Admiral King during the war in Washington. He was a Japanese-language student. His early days in the Navy, if he can remember them - he said his memory wasn't very good, would be interesting.

Anyway, Bill Sebald was in the Fire-Control Division

and I was assigned to help run the Ford range keeper. And another classmate of mine, Fred Bell, who was much brighter than I, was in the F Division. We had a group of twenty-four ensigns aboard the Texas, quite a large number, who were on the whole very compatible, and we had a junior officers' mess which was separate and distinct from the wardroom in those days.

Q: That tended to offset the coaling, did it not!

Mr. B.: Oh, yes. Well, we didn't mind the coaling too much after we got used to it. I rather got a challenge out of it, as I said before, and keeping the steam up in the boilers.

We lived under what would be considered primitive circumstances, which might induce a mutiny today, but Joe Worthington and Dick Johnson, R. F. J. Johnson, Jr., who's a captain, retired, and I, lived in a three-man stateroom on the Texas which had canvas-bottomed bunks with rope along steel frames. I remember Dick slept in the bottom bunk and I was in the middle and Joe was on top. Dick used to be able to sleep no matter where and we always kidded him about that. His bunk was half-unlashed so he was on the deck most of the time but he never knew the difference, we said!

Joe was in a turret division I think and Dick was in the Engineering Division. Dick's speciality was always engineering.

We had a very compatible group and we started to make friends in Portsmouth. The JO mess in those days was exceedingly good, I think, warm, and it induced a group-consciousness which you don't get as much nowadays. This was helped later on - I'm taking this a little bit out of context because I don't remember dates, but it was helped later on by the steward we had. The captain, when we came aboard, I. C. Wettengel, had a Chinese steward, a carryover from the old China Station - they allowed a certain number of these people to enlist and stay in the Navy, and this man had become a chief steward. His name was Tip. That's all we knew him by, Tip, and he was a really superb cook at his best and a wonderful steward. He had one failing. Every once in a while he'd go on a bender. It wouldn't be very often, but it would happen occasionally - and this was very unusual for a Chinese because most Chinese don't do this.

Q: They don't drink alcohol.

Mr. B.: No, but he would really be "out," and he would

show up at any time, anywhere. I remember the thing that really ended his glory as the captain's steward was when the captain was planning a very special party and this party was, I think, in the Portsmouth Navy Yard. He had a lot of guests coming aboard and he told Tip in the morning to go ashore and get some good food and left it up to him to prepare for the dinner.

Tip came back long after the guests had arrived. He had nothing. The captain finally had to send down to the wardroom to get some food. Tip appeared bearing one egg and a broken French ice cream freezer and about two sheets in the wind. So the captain broke him. He had this court-martial and broke him and sent him down to JO mess, which was much to our delight because we never ate so well in our lives.

Incidentally, I came across this man later on, strangely enough, on the destroyer to which I was assigned and we had equally good things to eat and I had the same experience. I had to have him court-martialed, unfortunately.

Anyway, the food that we got from Tip and his - very pleasant personality (when he wasn't drunk and he wasn't drunk that often) added a great deal to our JO mess.

Q: These Chinese in the Navy predated the Filipinos, did they?

Mr. B.: They were an outgrowth of our Yangtze Patrol and the Asiatic Fleet. There were special provisions made for using Chinese stewards on the Asiatic Station, and the Yangtze Patrol, of course, as you know from the book, had Chinese boys on these ships all the time. They did all the dirty work. That wasn't so true of ships that did cruising at sea, but they did have Chinese stewards. I ran across one much later in life, when I was with The New York Times, a Chinese who had been a mess boy for Admiral Ingram out on the China Station. Some of these, a few of them who had served for a very long time, were allowed to enlist and were given a permanent rank in the Navy. There were a number of them in the Navy at that time, not too many. There were more Filipinos, of course, who had a special legacy by law. I don't know what the legal requirements were, but I know Tip was fully and completely enlisted in the Navy, he was a Navy enlisted man. I guess he had become an American citizen.

Q: Were they able to become American citizens at that point?

Mr. B.: Well, as you remember, there were exclusions.

Q: The Exclusion Act of 1924, I think.

Mr. B.: Yes. There were a number of these acts from 1921 on, but Tip would have predated that. He must have been in the Navy when I first knew him on the Texas about eight or ten years because he was not a young chap even then. I think he probably came in sometime maybe in World War I, the latter part of it.

In any case, the Texas was assigned for a while to Portsmouth for, I think, some repairs or upkeep, not for a lengthy period and then, as I recollect it, we went out to sea and did some maneuvering with other battleships in the Atlantic. One of my chief recollections of being a junior officer of the deck was that Wettengel constantly required meticulous attention to station-keeping and he had JOs day and night just on the stadimeter, getting the distance to the ship ahead. The stadimeter is a simple instrument that measures the masthead light down to the waterline and gives you automatically the distance. If you know the height of the masthead light of the ship ahead of you, you can get the exact distance in yards. It's a little hard on the eyes, if you keep on using it. You squint through one eye and turn the screws and get the distance. It's particularly trying at night when you see nothing but the lights and you have to match the masthead light with the stern light. The captain would be asking for distances about once a minute for four hours and you almost became blind!

When Wettengel was on the bridge, it was always "stadimeter reading, stadimeter reading, and hurry it up."

Q: He was very apprehensive, was he?

Mr. B.: I think apprehensive and insistent on proper station-keeping. It was a very important thing in those days. If it was a 250-yard interval, you had to be 250, not 260 or 300, and that meant constantly taking the turns off the engine and putting them on. It was a trial for the officer of the deck and the JO and everyone concerned. What was, of course, more trying was when you were in fog and you were following a buoy. You had to keep right on top of that towing buoy, which was trailed from the ship ahead at a distance of 250 yards. This towing buoy had vanes on it so it would just break the surface of the water and create a white wake which you could see. You were supposed to keep your bow almost on top of that towing buoy, and in a fog you're always afraid the ship ahead may take off turns rapidly and you're going to close up on her, which sometimes happens. You're afraid of collisions, and that was very trying. There was no radar in those days, so you were blind.

I've often wondered how we got in and out of Newport in fog, but we did.

I think our first duty after some of that routine duty along the coast was rather interesting - no, wait a minute, I'm getting out of context here.

There was some battle torpedo practice because I see here as assignment for observers of the battle torpedo practice with the USS Utah, and assigned were Ensign Worthington and others.

Q: The battleships took you to . . . ?

Mr. B.: The Utah did. I'm trying to remember. I think the Texas did too, at the time. But we were assigned to observe for her. We were not firing. That must have been one of the exercises that took place, as I remember it, off the Virginia Capes somewhere. We used to call these things the southern drill grounds, anywhere from the Delaware Capes down to the Virginia Capes well at sea were called the southern drill grounds.

Shortly after that we were all shocked by the radio news we got, which I guess we got while we were still at sea, about the death of a classmate, Henry Clay Drexler. A turret explosion took place in the cruiser Trenton and

I still have that radio press we used to get that told of that explosion. I remember my father wrote an editorial for the Baltimore Sun about Drexler. Drexler tried to get the burning powder out of the turret and was killed in the attempt. There's a tablet in Memorial Hall to him. Drexler was very handsome, not one of the leading members of his class academically, but he was well known. This was our first death after graduation and it affected us all quite a lot.

We were then ordered to rather unusual duty. This was in the period between the Washington Disarmament Conference we had agreed to sink or scrap or destroy a great many battleships and other ships that were then being built, and the Texas was assigned to participate in tests against the hulk of the battleship Washington, which was never completed. The hull had no turret guns in it but the hull was finished and the turrets were in place and so on. She had no power, no steam. The Washington was taken out to the southern drill grounds, as I remember it, just inside the 100-fathom curve, off the Delaware Capes, and anchored and then made a sort of guinea pig for various types of tests.

I notice that Clay Blair in his book about the

submarine war in World War II says that she was sunk by a mine. That isn't strictly true. She was sunk by the 14-inch guns of the Texas ultimately, but she was subject for a period of days to all kinds of tests to investigate her watertight integrity and the strength of her armor and underwater hull. Those were the days, remember, when the Battle of Jutland was being very thoroughly studied.

Q: Yes.

Mr. B.: It was recollected that the Germans were the first to introduce the concept of damage control, and they had made quite a fettish of this and saved a lot of their ships as a result. We were commencing to become very interested in damage control. In fact, I think a damage control officer had been assigned in the Texas at that time.

So the Washington was to serve as a guinea pig for simulated torpedo explosions, simulated mine explosions. There were actual charges detonated underwater close to her, but they were deliberately placed within certain distances by spars or other means rather than firing torpedoes at her. They wanted to see the exact effects of a torpedo explosion or a mine explosion within certain distances, and at certain places, and they were put at different positions around her hull.

As I understood it, though I never got aboard, she did not have watertight integrity because some of her watertight doors and hatches had not been fitted or were deliberately left open. I never knew which.

I was in the fire-control division and running the Ford range-keeper. We fired some shells at her at different ranges at first, and she still survived. Then a very heavy storm came up. She was anchored and we were anchored. I think we steamed to our anchor. She was making very heavy weather of it. She was moored with, I guess, two or three anchors. You could see the waves breaking over her, I remember particularly at night. We kept the searchlights trained on her at night because people thought she was going to sink after a lot of punishment. It took us almost a week to do all these things - over a week. She didn't sink and then the next morning we were told to finish her off with our 14-inch battery.

I was running the plot on the Ford range-keeper down in the fire-control room, way down in the bowels of the ship, when we did this and I remember the word over the telephone that she was sinking and to stop plotting. So I did, and we all went topside and she was obviously settling. The bugler sounded Taps and, here, in this rather stormy sea she rolled slowly and settled under the water. A lot of us almost cried. Here was an unborn ship going down.

Q: General Billy Mitchell wasn't involved in this, was he?

Mr. B.: Oh, no, he didn't have anything to do with this. This was strictly a Navy test and it was secret. I see here a notice from Captain Wettengel saying the tests to be conducted on battleship No. 47 are of a strictly confidential nature and the officers and men of the Texas are warned not to disseminate any information either by word of mouth or letter concerning the tests on the above battleship or any details thereof.

Q: Was there anything of particular merit learned from this?

Mr. B.: I can't answer that. I never knew. They did not disseminate anything to the Texas or, as far as I know, to the Navy, but I imagine that the results were incorporated in future building programs. You see, we didn't build any more battleships until just before World War II, so that was a long time afterwards, and we had had other tests since then. This was, I think, chiefly valuable from the point of view of vertical armor and also underwater vulnerability.

Again, you remember, that Jutland showed that plunging shells fired from a long distance and coming in at a diagonal often did the maximum damage. That's what happened with the

Lion and the various British battle cruisers. This lesson was incorporated later in the Texas. I was coming to that in a minute, but as far as the Washington tests are concerned, I never knew the specifics of what was learned. Every time they made a test, the Board of Observers, who were high-ranking ordnance and construction people from Washington who were based on the Texas, would leave the Texas and go over in small boats to the Washington, get aboard and examine her and see what had happened. Of course, they couldn't do this at the very last when we were sinking her but they did up until that time.

We finished that, as I recall, in late November; this notice is dated the 20th of November and I don't think we started the tests till two or three days after that. I think I missed the Army and Navy game as a result. Then we returned to Norfolk, as I recall it, and I was then ordered along with Ensign William J. Sebald to the Ford Range-Keeper School in Long Island City for a two weeks' course of instruction. This was the firm that built the Navy's fire-control instruments in those days, and it was a two-week interval with my uncle in New York while I was doing it. Bill says he barely remembers it, too. I mentioned this to him because I found his name on the orders - Bill Sebald. He also said, which delighted me because he's a much brighter chap than I am, that he had earlier attended a range-keeper course and had sketched and described the thing many times but it was always a mystery to him! It is to me, too!

But somehow we managed to keep the thing working.

I believe that the routine after that in the Texas was that we went after Christmas, almost immediately after Christmas (I think we had some Christmas leave and we spent that around the Norfolk Navy Yard) - I think we headed south to Guantanamo. That was the usual routine for battleships. In fact, many of the ships of the Atlantic Fleet did that in those days, they would go down to Gitmo and base there and stay there a good part of the winter for various kinds of firing, antiaircraft, very primitive antiaircraft, and long-range battle practice and short-range battle practice, and all sorts of drills of one sort or another.

Q: What was the status of Guantanamo at that time? How elaborate was the base?

Mr. B.: It was primitive, very, very simple, and much more charming than it is now simply because of that fact, and there was a very good relationship with the Cubans.

We spent a lot of time in Guantanamo and there was absolutely nothing to do. The routine for the young ensigns often was to get their heads shaved when they went to Guantanamo. It was so hot and you could practically never sleep below the steel decks, so we'd all try to bring our mattresses up on deck when we could to get a breath of air. We were swimming a great deal and also we had to use a certain amount of salt water. The fresh-water supply was not plentiful. So we often got our heads shaved. This was the thing to do, and we'd be bald as an egg for a while. Then our hair would grow out in a sort of a fuzzy outcrop, and that signified that we were veterans of Guantanamo.

There were a couple of bad concrete tennis courts and a literally open little officers' club - or more properly, shack, up on a bluff, not far from where the fleet landing now is. Then there were rifle ranges and we'd use those quite a lot. We took the ship's company ashore. In those days it was routine for the sailors to be part of a landing force and each officer on board ship - not each officer but many officers, particularly junior officers, were assigned duty as battalion or company commanders of the landing force. The Marines, of course, would be a spearhead, but we'd go through a lot of routine to teach these people how to get into boats, very primitive amphibious doctrine, but it was practice, and a lot of marksmanship. So we spent a lot of time on the extensive rifle range at Guantanamo.

Part of the routine was that the sailors, having no real satisfactory uniforms for foot duty ashore, would boil their white works in coffee. So they dyed them brown and would wear those ashore with leggings. They wore leggings and boots. The business of spending hours and hours on the rifle range was part of the routine in the Guantanamo winter. Guantanamo had at that time and as far as I know may still have a great pile of coal that was kept under water, just dumped in the bay, salt water for preservative, dating back almost to the days of the Spanish-American War. We never used it but it was still there and still preserved.

The recreations were chiefly sports, swimming, and then, of course, the famous Caimanera, which was up the bay.

Q: That was another kind of recreation!

Mr. B.: That was a different kind and then was considered so wicked and so forth that it was off-bounds to most - well, it was off-bounds to all except officers, and usually only to division officers. There were one or two places up there where it was possible to get a good meal. When any officers did go to Caimanera with the captain's permission, there was always a boat officer assigned to the motor boat and the motor boat would wait until they'd had dinner and then bring them back to the ship. Sometimes there was good reason for that because sometimes the officers would get a little tight!

I was the boat officer on one occasion, which really brought me to fame with my classmates. I didn't drink then at all. I thought I was becoming very literary and I was reading, I don't know, some deep tome, Plutarch's Lives or something, and I was assigned as boat officer for this particular trip where Miles P. Refo was going to Caimanera. While not my division officer, Refo was the Gunnery Officer and hence in charge of the fire-control division, too. He and some other officers, heads of departments, were going up for dinner. I took them in the motor boat and we moored to a very small dock in Caimanera and waited there. I was supposed to see that the boat crew kept in order and didn't sneak ashore. I sat down in the lighted cockpit to read Plutarch's Lives while we waited for Refo and his friends to have dinner. It took quite a long time. I was trying to be very smart and act as a boat officer should. The coxswain reported that Commander Refo was returning to the boat, so I stepped out onto the dock, one foot on the dock and one foot on the motor boat. We prepared to shove off and I had this book with my place marked, put my fingers in it. I got Refo and his companions aboard all right and then I turned to the coxswain to say "Shove off," and I stepped right down into the water! My cap floated off on the tide and my dignity was ruined. I was so astonished I still held onto the book! I was sort of fished out by the coxswain very ignominiously. Refo was almost splitting his gut. I sat huddled against the engine trying to dry out before I got back to the _Texas_. It was quite a long ride, about three-quarters of an hour or so, and I finally ended up crawling up the ladder of the _Texas_ and dripping profusely. My classmates never let me get over that. They said I was drunk and disorderly on duty!

I do remember another occasion though, in which the commander and executive officer played the lead role. He was coming back either from Caimanera or the Red Barn, which was about half-way up to Caimanera, which served liquor and rum in great quantities. I wasn't aboard the boat at the time but I was junior officer of the deck and I heard the Bo'sun call out, "Executive officer returning to the ship, Sir," I saw the motor boat coming back. Then, suddenly, after a considerable interval, Commander Michaels appeared crawling up the gangway, dripping wet and absolutely naked! He'd taken off his clothes and swum back to the ship from the motor boat!

Q: He had indeed been to the Red Barn!

Mr. B.: Yes. Those things I remember most vividly about the sojourns at Guantanamo.

There was one other thing, I think, of note about my days aboard the Texas. We did participate in some fleet maneuvers, as I recollect, but perhaps of more interest still and I don't quite remember when this was, the Texas was assigned to participate in antiaircraft exercises in Naragansett Bay in Newport, Rhode Island, with the Shenandoah, the old lighter-than-air ship.

Q: Oh, yes.

Mr. B.: She was supposed to tow a target and we were supposed to try out the new range-keeping equipment against her. Of course, she towed at such low speed that it would have been considered ludicrous nowadays. My chief recollections about this are humorous, although apparently the tests pleased the Navy Department greatly, I know I have somewhere some sort of a letter commending the Texas for the work it did. We did some actual firing at sea against this towed target and I guess we had some good results, but my chief recollection about this is that in a practice run in Naragansett Bay itself when we were at anchor and the Shenandoah was flying around towing this target, I suddenly discovered, and I think I had been assigned at this time topside to help with the antiaircraft director - I'm not quite sure of this, but I know I was somewhere up above decks - and my chief recollection is suddenly seeing all our AA guns depressed, which just didn't make sense! All the telescopes were training on a very beautiful girl who was skiing behind a motor boat that was towing her around the harbor. It was the President of the Naval War College's daughter who apparently deliberately did this. She would shoot around the Texas as close as she could get.

Q: She knew she was a distraction!

Mr. B.: Oh, she knew she was a distraction. Actually, we got back to business very rapidly.

Q: Would you talk about the status of morale on board the Texas and the Navy as a whole in this period of treaty limitations and so forth? For the young officers the prospect of future careers in the Navy in a time of curtailment?

Mr. B.: I think they were dubious. I think that's shown in part by the resignation rate of my class. Of course, my class was one of the few, and I should have mentioned this on graduation, that was permitted to resign on graduation if they wanted to, and a good many of them did. There were too many officers in the Navy and they didn't need all these young ensigns. In my class and I think for a number of others at that time resignations immediately after graduation were permitted, in fact, somewhat encouraged. I could have resigned at any time I wanted but I didn't actually resign until some years later.

Q: Did this entail a Reserve commission then, when they did resign?

Mr. B.: If they wanted it. They had to apply for it.

Morale on the whole was good. Of course, it would be hard for me to judge it for the Navy as a whole. I don't think the enlisted personnel were nearly as bright, on the whole, or as responsible as they would have been when you were getting a higher-class, better-educated personnel. Many of these people were stayovers from World War I. Some of them were bad. I mentioned that in the cruise to Lisbon and elsewhere. But, on the other hand, there were some very fine Navy petty officers. I remembers some of them vividly in the Texas. A man named Rogers, who was a first class petty officer. There were also some young chaps. We were assigned among other things in the fire-control division - and again this is an outgrowth of the Battle of Jutland - a stereopticon range-finder, which the Germans had used in the Battle of Jutland with great success, and we were to try to experiment with this. All of our range-finders were coincidence types. When you brought the two images together in the stereopticon range-finder, if it could be used, it was supposed to be much more accurate. The problem was to find the man or the men who could use it. It entailed considerably longer training. The coincidence type was much easier to use. My division, the F Division, was charged with this job. This went on during the latter part of my stay in the <u>Texas</u> and I really ended up, I guess, with being in charge of this test.

I tried every man in the division and all the officers. I couldn't use the stereopticon range-finder myself. I didn't have the sense of depth that it took. And I couldn't find anybody in the division who could except one kid and he was about sixteen. He'd lied about his age and enlisted from the Tennessee hills. He'd had no education at all but he was naturally bright, and he could use this thing perfectly and get extremely accurate results. We tested the results and we did it to a known range, you see, to find out what readings we'd get with the coincidence type and the stereopticon type. We made reports to the Navy about it. They never did adopt the stereopticon range-finder, I think chiefly because of the difficulty of training and finding the people who could use it. The Germans used it with great success both in World War I and World War II. It supplemented their radar gun-ranging in World War II and had a lot to do, I think, with their extremely accurate gunnery. They were much more accurate than the British.

Q: Does that say something about the superiority of their ratings?

Mr. B.: It certainly said something about the longer period of enlistment. I don't think they were naturally any brighter than our people, but many of our enlisted men, except for those who became petty officers, did not reenlist. They went in for one four-year enlistment then went out again. Later on when the Depression came, of course that changed. You got a higher educated and better qualified group of personnel.

I think the German enlistment was much longer than ours and they had more time to pick and select and train these people, and our training was cursory. It had to be because you got constant changeover.

The only other things I remember about the Texas that might be of interest were that we were called upon to perform a lot of ancillary duties in addition to our regular duties. For instance, I was assigned as assistant in baseball, of which I knew nothing. I'd never played baseball but I had played football and crewed. I did become interested in both of those and I helped with both the Texas crew and the Texas football team. Later, when we were in Portsmouth Navy Yard, a Marine officer and I played on the Texas football team for a long time and had a lot of fun together, Captain Moss. And I was really the editor of the ship's paper called the Texas Steer. That was my second exposure to writing. The first was after we'd sunk the battleship Washington and I wrote a poem about it, for which I got the magnificent amount of five dollars. It was published in Our Navy. It was a god awful poem, it was really the worst poem you could possibly imagine, but I guess it gave me the bug.

Q: There was a literary stirring, however, at this point, was there not?

Mr. B.: I suppose.

We had these ancillary duties and those were to me pleasurable and enjoyable. But another one, which was not so pleasurable, was that you always had to sit as members or recorders on summary court-martials and things of that sort. That was part of the duties of a young ensign. You were not members but you were what was known as recorders, which really meant that you were a combination clerk keeping track of all the paper work and the charges but also a prosecutor.

You were supposed to prosecute these cases. The accused could have a defense counsel if he wanted, but often they didn't just bother with this for a summary court-martial, which was the lowest form of court-martial. There was a board of three officers.

I remember one occasion where I really got a good lesson in how to temper discipline with justice. A chief watertender in the fire room who'd been many years in the Navy and was a fine chief had gotten completely drunk one night and had come back to the ship and smashed the water gauge glasses in the fire room. There was no question that he had done it. He was just on a rampage. He was brought up on charges of deliberately destroying government property and so forth. The court knew this man's record. Miles Refo again was on the court. They were inclined to be merciful to him, instead of breaking him. Apparently he had a pretty good record and I, in my ardent youth, was certain that I had proved all the charges beyond doubt, and I had. There was no question about it that he had done it and I had proved them. They found him not guilty. It taught me a lesson which I needed to learn, and Refo later took the trouble to explain to me why they found him not guilty. They said they didn't want to ruin the man's record; he had a good record and this was a rare offense on his part and so forth.

Q: That type of duty for a young ensign was a part of his training, wasn't it?

Mr. B.: Yes, oh yes.

Q: And salutary, too.

Mr. B.: Yes. When you come out of the Academy you're taught or were taught then that you stick pretty much by the book; you live up to the regulations, and I've always believed that you ought to live up to the regulations if you have them, but they ought to be administered with some sense of justice and understanding.

One of the duties of the junior officer of the deck in port was to make inspections of the ship periodically when the ship was at anchor or alongside the dock. You were supposed to leave the deck, you would report to the officer of the deck and say, "I'd like to make an inspection." You were supposed to do this once or twice every watch, every four hours, and you'd go down the bag alleys. The idea was to see that there was nothing illicit going on, no gambling or drinking or what.

On this particular occasion I went down what they called the bag alleys, big, long, longitudinal compartments on either side of the ship, just inboard of the armor, where the men stowed their hammocks and also their sea bags. The idea of this dates back to Manila Bay, I guess or it dates back to wooden sailing ship days. You put your hammocks and sea bags outboard in order to catch splinters or round shot when they came in the hull! In any case, the sailors would often get dressed for liberty down there. They'd get their bags out and put on their blues. I was going down a bag alley and these two sailors were getting dressed for liberty and they didn't see me coming, and they said, "Who's got the deck?" "Oh, that son of a bitch, Baldwin. Get your hair cut." I often wonder how I would get along today with Zumwalt's haircuts.

I pretended I hadn't heard them and walked on. They looked a little startled.

These were good lessons for a young officer. You learn to temper discipline with justice, and I think all of us gradually learned these vital lessons in leadership. Sorting out who was a really good man who makes a mistake and one who is just a bum and you can't use him at all.

On the whole I think in the Fire-Control Division, the F Division, the men that I was most intimately associated with were quite a high type, but of course, they were hand-picked. They had to be brighter than a lot of the rest of the ship. They got some of the dregs in the fire room . . .

Q: Where you needed bodies and brawn?

Mr. B.: Yes, and they sometimes got some pretty bad ones, too, down there.

I should think generally speaking that the Navy was somewhat more stable in a sense, particularly toward the end of the twenties, when you'd gotten rid of a lot of the people who stayed over from World War I and who were not good and when you still had many of the old type petty officers and when many of the officers decided to stay in regardless of the Washington disarmament conference.

Q: What were the prospects of a career, advancement?

Mr. B.: Among the officers no one was sure. In the enlisted ranks I think they felt that there was a fairly good prospect of getting up to chief, and the idea of a chief in the Navy in those days was attractive. The pension seemed to be good.

Q: We'd entered an era of everlasting peace after World War I!

Mr. B.: I'm trying to think back to think how we felt about this. I don't think most of us felt that it would be everlasting peace. I also think that many of us were really enjoying just going to sea and enjoying cruising and weren't thinking too much about the future in detailed terms. I think the majority of those who certainly didn't want a naval career, had found out that they didn't want a naval career, found it out either on graduation or very shortly thereafter. Some, like myself, resigned as much as three and a half years later or four or five years later, but I would think the majority had already done that.

So I would think the morale was not bad. It depends so much on the ship you got and the division officer you got. There were some terrible sundowners in the Navy in those days, rigid, rather stupid people and sometimes they could make or break a ship and they could make or break your own division. I was very fortunate in having a really top-notch officer in Ted Wirth and, although Captain Wettengel was a pretty Prussian type, he was, I think, fair. This was part of his personality. He just couldn't unbend, he was that type of a person. We had some fine executive officers, particularly after Michaels left. We had Commander Blakeslee who later became an admiral. He was really highly loved, I think, on the ship. He was a fine man. And Miles Refo who had this sardonic twist to him was nevertheless a fair officer.

Q: He seems to have had a certain amount of compassion, didn't he?

Mr. B.: He did, although you wouldn't guess it to talk to him the first few times. He liked to be sardonic. I remember Joe and I went out to his house at his invitation once. Joe was in a turret and he was therefore under Refo, who had the gunnery department. We were invited out to play bridge. Neither one of us played bridge, we didn't have any use for it. We didn't like it. This was one of these compulsory things because Mrs. Refo asked these young officers and they'd have to come. We trumped our partners' ace and were never asked again! We didn't do it deliberately, either, we just didn't know any better. Joe still laughs at that to this day.

But despite that I think Refo saw some good in us.

So I would think between Tip, the steward, the happy, warm junior officers' mess feeling, a very good division officers and an excellent exec, we had a good ship.

I should have mentioned one other thing. The Texas had served with the British battle squadron in World War I and she had been presented with a British bulldog by Admiral Beatty whom we called Jim Texas, and he was still on the ship. He was the mascot of the ship and he used to alternatively have Marine caps and Navy caps to put on his head and pose for photographs. He was the epitome of the Texas.

The Texas was a good ship. She always had that reputation and when you got into port and the sailors got into a scrap they had a call, "Come on, Texas, wahoo." That was telling all the sailors from blocks around to come join in the scrap! The reputation of the ship was good and that helped greatly. She was also a good shooting ship. We had some fine comments from the Navy about some of the long-range battle practices we carried out. I don't know whether this sort of thing is interesting or not. Here it is, performance of main battery.

Q: Were Es awarded in those days?

Mr. B.: Yes. In the short-range we didn't do so well, but the performance of the Texas was excellent in other practices. Firing battle practice used to be a very elaborate business. We would send observing parties to other ships. We'd have observing parties on our ships. We'd take motion pictures of the fall of shot and we'd have different colored splashes to denote which guns and so on. We took a lot of pride in this.

The latter part of my stay on the Texas . . .

Q: This was for how long a period? It was in January 1926 that you left the Texas to report to the destroyer Breck, and this was the usual procedure, was it not, to go from a battleship to a destroyer?

Mr. B.: Yes, but it was a little different in this case. I might still have been aboard the Texas. In the latter part of 1925, the Texas was ordered into the Portsmouth Navy Yard for what they called modernization. She was to be converted to an oil-burner from coal and she was to have her old cage masts taken off and tripods put on and, above all, she was to get more horizontal armor as a result of the lessons of the plunging fire at the Battle of Jutland. This had been scheduled for some time and they were gradually doing it to some of the older battleships and it came the Texas' turn. When that happened they started to transfer officers.

Ted Wirth, my division officer, was transferred. Others were transferred and gradually I found myself as the F Division officer. I was in charge. Some crew and some officers were kept aboard during the modernization. There really wasn't a place for them to live. The ship was all torn up. The JO mess was gutted because they put another six to eight inches of armor down on the deck of the JO country and this meant, for me, at least, and for a good many others, that you couldn't possibly walk down there without ducking all the time because you hit your head on an overhead beam. The ship was filled with cables. She was torn up completely. There was a mess alongside the dock in the Navy Yard.

Though I enjoyed the responsibilities that accrued to me by virtue of the fact that the senior officers had been transferred, I didn't like just living through all this hubbub and also being alongside of a dock. I wasn't there too long because, as I recollect, it was only a period of about three or four months, maybe a little more than that. Sometime toward the end of that year I was detached and ordered to report to the destroyer Breck.

We had a good time even while we were modernizing, and it was during this period when the Texas was starting her modernization and was in the Portsmouth Navy Yard for a long time that I played with the Texas football team. And with this old Marine captain, Captain Moss, who was a fiery sort of a chap. His ideas of calling signals when he got all worked up in the midst of a football game we'd have a huddle, he'd say, "To hell with the signals. Give me the ball!"

One of the interesting things about this in those days was that the fleet and the services generally made a great deal more of athletics than they do now. The race boat races, I've mentioned these already, were fantastic events and usually held at Guantanamo. The football season was always regarded as a very competitive one and you'd have teams representing the Scouting Fleet, which was really the Atlantic Fleet, and teams representing the Marine Corps play each other in stadiums like Yankee Stadium. The Marine Corps had a tremendous team in those days. Frank Goettge, who was subsequently killed on Guandalcanal, a former University of Washington player, and Liversedge, a great big man. They could beat most college teams of that day.

My recollection is that in preparation - this would have been 1925 - for their season, they - a Marine Corps team was assigned to the Portsmouth Navy Yard. There were barracks there and a small Marine detachment and there was a football field, and they used the Texas team as a sort of tackling dummy. We, of course, couldn't in any way compete with these huge powerhouses, but I remember scrimmaging with them once or twice and just being broken in two. Liversedge and Goettge were merciful to us. They knew they were just practicing.

These people had a great reputation in the service, partly because of the football, but in those day all services, Army - there wasn't any Air Force - and everyone else featured athletics and particularly big football teams, and they collected these players from all over the

the service and assigned them to training camps.

Q: In a way, that was a tremendous asset, was it not, to morale?

Mr. B.: It was to morale. You were asking about morale and athletics was one of the great morale-builders of the old Navy. There's no doubt about it. We had an awful lot of it and a very competitive ship spirit, pride of ship, as far as athletics were concerned.

Q: Wrestling was a feature, wasn't it?

Mr. B.: Not too much wrestling. There was a lot of boxing, but not too much wrestling that I recollect.

We played the New York, for instance, which was our sister ship down at the Norfolk Navy Yard. I distinguished myself by trying to intercept a pass and just deflecting it into the hands of an opponent who scored a touchdown!

Q: You and Spinola!

Mr. B.: We had a lot of fun. The rules were a little different. You were allowed two officers to play on the football team, all the rest had to be enlisted men. I think a race-boat crew had to be, as I recollect it, all enlisted - perhaps one officer. An officer, however, was in charge of each particular sport and he would be entitled to ask sometimes some special privileges for the men who were participating and would go out and practice. You got to a place like Guantanamo and could row for miles up the bay and maybe go ashore and have a beer or something like that, the enlisted men. This was all part of the aura of sports and added to their interest in them. It also created a better officer-man relationship.

Q: Why was it dispensed with, then?

Mr. B.: I think the Navy became too big and too busy. You don't keep enough people long enough on a ship now to develop a ship team. Then again the pulling boats have gone out of the Navy. That was the big race-boat thing. There are no pulling boats now. I suppose you could create them. In addition to that, the idea of hauling football players from all over the service to represent one particular service is frowned upon, for good reason, I guess, because, Number One, it's costly and expensive, it eats up a lot of time, and Number Two, your people are too tied down with a great deal more technology than we ever dreamed of and a great deal more hard work. The Navy today has so many duties it's spread thin. That's the problem. It just really is incredibly thin. We didn't have all those duties. Part of our duty was to show the flag. It was a relatively simple navy.

But there's no doubt that these things added a great deal to morale, improved morale and also helped greatly in officer-enlisted relationships.

Q: You had golf down there?

Mr. B.: They had a golf tournament, usually officers only. Enlisted men didn't play golf in those days. But you had all sorts of sports going on - swimming, boxing, we had fleet boxing championships. The champion boxer in the fleet was usually Something. You had inter-ship competition. I remember one of my first tangles with the Navy in Panama - this was after I had resigned and was covering the fleet maneuver for The Times - and I started reporting the score of the fleet golf tournament. A zealous officer on the staff of the commander in chief said, "That hasn't been released yet!"

Q: That was confidential information!

Mr. B.: He tried to pull that on me. I had a lot of tangles in that way from time to time. The Navy was very backward in those days about public relations.

Q: It was the silent service!

Mr. B.: Yes. I guess that finishes the Texas pretty well.

Q: Then let's go to the destroyer Breck, shall we?

Mr. B.: I reported aboard the Breck in the winter and I think at first we followed the same routine the battleships did. We went down to Guantanamo for part of the winter of 1926. We were scheduled for thirteen months abroad, a year's duty in what was then called the European Squadron, and the United States at that time kept a squadron of destroyers and a light cruiser as the flagship. They cruised around various ports of Europe, not just the Mediterranean but other ports, too.

Q: No particular base?

Mr. B.: I was coming to that in a moment. They usually based when they needed repairs on British ports. In our case it was Gibraltar chiefly, and Malta, but more Gibraltar. But you were more or less a free agent.

We participated, as I recollect, in 1926 before we went to Europe - we went to Europe in June - in some fleet maneuvers down in Panama on the Pacific side. I immediately found a different sort of a navy when I went to this destroyer.

There were only about four to five officers aboard plus the captain, I think, for a total of six, and it was a small crew. These were four-stacker or four-piper, destroyers built in World War I, only 1,215 tons. (Incidentally, we used to call them four-<u>stackers</u> but I see the modern terminology is four-<u>pipers</u>.) Many of them were hurriedly built. The Cramp boats were notorious for breaking down. She was known as the USS <u>Break</u> as well as the USS <u>Breck</u>. It was difficult to keep the engineering plant going because it developed very simple things like steam leaks and evaporators going out of order and things of that sort.

I was assigned many duties when I first came aboard. First, I had to qualify as a watch-stander and then for officer of the deck watch. I had qualified on the <u>Texas</u> as OOD but actually hadn't had very much responsibility under way, and you really had to qualify in those days. You kept journals which were approved by the officer of the deck and your division officer and others and, at the same time, you had to prove your competence actually under way.

Well, I was assigned as potential officer of the deck on the <u>Breck</u> and then as an assistant communication officer, assistant engineering officer, torpedo officer, commissary officer, and two or three other things. You all had multiple duties and you had to learn as you went along because nobody knew much more about some of these things than you did. Of course, the captain and the exec were more senior people and, as I recollect, there was one lieutenant and one lieutenant, junior grade - one of two lieutenants, and the rest of us were ensigns.

I had one classmate aboard and another ensign who was a class ahead of me, and I guess that was it.

I remember our visits to the Canal Zone in those days. It was a sort of fraternal, getting-together place, particularly when the battle fleet, as it was called, of the Pacific fleet came down from the West Coast and we came down from the East and sometimes met down there for maneuvers.

Q: In the Pacific or in the Atlantic?

Mr. B.: It would be alternately, off and on, both sides of the canal. Sometimes it was a problem of defending the Caribbean, sometimes an imagined attack on the West Coast entrance - on the Pacific entrance. This particular one in which the Breck participated when I was there, as I recollect it, was in the Pacific and we had the task of penetrating the screen of the battlefleet and delivering a torpedo attack. Supposedly we sort of did this on our own at night.

As a communications officer, which I became later, I had the onerous duty with one other officer of decoding the messages which were put into code for maneuver purposes. This was an endless proposition. You were up all night and then stood watch because many of the messages were garbled and they just used code books in those days, we didn't have the machines they use now. You'd have to try to guess at what the message implied and if you got the wrong entrance to the code - I've forgotten what they call it - the first two or three letters, the first key words, then you were all off and you had to guess at the rest of it.

Sometimes we'd have these messages - I'd usually have the other ensigns to help and we'd be sitting around the wardroom table working all day and all night, and sometimes these messages piled up so thick and heavy that many, many messages were -

Q: It sounds like there were many opportunities for error?

Mr. B.: There were indeed, and there were a lot of errors in the messages themselves.

We claimed that we were quite successful when we penetrated the screen and sunk a battleship and so forth, but I think the umpires ruled we'd been sunk ourselves!

We used to go to the Strangers Club in Panama City and to another club. There was then a very friendly feeling between the old canal-diggers and some of the Panamanians and the Americans. Quite different from now. It was a general meeting place and a happy one.

We left for Europe, as I recall it, from Newport in June of 1926 and our first port of call in Europe was Gibraltar. We were to spend most of our time in the Mediterranean. The routine was that we relieved a destroyer that had been over there the previous year and they were supposed to tell us what to look out for and so forth, but it was a very informal relief. In our case, the Breck used Gibraltar as a base if necessary for docking, for machinery repairs, and so on. We also, I think, once used Malta. We visited Malta but I don't think we had very much done there, just of a minor nature.

Q: The British had adequate repair facilities there then?

Mr. B.: Oh, yes. The British at that time, of course, were still - at least psychologically, the king pins in the naval world, particularly in the Mediterranean. They always had a lot of ships in both Gibraltar and Malta, and the French were sort of out of sight.

Q: Did they not have Bizerte then?

Mr. B.: Yes, they had Bizerte. I was coming to that in a minute. We visited numbers of ports, some that are not visited very much today. We were more or less independent. We cruised individually most of the time. We sometimes met in other ports other ships in the squadron. We practically never saw the flagship. In my time, the flagship, I think, was the *Memphis*. We were supposed to show the flag. That was our duty, and that meant really only about half a day's work. It meant cruising from port to port and when we were in port we were supposed to go ashore and supposed to make the American presence visible.

Q: Was the crew adequately prepared for these visits? Did they have some knowledge of the ports and the people?

Mr. B.: Very little indeed. Our ships spent much time at Villefranche on the Riviera, that was supposed to be the headquarters. We weren't there too much, but the *Memphis* was and some of the other ships were. We based on Gibraltar, started at Gibraltar, visited a number of Spanish ports, Villefranche, Italian ports, Naples, and then we were up the Adriatic to Trieste and some of the Yugoslav ports, Sebenico, and around the eastern end of the Mediterranean. I remember Haifa where I got my first experience of a levanter, I think they call it, that easterly wind that blows on the rocks and comes up very suddenly. Haifa in those days was an open roadstead with no protection, really, and there were some very uninviting rocks close in to shore. All the officers went ashore, except me! I had the duty. They went to some sort of a dinner party ashore and about half the crew was ashore, and I remember that suddenly I saw this cruise liner which hadn't anchored at all, as we had done, cruising up and down the bay, get up and depart. Then I saw clouds forming and suddenly the wind started to blow without any warning at all, blowing us almost on the rocks. We had awnings up forward. Here I was a young ensign and the only officer aboard scared to death.

I got Cooper - I remember his name still - who was the gunner's mate and a fine old chief petty officer, got him up immediately and told him somehow he'd have to get down in the engine room and get up steam. We didn't have steam up except for in-port boiler needs.

Q: So you were at the mercy of a blow.

Mr. B.: I got Cooper up on the fo'c'sle and I got a fireman down in the fire room, and I veered chain, which was the first thing you were supposed to do, and dropped the other anchor. Meantime the fo'c'sle awning was carried away and was flapping around in the wind! We finally stopped dragging. We were dragging anchor all right, towards the rocks, and we stopped. We had steam up and in an interval in the blow the captain managed to get back aboard, which relieved me greatly, and he gave me a pat on the back for doing the right thing so I felt very good about it. So I learned that these tricky winds in the Mediterranean can't be tampered with in an open roadstead.

Among other places we visited the port of Bizerte and we had an interesting experience there because, in those days - 1926 that would have been, I think we visited there in the fall of 1926, the remnants of the White Russian fleet were still in Bizerte, those that had been evacuated or fled from the Black sea at the time of Wrangell's defeat, the defeat of the White Russians. There were a few old Russian ships rusting, anchored way up the port, and it was routine for visiting naval officers, the French told us, to pay a courtesy call on the senior Russian officer. There were still some Russian officers aboard these ships. Those who had any get up and go had left and were doormen in Paris or whatever they could learn to do, but some of the old-timers just weren't able to do anything.

I remember I went with our captain, a man named John Magruder, to call on the senior Russian captain, I guess he was, and it was really a pathetic occasion. I think there were two officers, or three, on board this ship, living in kind of a shabby state but managing to exist.

I think the French gave them a little bit of money to get along on. They received us with all the naval courtesies of the past and were glad to see us. I think we took them some cigarettes or something when we paid our respects. I've never forgotten that. I wish I remembered it more clearly but it was something that impressed me. We were only aboard for about ten minutes, I think, but it impressed itself on me very vividly.

We did very little cruising to ports other than the Mediterranean. Some of the other ships did but we did get up to British ports or to French ports, particularly towards the end of our cruise, and to an Irish port.

I should have said that along the way one of the problems of cruising as an individual ship in the Mediterranean was that you had to arrange for all your own provisions and you had to buy them in each port. The old four-stacker destroyers couldn't carry much fresh food. I was the commissary officer in addition to the other duties I had. I was responsible for getting the food and for seeing it was properly cooked, and these galleys were very primitive. You had to store up potatoes in a spud locker on deck and if you got a sea aboard that ruined the potatoes. There was no real provision for keeping fresh meat, or very little provision for it. So we were constantly replenishing stores.

I remember my ardent desire to try to improve the crew's diet and I tried to get greater variety in their food, and I almost caused a mutiny on one occasion when I was very green because the crew would occasionally (when we had fresh eggs) have omelettes or scrambled eggs for breakfast with jelly on the side. I thought we'd try a jellied omelette, and, my God, a delegation came up to the bridge and said, "Mr. Baldwin has ruined two good dishes." I quickly found out that the sailor's appetite for something new is strictly limited.

In any case, the problem in a lot of these ports was that for years the ship chandlers had gotten together and ganged up on the prices. We'd get a list of ship chandlers from the U.S. consul and we'd find that all their prices were the same for all foodstuffs.

Q: Collusion!

Mr. B.: Yes, and sometimes their food wouldn't be very good. I found that out particularly in Marseilles and in some Italian ports. We spent a lot of time in Marseilles, in the old port, moored stern to the dock down at the foot of Rue de Canabiere, which the sailors used to call the "can of beer," a very picturesque street. The sailors loved Marseilles. They all got girls there and never wanted to leave after we were there any length of time.

I found I think starting particularly in Marseilles that all these prices were the same. We wanted to get quite a large supply of provisions there because it was known as a good place to stock up. Among other things we wanted to get some canned hams. You could buy these canned Polish hams which would keep on board the destroyer and were quite good. So I took a look at all the ship chandlers the consul had provided and they were all the same price. I asked for quotes on all these different things and they all came out the same. I went to see the consul and said, "Look what's going on here? This doesn't sound right." He said, "Oh, that's been going on for some time. These are the people we have and the Navy doesn't seem to do anything about it." I said, "Can't you give me the names of some other people who are not on the list who also are reputable." He did and I went out to them and got bids and some of them were very much lower.

That outraged the regular ship chandlers and they came down in price immediately.

Then I did another thing. I inspected the food when it came on board. It was supposed to be done but it often hadn't been done. Among other things that really outraged one of the ship chandlers was that I made him open a canned ham, several of them actually, spot checks, and found one or two of them were bad. So I took a small step in trying to reform the system of buying supplies. I did that in other ports, too, and I found it did have very definite results, particularly when we got to the eastern end of the Mediterranean. They were really a bunch of cutthroats particularly in places like Alexandria where you'd be completely at their mercy unless you took a lot of pains and effort to try to change this.

That took a lot of time, more of my time than I guess anyone else's because I was the commissary officer, which was a pain in the neck anyway. But here on this destroyer our life was aided again by this same Chinese steward who'd been on the Texas, Tip. He came to us as the chief commissary steward and he took care of the wardroom. He did the same thing on the Breck that he had done on the Texas. He went ashore in Marseilles and got raving drunk, then was broken to first class by a summary court. In any case, for a long part of our time on the Breck until he was transferred when a man was broken from chief to first class it was routine to transfer him to another ship. Until he was transferred, toward the end of our stay in Europe, he kept the wardroom well fed and very happy indeed. I remember particularly his bacon, lettuce, and tomato sandwich which he seemed to have for you any time of day or night when you came off watch.

These little old four-stacker ships were very rough-going ships in the sense of creature comforts. Also they were so light that in any sort of a sea they were constantly bouncing around.

Q: Were you a good sailor?

Mr. B.: I was reasonably good. My experience has been that it is normal for anyone to get seasick at sometime or another. It is abnormal if you're never seasick or if you're always seasick. We had a man on board who was always seasick. He had to be transferred. He couldn't possibly stay. He was always seasick, not only when we went to sea but sometimes even a passing motor boat in port, making the ship rock a little, would make him seasick. We had an officer who was seasick a good part of the time but nevertheless kept his watch. We had an executive officer part of the time, I was aboard, who was never seasick under any conditions. That was Vince Godfrey. It used to make us mad as the devil when the rest of us were retching into the night!

About half of the crew at any one time - most of the officers - would be seasick if the conditions were bad enough. A lot depended on two things - two or three things really. What you had been doing in port if you were just going to sea, if you'd had a lot of alcohol, too much rich food, or something of that sort you were more prone to be seasick; secondly, "sea legs" when you had gotten used to the ship's motion to a certain extent. But they were very rough ships and I remember one occasion when we crossed the English Channel we rolled our whaleboat under. Our motor whale boat was kept in davits over the side, ready to be lowered in case of need, and to roll that much meant about 50 or 60 degrees roll, and we actually sprung the davits. They bent right in two, the whale boat was filled with water and had to be bailed out later and some of the equipment in it was wrecked. It was an unpleasant ship to be in in a sea way, it was hard to keep your footing, you soon found your muscles aching from hanging on, just hanging on because you couldn't keep your footing if you were rolling heavily or pitching up and down unless you did hang on to something. We always rigged lifelines on deck in rough weather and you were very careful about going from bow to stern. There was no way in the old four-stackers to get under cover from bow to stern, you had to go out on the open deck, the main deck, because immediately underneath the main deck were the fire rooms and the boiler rooms, which had solid, watertight bulkheads between them.

It was often a wet ship. They had portholes, unlike many of the modern ships. Anything near the waterline in a modern ship doesn't have a porthole. That's part of the watertight integrity of the ship. But the old ships had portholes and the portholes from my cabin - I shared a cabin with another ensign, there were only four or five cabins, the captain's cabin and four officers' cabins. The captain had one, the exec had one, and then the other cabins were double cabins in which you doubled up. The portholes were pretty close to the waterline and in any sort of a sea way they'd be under water. Water would come up over them all the time. They didn't dog down tight enough and you'd get water slopping in. Some of them didn't dog tight enough and water also came in over the combing of the hatch. The men would be slopping around in water and it would be cold. Your problem of eating at a time like that was very considerable because you would have - the table, of course, was screwed into the deck, the wardroom table, but to keep anything on it you not only had to have sideboards which were put up around the table to keep the china from slipping off, but you'd have to wet the tablecloth to provide friction for the dishes to stay on it. The chairs, unfortunately, were not bolted to the wardroom floor, so we usually ran a line around the chairs and roped them to the cabin table so you wouldn't go sliding across the wardroom.

The same thing held for the crew. And you couldn't really cook anything hot in the galley in extreme conditions. You could get coffee in the coffee urn and usually you'd subsist on cold meat sandwiches or cold sandwiches of some sort until the storm was over.

We had a particularly rough crossing of the Bay of Biscay one time. I remember that vividly because that was when we'd left the Mediterranean and were on our way up to Portsmouth, England - or to London, I guess, up to London, in the latter part of our cruise. I had become enamored of an English girl in Gibraltar who was the daughter of a British naval officer. They were being transferred back to England and she had asked me if I could take her beloved dog back to England. Well, it was a very foolish thing to do because the British have very strict quarantine laws on dogs . . .

Q: They do now.

Mr. B.: And they did then, but love was blind so I said that I'd take the dog. That was about the worst trip I ever had. First because it was the roughest, it was very rough and the poor dog couldn't keep its footing on the steel decks. I tried to keep it down in my room. Second, the dog got seasick on the captain's bunk, which didn't do me any good. And third, the captain later fell on a slippery deck and chipped the end of his elbow and he had to lie in considerable agony for the rest of the trip while the exec ran the ship.

Then, when we got to London, we found that despite all these efforts the quarantine officers very politely took the dog off the ship and put it in quarantine for six months! But despite all these things, the experience in Europe was fascinating and a young officer learned a great deal because there's a lot more responsibility than you could get on a big ship. You had to do things yourself.

Again we participated in a lot of athletics. One of the things that struck me about the British at that time, I began to feel the British were getting a little soft, maybe wrongly, but, as a destroyer, we competed frequently with British battleships and our easy victories were sometimes embarrassing. For instance, in Malta when we came into the Grand Harbor and we were the sole American ship there, 125 men, we were challenged to a race-boat race, a whaleboat race, by the crew of, I think, the Royal Sovereign or one of the British battleships and we accepted.

I didn't row. I had rowed with the crew, but I think under the rules there were no British officers rowing so I didn't row. It was embarrassing. We finished so far ahead of them, there was about a half-mile lead at the end. We also won some overwhelming victories in Gibraltar where we competed in track and swimming and a different kind of a rowing race there. They had a kind of a shell. Up until almost the last we had defeated by far the best they had. They didn't seem to train at it as we did, at least in the Navy. They didn't seem to have the same kind of enthusiasm. These races and these competitions would really enlist the Breck's wholehearted enthusiasm and they'd get out and yell for their crew.

Despite the traditional enmity between the American sailor and the Limey, they got along quite well, I think, chiefly because the British were very hospitable. They did their best to try to make you feel at home. They had a slight sense of superiority but they tried to make you feel at home, and they went out of their way to do that.

We were in Plymouth, England, in 1927 when Lindberg flew overhead to Europe on his initial flight. We were then ordered to Cherbourg before returning to the United States. I have learned since then, though I didn't know it then, that the Breck was originally scheduled to bring Lindberg back to the United States. We were the closest destroyer. But the Memphis, the flagship, could take a plane aboard and we couldn't have and also she could maintain much higher speed than we could because we would run out of oil very rapidly if we tried to go at high speed across the Atlantic.

Q: And I suppose the tumultuous reception and worldwide interest had something to do with changing the plans?

Mr. B.: Oh, yes. It was fantastic the interest in that at the time. I actually saw the plane fly over Plymouth, so did several others, and it was Lindberg's plane, as we later discovered. He was very, very high.

We were ordered to Cherbourg, anyway, originally I guess for this reason and we were there when the Memphis came in and when Lindberg came down from Paris. He was taken aboard the Memphis in a motor boat and cruised around the Breck. We had the rails lined and he waved to us. He's supposed to have said - I didn't hear this at the time but again I've been talking to the man who's doing Lindberg's biography and he tells me that Lindberg said, "I'd rather go back with you. I like a small ship." I don't know whether he would have liked it if he'd gone in it, but anyway he was very gracious. He was very boyish and we were tremendously enthusiastic about him.

I should mention one thing in Cherbourg about the duties of a young officer. I was assigned to shore patrol. I guess that was one of the few times I was assigned, because usually when we got into port I had so much to do with the commissary I didn't have time for it, but I was assigned to shore patrol in Cherbourg. One of the duties of a shore patrol officer was to go around to check at all the French houses of prostitution, which were perfectly open in those days, they were legalized.

Q: Checking for what, for sanitary conditions?

Mr. B.: To see whether the sailors were behaving themselves and getting them out of there if they weren't. You'd go in with an enlisted man and the Madame would meet you graciously and you'd say, "Is everything all right?" and go out again.

Our final port in Europe was Dublin. We went to Dublin and I think were there relieved by another four-stacker destroyer. My chief memory of Dublin is seeing an Irish horse race and doing a bicycle trip with the skipper in County Wicklow. I haven't been back there since. It was a beautiful, lovely place in those days, simple.

We came back to the United States after about thirteen months in June of 1927, and came to Charleston, South Carolina, which was then being developed as a kind of destroyer base. There were a few other ships there, minesweepers principally. It was a very sleepy, small naval base. We may have come to New York first or to Newport, I'm not sure, but in any case we ended up at Charleston.

During this period I was deciding that I would resign

from the Navy.

Q: You had been advanced to lieutenant, jg, in June of that year?

Mr. B.: Yes, and I should have mentioned that while I was aboard the Breck and while we were still in Mediterranean waters, actually in the very delightful harbor of Villefranche, I was ordered along with my classmates to take the examination for lieutenant, junior grade. In those days every officer had to take an examination in every subject before he was adjudged fit for advancement, and these were very stiff day-long examinations. It almost broke our hearts to have to sit aboard the Breck in that very delightful harbor and spend I think about ten days while we were there, day after day, taking examinations in seamanship and gunnery and ordnance and navigation, engineering, and military law, and what not.

I didn't know what marks I'd gotten until much later when the former executive officer of the Breck was on duty in Washington and at my request he dug out the marks and I did all right. As a result of those exams I was duly after three years advanced to lieutenant, junior grade. That's what you were supposed to serve - three years as an ensign and four years as a lieutenant, junior grade, and each time before you were promoted you had to take an examination. The examinations went on up to lieutenant commander, through lieutenant commander grade, and they were stiff exams, they were written and detailed.

Q: In retrospect, was that a good system, do you think?

Mr. B.: It was for the navy of those days. I think it would be impractical today. The navy in those days only had about 7,000 officers. I don't believe that you could do that with I don't know how many thousands that there are now. I do think that they're advancing too quickly from junior ranks today. I don't believe that we're getting very experienced officers as lieutenants, for instance, or for that matter as captains or admirals. You may get them somewhat more experienced in certain specialized fields. There may be much better electronics officers. I've found this is the problem in the modern Navy. They are too specialized in some sense, in the narrow sense, because they don't know anything about the rest of the navy or anything else, except about their own specialty. This is particularly true of pilots, particularly true of fliers.

Another thing I should have mentioned in connection with examinations is that the Naval War College in those days, as they do now, gave a correspondence course. I started taking that almost as soon as I graduated.

Q: That was completely voluntary, wasn't it?

Mr. B.: Voluntary. I got most of it done aboard the <u>Texas.</u> I think I had a few installments to finish aboard the <u>Breck</u>. It was a course that involved not too much reading but a great deal of chart work and a great deal of plotting, estimates of the situation, and that sort of thing. I finished it with credit. They disagreed with some of my solutions but I finished it with credit and rather enjoyed it. A lot of it was focused, as you would have expected, on World War I and the Battle of Jutland, and nowhere near enough, in retrospect, on submarine warfare or antisubmarine warfare. Most of it was big-ship actions and night torpedo attacks and things of that sort.

I think the chief value to me was kind of inspirational. I got a lift from reading a lot of books, some of which were required, some were about World War I. I got a lot clearer knowledge of the naval history of the period and also of some of the very gallant deeds.

I noted a moment ago that we came back to Charleston. I'm not sure in retrospect that we came immediately to Charleston. We ended up there. I see here I applied for some leave from Portland, Maine, so we were in Portland and

I think we were in New York. In fact, I know we were in New York because we had changed skippers in the _Breck_ soon after we returned to this country, and the new skipper was in command when we came into New York Harbor and were supposed to moor alongside a dock up at 96th Street, which was then a New York yacht pier. It wasn't a New York Yacht Club pier but there were a lot of yachts near there. The new skipper was not too expert at destroyer-handling and he unfortunately had come alongside and didn't allow enough for the very considerable current in the river and he ended up smashing into a couple of yachts and half-sinking one of them. I spent a lot of my period - I've forgotten what other collateral duty I had then, but it involved the ship's carpenter and so forth, and I spent a lot of my time in New York with the ship's carpenter repairing the damages to these boats. Actually, we'd gotten something stuck in our underwater intake and I remember diving in that murky water of the river with somebody else with just a light helmet on, you know, without any suit, to see if we could free it. We finally got squared away, but this wasn't a very good introduction for this skipper, who was a nice guy . . .

Q: Did he continue on as skipper?

Mr. B.: Yes. I don't think any report was ever made about

this. The yacht owners were very sympathetic. I don't think so.

In any case, after some of these visits to New York and Portland and I think to Newport we did end up in Charleston. I had submitted my resignation, I guess, around September or August. Initially, I didn't give any reason and the Bureau came back, "What are the reasons for resignation?" As I recall, I said, "Too much paper work," which was true, "incompatibility" . . .

Q: In what sense?

Mr. B.: I think basically the reasons were that I liked and enjoyed the work with men and I liked going to sea. I hated the red tape and I disliked thoroughly the time I had to spend on reports and paper work. I also was beginning to see a new world. My mind hadn't really opened at that time. Frankly, I was pretty narrowly confined to the Navy and to getting ahead in that, and I was beginning to see a little of a new world.

While I was abroad - I guess I should have mentioned this - I did some travel articles for the Baltimore Sun, my father was on it. I wrote a few pieces about the Azores, where we stopped on our way over, and about Gibraltar, and about various other places, and I began to have a vague idea that maybe I wanted to write. I wasn't sure what I wanted to do when I got out of the Navy. I just was sure I wanted to see more of the world, wanted to get more experiences, I wanted to broaden myself a little.

Q: You said earlier that you were reading Plutarch's Lives and so forth, so you had an idea that you wanted to be more literary?

Mr. B.: I think so. I was very immature emotionally and otherwise. Even at that time I wasn't really in a position to evaluate myself very accurately. For instance, it was a matter of pride to me that when we went through Europe - I didn't drink - I said, "I will bet you I won't take a drink in Europe." I said this to one of my friends and classmates. Well, I didn't, but it was awfully stupid because that included wine and everything else and I was in the invidious position of trying to get Cocoa Cola or something like that!

Q: With all these gorgeous French wines around!

Mr. B.: This was a rigidity which was rather silly.

There was another factor, although it didn't come to be a factor - a real factor - until later. My father was quite old. I was the son of his second wedding and he was in his eighties at this time and not too well. But that really didn't become a decisive factor until after I'd gotten out of the Navy. But I decided that I wanted to get out.

Q: Did you consult your father in advance?

Mr. B.: I talked to him about it but he didn't try to influence me one way or the other. He was very good that way. He urged me to think about it very carefully, and it was a wrench, there's no question about it. A number of my classmates, and I think this was one thing that gave the Navy pause, as I recollect several of them resigned after the trip to Europe was over. I said if I have to face routine duty along the Atlantic coast or along the Pacific coast, I just don't want to stay in. If I can get the Yangtze Patrol or the Asiatic Fleet, I would stay in. I'd love to see that part of the world. I applied for Asiatic duty and was turned down. I did face a long period of routine duty along the Atlantic coast, doing much the same thing I'd done for three years because I had to be a lieutenant, junior grade, for four years before I could be a lieutenant.

Q: Advancement was slow.

Mr. B.: Yes, and so I decided finally I didn't want to go through that again and spend these long months at Guantanamo, which I liked and enjoyed originally but I wouldn't have wanted to keep it up indefinitely.

So I did submit my resignation with a request for all accrued leave - I had about a month's leave coming to me. I remember when I was at home in Baltimore on this leave trying to decide what to do, really getting a little panicky. It's quite a wrench, you know, when you decide to resign, and wondering whether I should try to rescind this. I decided, no, I'd stick to it.

I think I can honestly say since then I've never regretted being in the Navy. I'm very proud of that. I've never regretted resigning. Probably I did the right thing although I wasn't sure about it at the time.

Q: Certainly, in the light of your career, you did!

Mr. B.: I don't know whether there's anything else we ought to go back and pick up.

Q: Had romance entered your life? I mean was there any idea that you didn't . . . ?

Mr. B.: Oh, yes, I was engaged for a brief time to this English girl whose dog I took up to Gibraltar. That was broken off and that affected me emotionally and probably had something to do with my desire to resign. But looking back at it I don't think so. I was too young, too uncertain to be sure. Looking back at it, it's a very good thing we didn't get married, but at that time you can't see those things as clearly.

Q: How did Joe feel about you getting out of the Navy?

Mr. B.: I'm not sure. Joe was on a different ship, you see, after the Texas, he went to the Nakomis, the old survey ship which spent its time in surveying the depths of the oceans. Entirely different. It was then a Navy duty, it's now a Coast and Geodetic duty.

Q: The hydrographic business.

Mr. B.: Yes. I hadn't seen Joe for quite a long time. He got assigned later on to China. I didn't see him there, so we weren't then as close as we had been.

There were a lot of people feeling the way I did at the time. As I say, several of my classmates or the class just after me resigned after they returned from Europe, not only from this squadron but in the subsequent year. I think this gave the Navy pause. They said well, is this duty really helping the Navy or is it hurting it. There were a considerable number of resignations in the 1927, 1928, 1929 period. Of course, there was a great deal of talk in those days about another disarmament conference. There was the Geneva one at the time, which was fruitless. And there seemed to be opportunities in civilian life which seemed to be lacking in the Navy. So I think all those things had a place.

My principal feeling, as I recall it - it's very hard to recall - was that I wanted broader horizons. That seemed to be the feeling I had.

Q: The response you made by dispatch to the Bureau of Navigation when they made inquiry as to the reasons for resigning:

> Lieutenant, junior grade, Hanson W. Baldwin states the reasons for resigning are limited opportunity, incompatible work, and personal reasons.

Your resignation was submitted at the end of August, it was accepted as of the 1st of October to be effective the 5th of November.

Mr. B.: The 5th of November, after accumulated leave.

Q: Yes. You went into the Naval Reserve so I think you

want to deal with that aspect of your career.

Mr. B.: Yes. You had to apply after you resigned to the Naval Reserve, and I was commissioned on 29 November 1927 as a lieutenant, junior grade, for what they called deck and engineering duties for general service, United States volunteer Naval Reserve. "Volunteer" meant that you were not assigned to a specific unit. I continued in that for some time.

Q: What were the requirements?

Mr. B.: This is not clear to me at the moment. You were supposed to take periodic cruises and keep up, and I did take one such cruise aboard the USS Childs, an old four-stacker destroyer which was one of the same type I'd been on, in 1930. That was after I'd come to The New York Times. It was a two weeks' cruise up along the New England coast and it did not add anything to my knowledge, in fact it was quite a comedown after having been officer of the deck on a four-stacker and having more responsibility because I found that on these ships you were not trusted as a Reserve officer and also you were sort of a fifth wheel. So there was not a great deal of inducement to go on a cruise like that. You were paid for active duty but that's all. The rest of the time I guess that I was supposed to intermittently study, but I had no regular duties. That's what "Volunteer" meant.

I do see here that later on, when I was eligible for promotion to lieutenant, it stated that I must take those examinations by a certain period or I would have to be dropped from the Naval Reserve. And it was about this period in 1932, two years later, that I requested transfer from the general division, Volunteer Naval Reserve, to the intelligence division, and the reason for that was that I was a reporter for The New York Times, specializing in naval assignments.

Q: You might read that onto the tape. It's a letter of January 27, 1932, a letter from you to the Navy Department by way of the Commandant of the Third Naval District, a request that you be transferred to the intelligence division.

> "I am a reporter for The New York Times and am specializing in naval assignments. My work frequently takes me away from New York City and I am at all times required to work at night and other unusual hours. Because of this irregular schedule and the pressure of business, I am unable either to go on summer training cruises or to participate in other activities of the Naval

Reserve. Some time ago I was eligible for promotion but have been unable to take the examinations not only because of the lack of time for study but because of my absence from the city and irregular hours. I feel that my work in civilian life naturally fits me for duties with the intelligence section and that I am more qualified for this than for any section in the Naval Reserve.

I am making this request because I desire to maintain my association with the Navy and yet am unable to perform the duties of the division to which I now belong."

Mr. B.: That continued then for two years during which I was . . .

Q: You mean that was granted?

Mr. B.: That was granted and I transferred to class I, intelligence, - V, Voluntary, U.S.N.R., and at the end of about two years without any examinations I was promoted to lieutenant, which is the highest I ever got! However, in this two-year period, there were one or two occasions - one occasion, I guess, when the - I've forgotten now who it was, whether it was Randall Jacobs who wasn't the head of the Bureau of Navigation but was I think in it, it was someone in the Bureau of Navigation who was objecting to some of the things that I wrote and took me to task and tried to tell me to reveal the sources of my stories.

I didn't like this.

Q: That's a sore spot with a reporter!

Mr. B.: Yes, very. In any case, I can't find the correspondence that dealt with that. I think I must have given it to   . In any case, I wrote quite a spirited letter and I won the immediate battle. I answered the report in very definite terms and told them that this was an infringement on the freedom of the press and on me as a person. I was a volunteer, after all, and they had no right to order me to do anything unless I was on active duty.

Then, finally, in August 1934 I submitted this letter which is self-explanatory.

Q: August 20, 1934 from Hanson W. Baldwin of The New York Times to the Secretary of the Navy, by way of the Commandant of the Third Naval District:

"I hereby submit my resignation as an officer in the Volunteer Naval Reserve, Intelligence Section.

The principal reason for my resignation is the

interpretation apparently put upon the term "Volunteer" by the Department. Various letters I have received from Commandant, Third Naval District, as well as from the Department within the past eighteen months definitely indicate that the Department considers Volunteer Naval Reserve officers to be subject to its orders and available for its service at all times, in time of peace as well as in war, and even when such officers are on an inactive duty status.

Such a condition is not acceptable to me, as I have previously indicated in letters to the Department. Furthermore, my commission if I had bowed to the Department's wishes in the past would have acted as a handicap to me in my work, which is the accurate and impartial reporting of the news without fear or favor.

Still a third factor in my decision, which I have reached with regret after mature consideration, is the possibility that my continued affiliation with the Naval Reserve might be considered in some quarters as too close a connection with the naval establishment to permit accurate and fair reporting of naval news. My connection with the Intelligence Section of the Reserve would possibly in some foreign countries, undoubtedly in others, prove embarrassing to me should I be called upon to report upon the military or naval news of those countries.

For these reasons I tender my resignation and return herewith my Naval Reserve identification card. Though I feel it definitely advisable to end my connection with the Navy after fourteen years of active and Reserve affiliation, nevertheless the severance of my official ties will not diminish my deep interest in the naval establishment."

Mr. B.: That last reference to the connection with the Intelligence Section of the Reserve proving a possible embarrassment in reporting the military and naval news of other countries should be read against the background of what was the growing danger of Hitler's rule in Europe and the fact that I was beginning to cover for The New York Times more and more naval and military news and that I felt I would probably be called upon to go to Germany and Russia.

Actually, my forebodings about this were borne out later when I did go abroad for The Times in 1937 and visited all of the dictator countries and went into Russia. I arrived there just in the midst of the great purge trials and I was met at the railroad station by The Times correspondent in Russia and he was a frightened man and very much on the qui vive. He said, "My secretary disappeared last night, my chauffeur has been picked up. They know you were in the Navy. For God's sake, watch your step." This was the atmosphere in the Russia of those days under Stalin.

Q: Naval Reserve and Intelligence Section!

Mr. B.: I think they had the whole dossier.

Q: Oh, I'm sure they did.

Mr. B.: In any case, I felt, as that paper you read into the tape indicated, that there was a built-in conflict here between my job on The Times and my commission in the Naval Reserve, particularly as it was interpreted in Washington. So I decided regretfully to resign, and looking back at it I think I **did** the right thing.

The only other part to this I think we might finish up is that when World War II came and when we got into it, I was very much torn as to what to do, because I had a Naval

Academy education, I had served in the Navy and I had more professional competence than a lot of officers who were being commissioned. I wanted to serve and really had a great desire to get back into the Navy, but I did not want under any conditions to be stuck to a public relations desk in Washington, which I was afraid would be my fate. And so I went to considerable pains to try to talk to a number of people and try to get their advice as to what I should do.

Of course, Admiral Nimitz was then the head of the Bureau of Navigation. This was before we actually got into the war, and he sent out this routine paper to everyone who had anything to do with the Navy.

Q: That would be of interest. Shall I read this?

Mr. B.: Yes, if you like.

Q: This was a routine notice to all people who had had some previous connection: it's dated June 4, 1941.

Dear Sir,

The great expansion which the Navy is now undergoing due to the unsettled world conditions and the critical situation confronting our country requires the service of many additional officers in the Naval

Reserve.

Your prior experience and training as a Naval Academy graduate have given you a foundation for naval service which is not available among other applicants in civil life. The Navy is in need of persons with such experience to meet the heavy demands which are being placed upon it.

The Bureau realizes that you may be called upon to make considerable sacrifices at this time by offering your service to the Navy, but this is the time when all good men should come to the aid of their country.

If you desire to apply, the Bureau will give favorable consideration to your application for a commission in the Naval Reserve, subject to physical and certain other professional requirements. Physical defects of a minor nature will not prevent your being granted a commission in the Naval Reserve for special service and your assignment to appropriate duty where you can best render such service. Your eligibility for appointment will depend upon the length and nature of your prior naval service, the reasons for your separation therefrom, your age, and to a considerable degree the work you have been doing in civil life.

If you desire to serve your country in the capacity of a Naval Reserve officer, you are requested to contact the Director of Naval Reserve in the office of the Commandant of the Naval District in which you live, who will be pleased to give you full information and to assist you in filling your applications.

        Sincerely yours,
         C. W. Nimitz

Mr. B.: I had already started talking to people in the Navy whose opinion I respected. This was before we were actually in the war, but of course there was the undeclared war in the Atlantic still going on.

Q: The Neutrality Patrol!

Mr. B.: Yes. So I followed this up, particularly after this appeal came, and as a result I talked to Admiral Hepburn and I talked to others, and this is from Admiral Ingersoll, who was Joe's great friend. You know him, don't you?

Q: Yes, indeed, still is.

July 17, 1941

My dear Mr. Baldwin,

This is to acknowledge the receipt of your letter of July 16.

I have talked with Admiral Hepburn . . .

Mr. B.: Excuse me for interrupting, but I think this was the result, in part, of my talking to Joe when I wanted to ask him what I should do and Joe suggested I write to Admiral Ingersoll, I believe, whom he greatly respected.

Q: I have talked with Admiral Hepburn, the Navy Department Public Relations Officer, with regard to you and I have also shown him your letter. He is of the opinion, and I concur, that at the present time you are far more useful to the Navy in general in your present capacity on the staff of The Times than you would be at sea or at a desk job in a public relations office or in Naval Intelligence.

I share your feeling that we would all rather be at sea on the firing line than sitting at a desk, but certain work ashore, as you know, has to be done.

With kindest regards,

Very sincerely yours,

R. E. Ingersoll
Rear Admiral, U.S. Navy

Mr. B.: Well, to make a long story short, I followed this up later, after Pearl Harbor, by talking to Jim Forrestal and to others in the Department and all of them urged me to stay where I was and I finally decided with some reluctance to do it.

However, in 1942 there were two specific offers of commissions. One from Tom Hamilton, who was then running the aviation training program, and he wanted me to come in for service. And another one was from Randall Jacobs, who was then Chief of the Bureau of Navigation. I suspected the latter a little bit, only because I had written some quite critical articles about the way in which the Bureau of Navigation was procuring naval officers. Remember some rather socially prominent people were getting rather high commissions without any particular qualification for them. Actually, I'd gone into this at some length up in New York with the Third Naval District in my capacity as a reporter and had written one or two very critical articles about the real confusion that existed up there.

So I suspected that Randall Jacobs' offer of a commission had certain strings attached to it.

But in any case, I talked about that again after I received it with various people whose opinion I particularly admired and with people in the Navy Department. I think

I talked to at least twelve or fifteen people and I sent him a telegram and later sent Tom Hamilton a declination, too.

Q: This is a night letter addressed to Rear Admiral Randall Jacobs, Chief of the Bureau of Navigation. The date is not apparent on here.

"Deeply appreciate honor and am very anxious be of maximum service but after previous consultation sometime ago with Admirals Hepburn, Horne, Ingersoll, Captain Lovett on desirability my returning to Navy it was decided I was of more value in present position. Though deeply honored by your offer I still feel I am probably of more use outside the Navy than in it. The war situation some day, of course, may modify this decision. Appreciatively and regretfully, Hanson W. Baldwin."

Mr. B.: This was often the case of the right hand of the Navy not knowing what the left was doing because I had talked to most of the people in Washington. Admiral Jacobs apparently didn't realize it and neither did Tom Hamilton. I had talked to Tom Hamilton's boss, Admiral Towers, as I told him in that letter. Unless you want to, I don't think it's necessary to read all those into the record. This was the aviation cadet program that Tom ran, you know. I'd known Tom not too well but slightly.

Q: He's the president of the class of 1927, isn't he?

Mr. B.: Yes. I think that concluded the various efforts and various chances I had to get back into the Navy. In some ways I regretted I didn't get back during the war.

Q: It was always tearing at your heart strings, wasn't it?

Mr. B.: Well, I had a debt to the Navy. There's no doubt about it. They gave me what I thought was an excellent training.

Q: But deep down in your heart didn't you feel that you were doing a bigger job than you could have done . . . ?

Mr. B.: Oh, I was absolutely sure of that, particularly later on when I really despised the thought of getting into public relations, which is almost certainly what I would have been earmarked for, or even into intelligence, in which I had some competence but not as much as I might have because I didn't have foreign languages and you should have.

I also found later that as I was going overseas quite a lot during the war that part of this feeling you were just sitting at home doing nothing was expunged by being able to get out where there was some action.

Admiral Horne was mentioned in that telegram and perhaps another time we can come back to him because I think he did a tremendous service for the Navy from the point of view of public relations which has never been recognized.

Q: I hope you will talk in some detail about the Navy and public relations and its development from the prewar days and the silent navy to something different now.

Interview No. 3 with Mr. Hanson W. Baldwin

Place: His residence in Roxbury, Connecticut

Date: Monday morning, 21 April 1975

Subject: Biography

By: John T. Mason, Jr.

Q: Well, Sir, it's good to see you. I'm disappointed that spring hasn't arrived here in Roxbury but we will look forward to some day when it does.

Mr. B.: It takes time up here. We usually don't get a real spring, unfortunately.

Q: Last time, you told me about your resignation from the Navy in 1927 and then you reviewed your status as a Reservist and brought us up to World War II, when you were offered a commission in the Navy and finally decided against it.

So, I think we want to resume our story this morning in the year 1927, with your resignation and the new career that was launched at that point.

Mr. B.: I left the Navy in Charleston, South Carolina. That is, I left my ship there, the destroyer Breck. My resignation took effect about a month afterwards, when I was at home in Baltimore, after I'd had my accumulated leave.

Before I left the Navy I had written a letter to Admiral Byrd —

Q: Richard Evelyn Byrd?

Mr. B.: Richard Byrd, who was then making his explorations in Antarctica and he was planning another expedition and I thought I would like to go with him. I left the Navy with no clear idea of what I was going to do. I knew I wanted to see more of the world. I knew I wanted to write. I wasn't sure what I wanted to do. So I had written to Admiral Byrd and had a letter from him which seemed to be receptive. It was not definite one way or the other, but he said when he commenced to select personnel for his expedition he would consider me, and, as a former Navy man, I thought I had a pretty good chance.

Q: What sort of a job did you anticipate on his expedition?

Mr. B.: Any kind of a job I was willing to take.

So I went to Baltimore and arrived there in October, I guess it was, or September, 1927 and had been home a month or so when my father became quite ill. He was rather advanced in years, so I decided I'd better not leave on a long expedition where I would not be available, to the South Pole. So with some reluctance I wrote to Byrd and told him that. I've forgotten when I did it, but I guess it must have been about December. In the meantime, I looked about for something to do and decided to try to get a job on the Baltimore Sun, where my father had been an editor and my grandfather before him for many years.

So I started as a cub reporter on the Baltimore Sun in, I think, January 1928.

Q: This must have pleased your father?

Mr. B.: Yes, it did, although in the early months he was ill a good bit of the time and was home. But it was the days when some of the Sun giants were still alive. Henry L. Mencken was still living. Mark Watson was the Sunday editor of the Sun, a delightful person, more of my father's generation, not as old as my father but Dad had known him for a long time. And a good many others who had helped to make the Sunpapers famous in their day.

I actually stayed on the Sun about eleven months, I believe, ten or eleven months and started covering police districts. As a cub reporter you're assigned to district police stations and you get all the bits of crime and nasty things that happen, you cover fires, and so on.

Q: And night court. Did you go to night court?

Mr. B.: When it was necessary, yes. They ran a different system in Baltimore. I don't remember that night courts were convened very frequently. But I worked twelve hours a day six days a week and I got $18 a week, to start with. I remember that.

Q: And rode the streetcars!

Mr. B.: Yes, rode the streetcars or walked. I didn't have a car.

I was assigned to the Northwestern District in the city, which was probably the worst district in the city because it was a Negro district and, in those days, the Negroes were not as militant or radical as they are now but they cut each other up with great frequency and there was a tremendous amount of crime. It was also an unpleasant district in a way to cover.

Q: Did you discover that you had a real aptitude as a reporter?

Mr. B.: I think I did. The one absolutely essential requirement for a reporter is a nose for news. If he doesn't have that he's not going to make much of a reporter. You've got to sniff it out, and nobody's defined a nose for news, really. It's an ability to ferret out news from seemingly uninteresting sources or unrelated incidents.

I made considerable progress, I guess, in a short time. I don't think it was due to Dad at all because my father was an editorial writer and I came up from a district reporter to what they called a general assignment reporter doing everything. One of the curious things of that period in my life was that there was a young English reporter named Rene MacColl who subsequently was a star reporter for the Daily Express, the Beaverbrook paper in London. Rene had come to America with Van Lear Black. Van Lear Black was then the principal owner of the Sun, a multimillionaire or millionaire, and he was one of the people who were prominent in early flying. He had his own plane and Dutch pilots, and he used to fly around the world a great deal and for those days that was very adventurous. He hired MacColl - I don't know how or why, but he hired him as his secretary and then brought him over to America and he got a job on the Baltimore Sun through Black. My last job on the district was to introduce Rene MacColl to the police districts in Baltimore, and that was very funny because he had this broad English accent and was very cultured. Police sergeants didn't know what to make of it. It was difficult enough for me because I'd just come out of the Navy, but when Rene got there they couldn't understand him and were puzzled by him. He was a very humorous fellow, he was always cracking jokes which they didn't understand.

I remember some of his assignments subsequently were to cover the American circus, which he'd never seen before, and baseball, and of course he did articles from the point of view of an Englishman and they were very well done and very humorous. We formed a lifetime friendship which persisted until Rene died some years ago. I used to see him in various parts of the world later on.

When I was assigned to general assignments, because of my Navy background, I got a number of assignments, I suppose, which were particularly favorable. For instance, Swede Mommsen, whom you may know, tested his escape lung down at Solomons Island, the deepest part of the Chesapeake Bay, in 1928 and I was assigned to that and had, I guess, one of the first stories about it. I don't think there was any other newspaperman there actually. I was there and saw him come up out of this depth.

Q: Did you have to have experience, too, in order to . . . ?

Mr. B.: No, I didn't do it. I couldn't have done it and if I had I probably would have been dead! Using that Mommsen lung in those experimental stages it took a lot of knowledge and guts to do it.

Then, when the <u>Vestris</u> disaster occurred down at Norfolk, my old stamping ground, I was assigned to go down there and interview some of the survivors.

Q: This was something that happened off the coast of New Jersey, wasn't it?

Mr. B.: Yes, she was heavily loaded in New York and the cargo passenger door, through which they loaded a lot of things, was ill-fitting, it wasn't completely dogged shut, and when they got out to sea in a fairly heavy sea she had a list and the cargo shifted a little more. She had a lot of passengers. She was a cargo-passenger ship. The cargo shifted a little more and this door came under water and water started to seep in there. In addition to that, she was a coal-burner and had these old ash ejectors like they used to have on the Navy ships, and the ash ejectors clogged up and the outlets of the ash ejectors were under water and the water started to come in through the ash ejectors into the fireroom. It went from bad to worse. They had a very ill-disciplined crew. She was a very badly run ship like many of the ships of those days, and she gradually shifted until she was in extremis, really.

The fires were put out by the rising water in the fireroom. The engineers had to keep the black gang at work with loaded pistols. It was a very nasty business. The passengers were left to fend for themselves largely.

Q: Later one of our very illustrious American women, was a passenger on that ship, Mary Lord.

Mr. B.: I didn't know that.

Q: Mary Lord and her sister, the Pillsbury girls.

Mr. B.: I've never forgotten that famous picture of the passenger who had broken both arms sitting on the boat deck - a picture of these passengers waiting for the lifeboats to be lowered. The lifeboats couldn't be lowered because of the list of the ship. They were jammed on one side and they couldn't get them down. He was a pitiful figure, with both arms broken, sitting there.

Well, anyway, a tremendous number of people died. Some were rescued and taken to the Naval Hospital in Portsmouth, where I interviewed some of them. Most of them were members of the crew, not passengers. Some of them were from the black gang who had deserted their posts.

I enjoyed that kind of coverage and tried to bring into it the language of the sea, which hadn't been done very much before in the American newspaper business. There were very few people who spoke the language of the sea. I tried to put it in nautical terms.

After about ten or eleven months of that . . .

Q: Did your interest in it go to the extent of trying to discover the reasons why this all happened on the Vestris?

Mr. B.: Oh, yes. Of course, you couldn't tell completely until you interviewed a tremendous number of people. But this gradually came out in the investigation afterwards, and I covered some of that.

Q: This is what you call now investigative reporting?

Mr. B.: No, I wouldn't say that's really investigative reporting. This was more a spot news story. Investigative reporting would involve a lot of consultation of available public records, deep delving into figures and finance, and that kind of thing, then pursuing for a long period of time just one story without anything in the paper while you're doing it. That I didn't do.

Investigative reporting is a new name for really an old trade. You could say that this was done many, many years ago. I don't think there's anything terribly new about it, except that you have new techniques because of new record-keeping and tools and so on.

During this ten or eleven months on the Baltimore Sun, my father improved. He had an operation and was much better, so I decided to start traveling again. I wanted to see more of the world. I'd taken a licence as a second mate. When I left the Navy I took the exams for it. I just wanted it under my belt. You have to spend a certain amount of years at sea in order to qualify. Well, I'd been at sea long enough to qualify as a second mate.

So I decided to try to get a job in the merchant marine but I deliberately sought one which would give me a taste of the enlisted man's berth. I got a quartermaster's job on the Munson liner American Legion bound for South America, and it was a joke. You had to take a so-called lifeboat test from the Coast Guard. That was the only real requirement. The lifeboat test was simply the lowering of a lifeboat with other men and proving you could row.

Q: Not very stringent regulations!

Mr. B.: Not at all, and it was lowered very sloppily somewhere over on Staten Island in calm water. The crew was entirely out of time in their rowing.

I ultimately, however, got the quartermaster berth and

started off I guess in late December or early January 1929.

Q: You had to join a maritime union, did you?

Mr. B.: No, no unions in those days were required. You didn't have to. You see, this was before the days of compulsory unionization. You do now. I got my grandson, with the help of Miller - you know Miller who's in the Department of Commerce, Admiral Miller . . .

Q: George Miller?

Mr. B.: Yes. My grandson had a job in the merchant marine two summers ago and he had to join a union. The union has done something in weeding out all these bums in the merchant marine to some extent. The unions have also forced the contraction of the American merchant marine because they have priced many ships and lines out of business. In any case, seamen can't get along today who are always drunk and things like that. They've been shoved aside and there is a better group aboard ship, I think, than there was in my day.

The Munson Line was a British-owned line, or partially British-owned, that plied back and forth from New York to South America. It was a terribly run line. It utilized cargo-passenger ships, big ships. The ship I was on was

was about 22,000 tons and carried a lot of passengers. It was one of the worst disciplined crews. I was shocked, having been in the Navy, to see what went on in the merchant marine. Also, the kind of companions you had to associate with. All they could think about was women and liquor and so forth. It was an eye-opener and a good one, I guess, for me.

Q: You got a little of that when you were a police reporter?

Mr. B.: Yes, but not so much because there you were so busy with what was happening and so forth. Here, you lived with them day and night.

I remember vividly that when we were cruising along the South American coast within sight of land, a place where I'd never been before, I was told to go up in the crow's nest and check on the lookout and I found him sound asleep. I so reported to the officer of the watch and he did nothing about it. It was apparently routine for them to go to sleep, and also routine for some of them to be drunk on watch. There was a lot of drinking deep down below decks. The officer of the deck was just as culpable because the first mate left the bridge entirely, left me in charge as quartermaster, and he didn't know that I'd ever been in the Navy, he didn't know that I had a second mate's licence. He just knew I'd come from the New York waterfront. I'd actually spent the night in a Hoboken sailors' boarding house before we sailed. He went down below to flirt with one of the women passengers. He actually spent a long time with her - two or three hours - while we were cruising. I was worried because I didn't know these waters at all. I was as meticulous as I could be about navigation, but it was a 22,000-ton ship with some 100 passengers, and this was the attention that was paid to their safety. The captain rarely came to the bridge. He did occasionally but not often.

Anyway, that was a sample. We stopped at various ports, Buenos Aires, Santos, Rio de Janeiro. At Santos, I had the watch in port, as the senior petty officer. Most of the passengers had gone ashore and, I think, virtually all of the officers. The master of arms was supposed to have the key to the brig aboard ship and was supposed to be aboard, as I remember. There were a couple of drunken sailors coming back to the ship down on the dock and one of them was chasing the other with a knife. We tried to find the master at arms and we finally got one of them aboard - I've forgotten the exact circumstances - and I guess we got the knife away from the fellow who owned it. There were only two or three of us available. We looked for the master at arms for a place to lock this man up until he sobered up, and the master at arms had gone ashore with the key to the brig without any permission or anything else!

Well, I came away from that ship with a very unhealthy respect for the discipline of the merchant marine as I saw it.

Q: I hope that was exceptional and not the rule?

Mr. B.: I think the Munson Line was particularly bad but then I think the <u>Vestris</u> - that wasn't the Munson Line, that was another example of bad discipline, too. Very poor discipline. I remember the Ward Line, the <u>Morro Castle</u>, which I covered later when I was on <u>The Times</u>. The Ward Line was a terribly badly disciplined ship. There was an awful lot of laxity. There was none of this tautness of discipline or seamanship which you found in Norwegian or Dutch ships or Scandinavian ships. You did not pick an American ship by choice if you were going as a passenger. You'd get a lot more feeling of security and also service on foreign ships.

That cruise finally ended after a couple of months, I guess, and I looked around for another part of the world to go to. Sir Wilfrid Grenfell was then running the Foundation in Labrador and I applied for a job up there for the summer, and he took me on as what they called a wop driver, in other words, a man who had graduated from college in charge of a group of college boys who were supposed to do volunteer work somewhere along the Newfoundland and Labrador coast for the summer.

In my case, the place selected was Cartwright, Labrador, which is about one-third the way up the coast. Sir Wilfrid was thinking of establishing a hospital at Cartwright, which is only a tiny fishing village. I went up there in the old steamer Kyle, which was a mail steamer. You had to get up to Newfoundland and then you went from St. John's, Newfoundland, by the Kyle and went along the Labrador coast stopping at all these fishing villages. The Kyle carried mail and freight.

We got to Cartwright and we had about ten or twelve college kids most of whom were not much younger than I was but they were still in college. We were supposed to prospect for a site for a hospital. We lived on the local economy with the Labradorians. There were very few there. This was an old settlement, settled, I guess, about two centuries before.

Q: Were they Danes?

Mr. B.: No, these were English. Labrador was settled by the

English. They still had some of the old English silver with the hall marks on the back, so worn down, the spoons, I remember, so worn down from use that they were just a little tiny segment of what they had been. Old names like Dorcas were still used, and they had these old expressions, "Have you made a good breakfast?" They talked a kind of vernacular. These were enclaves, they were cut off completely in summer, except by sea, because inland it was just impassable. You sank in during the summer up to your knees. The top snow melted but never melted beyond a certain depth.

Q: Is that the tundra?

Mr. B.: No, it's not. It was heavily forested, but you still would sink way in and you would get eaten alive by black flies.

In the winter, of course, you had some travel by dog team but there was nowhere to go by dog team, except from one settlement to another. And, of course, the rest of Labrador was more or less cut off from Canada. It was miles away. There was none of this iron-mine development then, you see, and none of the air bases which were built in World War II.

So they were isolated enclaves, living on fish, inadequate food. There was a lot of bone tuberculosis and a lot of other diseases which were really nutritional, I guess. And Sir Wilfrid had selected this area to establish his hospital and doctors. His main headquarters were down in Newfoundland, but he would make periodic visits up here.

Q: Did you have an opportunity to see him at close quarters?

Mr. B.: Yes, I did, and it was invaluable. I was coming to that. We spent the summer with, I didn't think, very much accomplishment, partly because the planning hadn't been too good for this particular hospital.

Q: Was it to be a general hospital?

Mr. B.: Yes, it was supposed to be a general hospital, not a big one. There were not many people there, very few, so you didn't need a big hospital. The big hospital was down at St. Anthony in Newfoundland, on the northern Newfoundland coast, and for serious cases they would transport people down there.

We spent the summer tramping around chiefly, looking for sites for the hospital and trying to mark them out with the aid of a local fisherman and we helped them with unloading fish and we unloaded a lot of supplies which were useful the following summer. I didn't think we accomplished much during that summer. Like all of these volunteer missions when you use volunteer labor sometimes the planning is not very good, and it was I think true in this case.

Q: More idealistic than practical.

Mr. B.: Yes. Then, when fall came on - oh, I should have said that we got infrequent baths in absolutely icy water. There was no running water there, of course, at all, except in the streams. We would go over to a stream that emptied into Cartwright Bay and try to take a very quick bath. The snow was still melting most of the summer so you can see how cold it was, but the great problem with taking a bath was not only the coldness of the water but the minute there was an exposed inch of flesh above the water, you were bitten to death by black flies. We all grew beards and we had head nets and everything else, but it didn't do any good. We'd double-wrap our pants and put heavy socks over them and they'd crawl up underneath and we'd come back with bloody shins every day from the woods!

It was a fascinating experience. I worked hard. We did a lot of hard physical labor. I guess I got to a larger weight than I ever had, 173 or 174, because I ate so much.

Q: The diet of fish was beneficial in that sense?

Mr. B.: But toward the end of the summer, Sir Wilfrid Grenfell had been visiting the coast and he came into Cartwright. He had an old yacht, it was a former yacht, called the Strathcona, named for Lord Strathcona, a Canadian, who had given this to the Grenfell mission. It was an old steam yacht which burned anything, coal, or wood, rags, anything at all. It was in pretty bad condition, really, but it moved. Sir Wilfrid wanted to take this yacht back down to Newfoundland to deliver him and Lady Grenfell to Ailhead in Newfoundland, and then for me to take it back to St. Anthony, where the Strathcona wintered. St. Anthony was the headquarters of the mission in Newfoundland.

Q: Your naval background had been discovered?

Mr. B.: He knew, yes. He knew that I'd been in the Navy. I said, "Look, I don't know anything about this coast and it's a very treacherous coast." In those days it wasn't even lighted and there had been a great many wrecks particularly between Newfoundland and Labrador. The tides and currents are very treacherous, and there are a lot of rocks, some of which weren't charted in those days. He said:

"That isn't necessary. I have an old boy aboard who's been with me for many years and he knows this coast like the palm of his hand. The only trouble is he can't see. If you will tell him what's on that headland, if there's a lone pine and so forth, he'll tell you which way to steer!"

I thought that was a little like by guess and by God.

Q: It sounds like the Munson Line all over again!

Mr. B.: One thing you didn't do up there, you did not steam at night. The _Kyle_, the mail steamer, never steamed at night. You laid up overnight. This seemed like it should be relatively simple so I took the _Strathcona_ - I've forgotten where I picked her up, but Lady Grenfell and Sir Wilfrid were aboard and we went down to St. Anthony first from Cartwright, stopping at a couple of places along the way. He would do the typical job of a medical missionary, he or his assistants, and they would see who needed some treatment in the villages and pick up, maybe, some patients for St. Anthony, and would work their way down the coast that way. He would also take an inventory of what was needed at a particular village, particular settlement.

He was a wonderful personality. I got to know him when I made this trip and particularly I got to know him after we left St. Anthony, before we got to Ailhead. We were going down the Newfoundland coast and had to go about halfway down, I guess. The _Strathcona_ only made about seven or eight knots at full speed, maybe a little more, so it was a very slow trip, and we came into a very heavy fog, which are very frequent over those waters, and decided to anchor and wait out the fog, which we did. So we anchored and remained all night in this fog-bound area, and Sir Wilfrid, who was not a young man then and had some heart trouble, came up on the bridge with me where I stayed all night, as I remember, to make sure nobody was going to run us down, and he just talked all night long. Lady Grenfell was always watching out for him. She thought he overdid and so forth, and she came up or sent up two or three times to ask him, tell him, to come down and so forth. I was in a delicate position because I didn't want to encourage the man to do anything he didn't want to do, but I was entranced. He had such a wonderful philosophy of life and such an optimism, tremendous optimism, and a sparkling personality which was really tremendously outgoing, and a deep and abiding faith in God.

He just talked to me all night long and I've always remembered that vividly as one of the highlights of that particular trip. I couldn't tell you now what we talked about except life and death and all the eternal verities.

In any case, I finally got the <u>Strathcona</u> down to Ailhead and Sir Wilfrid and Lady Grenfell left and I took her back up to St. Anthony, which was a short trip and we had no fog that time so there was no problem.

Q: And your pilot was able to . . . ?

Mr. B.: Yes. I remember my inglorious landing at St. Anthony. I was trying to come alongside the dock. I had discovered, of course, that the Strathcona did not maneuver very well and it was very different from ringing bells in a destroyer and then backing down rapidly. It took quite a long time before she answered any bells and I thought I'd allowed for this but I hadn't allowed sufficiently and we sort of crashed into the dock! Much to the delight of all those who thought this former naval officer didn't know what he was doing, anyway.

So I then hooked a ride down to St. John's in a sealer, which was part of the fleet of the Job Brothers, of St. John's, some of the famous traders and sealers of that day. One of them, the younger one, was aboard this trawler, really, converted as a sealing vessel.

Q: Did they process the Seals on board?

Mr. B.: Actually, I never saw this done so I can't answer, but it was described to me. This ship that he was on was really one of the smaller ones. They would use the crew from this ship, I guess, to kill the seals and then bigger ships would take most of the skins and carcasses. I was offered a job in the sealing fleet as a doctor, and I said:

"I'm not a doctor," and he said, "Oh, well, all you need is iodine and cc pills. We go out there when the ice is just melting," that would be in the spring, of course, and I was there in September, "and we're out there for six weeks at a time or something like that." And he described to me the bloody, gory, awful mess. And I didn't stay up there for that. I decided I had to get back and start to make a living.

I got back to Baltimore, I guess, about October 1929 and I decided to try to get a job in New York.

Q: Your wanderlust had been sated?

Mr. B.: Well, for the time being. I wanted to write more. I wrote something for the Baltimore Sun about some of these experiences, both in the merchant marine and also in Labrador.

Q: And they ran it?

Mr. B.: Yes, in the Sunday paper, I think it was. Also in experimenting with writing and enjoying it, I thought I wanted now to be a newspaperman. In any case, I thought I ought to try it for two or three years. I knew I liked to write. I knew that.

I went up to New York and first tried to get a job on

the Herald Tribune, which was then the mecca of the newspaper crowd. There were three newspapers that were really a mecca in those days - the Herald Tribune, the Paris Herald, and the Honolulu Star-Bulletin.

Q: The Star-Bulletin was?

Mr. B.: Well, the reason for that was that it was the land of the lotus-eaters, you see, just as Paris was the land of the left-wing intelligentsia, avant garde, and so forth. It had a kind of romantic appeal. But the Herald Tribune was probably at the head of the list. Also my father gave me a letter of introduction to - or wrote a letter, rather - to Carr Van Anda, who had been on the Baltimore Sun as managing editor some years before and who had been brought to New York by Adolph Ochs, who had taken the Times over and who was the genius of that paper. Van Anda developed it in World War I. Carr Van Anda was an amazing man. He had a brain which understood the Einstein theory and saw the importance of it, had it written as a newspaper story. He was responsible for the Times' superb coverage of World War I, and a more thorough war coverage than had ever been done before, I guess, and, as far as the news columns are concerned, he, really much more than Adolph Ochs, was responsible for the Times' success in news coverage.

Mark you, he was selected by Adolph Ochs, so Adolph Ochs knew a good man when he saw him. He was a minor genius. He was an astronomer, an amateur astronomer, and a mathematician, and so on. He had retired or virtually retired by the time I got to New York, although a permanent successor had not been appointed. The man who was appointed as his acting managing editor was Fred Birchall, a little Englishman with a white goatee, which always wagged like a goat, but he would never give up his English citizenship so he was never appointed full managing editor, which a lot of us thought was too bad because he was a delightful guy and a wonderful newspaperman.

In any case, after the Herald Tribune had said they'd consider my application but nothing happened, I got a call to come to New York to see Freddie Birchell. That was due to my father's letter. It shows that contacts are important!

Q: Within the fraternity, certainly.

Mr. B.: They are anywhere, really. Freddie talked to me for some time. He was rather frightening in a way. He was sort of gruff, but underneath nowhere near as bad as his bark. Carr Van Anda, I think, came in and Freddie said:

"I think this young man will make out all right," or something like that, and Van Anda allowed as how I might, so I was hired. I was hired to start work just about three days after the stock market crash in 1929.

Q: You got in under the wire, didn't you?

Mr. B.: I didn't know how lucky I was because if I had gotten a job on the Herald Tribune I almost certainly would have been fired. A great many people over there were fired who'd been hired recently. I think the Tribune took three 10 percent cuts during the Depression, one after the other, and the Times took one 10 percent pay cut. I don't believe anyone was fired from the Times. I don't think they did any hiring during the Depression, but I don't think anyone was fired.

In those days the Times was just the Times. It had no outside interests except partial interest in a paper mill in Canada and it was making very little money, but the publisher felt that the Times was a public trust and he believed it was more important to fulfill that trust than to make a lot of money. This was the heritage, in a sense, of Adolph Ochs, although Adolph Ochs liked money and made money, too.

I was a general assignment reporter on the Times and

hired first on a trial basis and then kept on. One of my first assignments, which I flubbed, was covering a cat which had gotten caught up in the spire of St. Patrick's Cathedral and firemen had to come and get it down. This is what they call a feature story which I'd done before.

Q: In the second half!

Mr. B.: I didn't do it very well and David Joseph, who was then the city editor, a nice guy but not very understanding as far as human nature is concerned. He was not very helpful and I didn't get such good assignments after that for a while.

Q: In what sense did you flub it?

Mr. B.: I just didn't write it in the right way. I reported it all right, but it was one of these stories that has to be reported with quite a sense of humor and a light touch and so on.

Q: Cuteness!

Mr. B.: I guess I've never been particularly good at that kind of story. I can do dramatic effects better, although later I got a great many feature assignments and did them all right.

In any case, the assistant city editor was much more inclined to help younger people, a man named Walter Fenton, who was much younger than Joseph. After about a month on the *Times* they said, well, I could stay on but they'd have to decrease my salary from I think it was $75 a week to $65 a week. That was a blow but it made me mad and I said, I'm going to show these guys. So I said all right and stayed on and I didn't get any very good chances, a lot of routine small stuff, attending dinners which never got in the paper, this kind of thing. You worked from about one or two o'clock until you were finished with your night assignment, eleven, twelve, one, or whatever it might be.

Finally, one day, I guess it was Sunday, there was a murder right there in Times Square and Walter Fenton told me to get over there fast and see what had happened. I got there before the detectives did and they thought I was one of the detectives until they found out I was a newspaperman and expelled me from the scene. But I got there first and got the whole story and did it acceptably. It was a front-page story, and from then on I started to get along better. Joseph gave me somewhat better assignments, chiefly, I think, due to Fenton's influence.

I did all sorts of general assignment stories, many of them features, very few political stories, but occasionally a political story. Many of them were crimes, many of them things like parades. I did the last of the GAR parades on Riverside Drive in 1932 when I became what they called in the office parade editor because I could provide some of the drama and pomp and circumstances of this in writing. I did a story of the eclipse in North America in 1932 and got a byline, one of the first bylines that I had. In those days, the Times did not give many bylines. There were very, very few.

This was one of the bad things that happened in the Depression. In place of raises, we started to get bylines. I think that cheapened the paper, made bylines much less impressive instead of a mark of merit for a very good story, and it became just a due, so that nowadays everybody on the paper has a byline. There are advantages and disadvantages to this but, on the whole, I think it has tended to hurt the product of journalism. When I came to town originally there were no bylines at all.

Q: On that particular occasion, though, was it merit?

Mr. B.: That's what they thought.

Q: You delved into the scientific background for the whole thing?

Mr. B.: Yes, and the writing, too.

Of course, there were some bylines in the Sunday paper, when you did a Sunday magazine article or something of that sort. I discovered an article I wrote in I guess it was 1931 or 1932 when Billy Mitchell's Army fliers tried to find and bomb the Mount Shasta which was anchored somewhere off the Virginia capes. I wrote a long, analytical piece on this, really quite anti-Mitchell and pro-Navy. It was quite wrong in many ways, but on the merits of the Mount Shasta effort alone, it was correct. They didn't even find the Mount Shasta. They couldn't find her. She was anchored somewhere 100 miles at sea or something like that. Those were very crude bombing days, of course. Nobody knew how to bomb or how to find a ship.

I retained my interest in the sea and the Navy, of course, and as military assignments came along I told Joseph and Fenton that I would like to cover naval assignments.

I started on my spare time to try to develop contacts in the Brooklyn Navy Yard and the Third Naval District, where I already had some -

Q: I guess you began to find this your aptitude?

Mr. B.: Yes, I enjoyed getting a good sea story. One of

the earliest assignments, I guess, where I got considerable publicity, mostly on the sports pages, strangely enough, was covering the rifle matches at Camp Perry, a big thing in those days, and in which there was some particular interest that certain year by someone high on the _Times_ hierarchy. I've forgotten who it was. I don't think it was the publisher but it may have been someone else.

Freddie Birchall assigned me to go out there and I spent two or three weeks at Camp Perry writing about these rifle matches.

Then I asked early for a chance to cover some of the fleet maneuvers, and I think I started covering these in the spring of 1932 because I found a letter here which I wrote to my sister - our first daughter was born in the summer of 1932 and I think I was away that spring. For the first nine months we were married, we thought there was a conspiracy because I was away more than I was at home.

Q: Maybe you should go back for a moment and tell me about your marriage because you did not do that before.

Mr. B.: I was married - we were married - in 1931. I had met Helen long before, when she was a student at Hollins College with my sister and I was a midshipman first and then an ensign. But I had not been, let's say, sufficiently impressed or she had not been sufficiently impressed! We then didn't come in contact again for quite a long time. I went to Europe in the Navy and then various other places. When I got to New York she was working there. She'd graduated from Hollins and had left Springfield, Ohio, her home. I've forgotten, really, how I met her in New York again, but I did and soon it became a certain thing!

So in June of '31 we were married. I'd been living before that down in Chelsea with another chap on the Times.

Q: At the old hotel down there?

Mr. B.: No, I never lived in the old hotel. We had an apartment down in Chelsea. The strange ways New York has changed. We would think nothing - I would think nothing of walking down to the 26th Street area from the Times at night, down 8th Avenue, at one or two o'clock in the morning and never be worried at all by any thought of anyone bashing me on the head. I wouldn't do it now for anything. Maybe it's a sign, of advanced age.

Q: No, it's a sign of common sense!

Mr. B.: We lived originally at 29 West 10th Street and lived there until our first daughter was born and for some months thereafter. We finally decided that we'd have to find another apartment. We had to walk up five flights and had to take Barby up to the roof in a basket to get sun, and that wasn't very satisfactory.

In any case, I started covering naval assignments and I covered the fleet maneuvers.

Q: Where? Down in the Caribbean?

Mr. B.: I hate to trust my memory on this and yet I don't find these immediately available records. They would be available in the Times clippings and the Times index - where the maneuvers were, but I think in 32 they were down in the Caribbean, around the Panama Canal, but I'm not certain.

I covered most of the big fleet maneuvers from then on till World War II - and after. In addition to that, having started covering the Navy and writing about things like the treaty cruisers, the Salt Lake City when she was commissioned and others, I started gradually to cover Army and Air Force assignments.

Q: Meanwhile, carrying others as well?

Mr. B.: Oh, yes. I was on general assignment all this time, doing everything for the Times, but when a military assignment or a naval assignment that seemed important came along generally the Times would assign me to it if it was feasible or they wanted it covered.

Q: Did this take you to the Pacific as well?

Mr. B.: It did later on, not immediately in '32, but I covered the fleet maneuvers at Midway, which was a replica of the attack on Pearl Harbor really, that famous maneuver whenever it was, '37 or '38.

One of the things I remember most and I don't know whether it was in these '32 fleet maneuvers or whether it was a later one, there were at least two of them down around Panama, was Admiral Pratt, who was then chief of naval operations. I guess it must have been '32 because his tour would have ended by that time or shortly thereafter. He came down for the critique and the final part of the maneuver and I remember interviewing him and asking him the old controversy which was still pretty strong about the aircraft carrier versus the battleship. He was very emphatic the battleship was still queen of the seas. He was a battleship man. I don't have a clipping but it's in the Times clippings.

I didn't get to know Pratt very well. I met him then and on a number of other occasions. He had a very good mind, there's no doubt about that, but, like Spruance, who was a battleship man, they were brought up in those days with the leviathans and it was hard to conceive that this new instrument of war was going to make them all obsolete.

Q: That particular maneuver was in defense of the Panama Canal, wasn't it?

Mr. B.: I think it was, but I'm confused about this because there were at least two of them that had about the same objective. On one of them, and I think it was a later maneuver, the Lexington and the Saratoga came in from the Pacific and did successfully bomb the canal without anyone detecting them.

Q: With Admiral Reeves in charge, yes.

Mr. B.: Yes, and I think that was a later one.

In some of these early reports on the Navy I encountered some of the traditional silent service problems that you had with the fleet. They didn't understand public relations at all and they didn't understand the role of the press. I had a great deal of difficulty in communications, first, because the Navy was not equipped to send press messages - their own messages were very brief and terse. You'd give them 1,000 words of press and it might take them twelve to twenty-four hours to get it off to a shore station. They would say they couldn't send it to a naval shore station, they'd have to send it to a commercial station. There was none of this automatic receiving equipment in those days, so a lot of it was tapped out. So, frequently stories arrived late and garbled. Always one of the big problems was to get permission and approval before you left on the trip from Washington so that the Navy could send direct to a Navy shore station, then have it automatically put on the wire to The New York Times. That always had to be done. It took a lot of doing. I had to arrange that in Washington.

And you encountered a great many garbles from inexperienced operators. I remember Admiral Willard had command of the Scouting Force. He was a very fat and heavy man, one of the fattest admirals I've ever seen in my life, and I wrote some really trite phrase about Admiral Willard's battleships being ponderous and mighty, and it came out Admiral Willard was ponderous and mighty!

Q: What was his first name?

Mr. B.: I don't remember his first name. I should.

One other incident that stuck in my craw was after a maneuver at Panama - I don't think it was this '32 maneuver, I think it was a later one - when the fleet had actually come to port and they had a succession of athletic events in Panama, including a fleet golf match. I reported the scores of the fleet golf match and the flag secretary attempted to censor these. He said that it hadn't been officially released! So I had quite a run-in with him.

I discovered that I could be very aggressive and tough in some of these things. I had to be because these people were really incredibly obtuse. In one instance, and I think this was the instance or maybe it was in another case, where I filed ashore, when the fleet came in to Panama, I always filed ashore because they were much faster and more rapid. In any case, when you were in port you were supposed to file through commercial facilities, and I filed with Cable and Wireless, I think. But in any case, in Panama in those days the government had an interest in Cable and Wireless and I'd file my dispatches. I think it was this same officer who came over to the Cable and Wireless station without my knowledge, took my dispatch, and attempted to change something in it. I got very angry at that and we had a go-round because I said:

"Look, dispatches are supposed to be - they're international communications and they're supposed to be completely private and no one is supposed to interfere with them. There's a law against that. Would you like me to take this up with Washington?"

He was very huffy. Well, it blew over. I took it to the admiral. I found you often had to take these things right to the top.

Looking back at it, this is really nobody's fault. The Navy simply had no experience in public relations and, even though I'd been in the Navy - they had this old absolutist idea that everything had to be done under their thumb.

Q: Did you happen to be the only reporter at that point?

Mr. B.: In some of the maneuvers I was the only reporter. I think I was the only reporter in the '32 one. Then people started to get interested, other papers, because of the obvious approach of problems in Europe and later on other reporters were assigned in much greater numbers.

For instance, the maneuver in the Pacific, the famous Midway Island maneuver, Floyd Gibbons, the famous one-eyed World War I war correspondent, was aboard - that was aboard the battleship Pennsylvania, I think, which was the flagship of the fleet then.

Q: This showed a lot of initiative and a very advanced point of view on the part of the Times, did it not, to want stories at this early stage on fleet maneuvers when none of the other papers were doing it?

Mr. B.: There's no question about that. I think they were anxious to improve their coverage in every field. The Times had never had a permanent staff member who specialized in the military. No other American paper had, to my knowledge. During World War I a lot of them had run the syndicated columns of Palmer, you remember, who was the Army man and wrote a biography of Pershing. The Baltimore Sun carried occasional pieces from Hector Bywater, an English naval correspondent. But none of them had had a permanent staff member who was writing about military affairs.

As time went on, and I'm capsuling this now, before World War II, Arthur Sulzberger, who was the son-in-law of Adolph Ochs with whom I more or less grew up at the Times - Ochs was still alive when I came to the paper but he died early in the thirties, as I remember. Sulzberger took over and Sulzberger saw, as I think all of us did or many of us did, that there was likely to be a war in Europe, and he said he wanted me to specialize and spend more and more time on the military.

I got direct access to him because he was interested in this. There's another reason he was interested, I think, and that was that Julius Ochs Adler was the Number 2 man on the Times. General Adler had made quite a record for himself as an officer in World War I and was at that time a

Reserve officer and very interested in the Army. He had been promoted by the time World War II started to a brigadier general in the Reserve and actually served in the Pacific during World War II. Adler had a knowledge of the military, particularly the Army, which Sulzberger lacked, and a great interest in it.

Sulzberger had an interest in it primarily, I think, because of his belief that war would start in Europe. I think there was another factor that contributed to the Times' decision to assign me full time to this, and this was that it wasn't completely clear when Adolph Ochs died, who would subsequently become the full heir apparent. It was probably going to be Arthur Sulzberger, but the duties at the Times were divided between him and Adler. Adler was in charge of the business end and Sulzberger was in charge of the editorial end. Soon it became quite clear that Arthur Sulzberger would be the top man, yet Adler's interest in the military undoubtedly influenced the paper's coverage.

I think for all these reasons there was an interest in more and more concentration on military affairs. There was a foresight involved on the part of Sulzberger particularly and Adler, too, who was very interested in the military. And his influence in that field was very considerable. When he died there was a pronounced change, later, after the war was over.

In any case, by 1937 I had covered a great many Army assignments - Army maneuvers as well as Navy maneuvers. I'd gotten a lot of instruction about the Army from Governor's Island, which was then the headquarters of the First Army and from two particularly good friends, the man who came to be Major General "Joe" Dalton - he was a colonel then, and Stanley Grogan who retired as a colonel quite some time ago, and also from Colonel Dupuy, whom you may have heard of. They gave me a number of books and I studied them and some of the Army Staff College procedures.

I also started covering some of the Air Force maneuvers. I remember covering one or two at Mitchell Field of what was then called the General Headquarters, Air Force, which was the predecessor of the Strategic Air Command, then under General Frank Andrews, who probably would have had the job Eisenhower had in World War II had he lived. He was killed, as you may remember, in a crash in Iceland just at the start of World War II. General Frank Andrews was a very fine man. He had a wonderful brain and a very fine personality.

In any case, we attempted to cover more and more of these things. I remember one amusing incident in the maneuver which included the Midway Island bit. We came in to Pearl Harbor after the maneuver was over and one or two of us wanted to fly in the Army Air Corps planes, which were, I believe, old Martin three-engined bombers, around the islands to see them from the air and also to see what the Army Air Corps could do. So several of us went up. They could only take one or two passengers apiece. I think there were three planes. There was one particularly unpleasant correspondent from the Hearst newspapers who was along on that trip. He was in one of the other Martin bombers. These Martin bombers were barely able to stagger off the ground. They were really old, old things with very slow speed. I think it was 90 miles or something like that. They gave you a good panoramic view of the islands and one of them, the one with the Hearst man in it, had a forced landing. It had to come down in a pineapple patch. We thought it was very fitting and nobody felt a bit sorry for him.

On that same maneuver, General Walter Krueger came along as an observer from the Army. He was one of the few Army people who had then ever attended the Naval War College, one of the few senior Army people, in any case, in fact, the only one, and, apart from the fact that he attended this maneuver, he, I think, really helped greatly with Army-Navy relationships later in World War II. Krueger was a very broad visioned man. A lot of people thought he was a German-Prussian type and he did believe in discipline, there's no doubt about it, but he was a delightful shipmate. I used to walk with him on the quarter deck of the Pennsylvania often and talk to him about the Army and about what might be coming. He understood the importance of the Navy too better than a great many other Army officers.

Q: It was more than a means of conveyance?

Mr. B.: Oh, yes. In 1937 after I'd covered a lot of these Army and Air Force maneuvers, Sulzberger thought that I ought to go to Europe and take a hard look. He said, "You've learned a lot about the Army and Air Force, you ought to take a good look at the armies, navies, and air forces of all the principal powers in Europe. War is certainly going to come over there sooner or later and you'd better get informed about that. Then, I think, when you come back from then on you'd better specialize and do only military affairs."

Q: That was really a great break, wasn't it, in the career?

Mr. B.: Yes, it was. I was then called the Military Correspondent. I think it was good foresight because no other paper had such a person at this time. I had made this point. I'd suggested it to Joseph and others but, of course, the publisher had to really approve that.

The British, you know, had had what they called "Our Naval Correspondent" - they always say "Our Army Correspondent" or "Our Air Force Correspondent," because they were all separate and distinct which I think was a disadvantage because I've always believed in the indivisibility of military force. The British sort of channelized it and didn't see the whole picture, I don't think.

Q: Before you go on with that, may I ask you to say something about the Army attitude toward public relations, as you experienced it at these various maneuvers?

Mr. B.: The Army was much more liberal than the Navy had been and the Air Force probably even - well, it wasn't an air force then, it was the Army Air Corps. The Air Corps had something to prove, something to sell. They wanted to sell the Air Corps, they wanted to prove that they could win a war single-handed, and they tended to welcome the press, hoping that they could convert them to their point of view.

Q: This was from the very outset then.

Mr. B.: The Army had lived a life which was closer to the people than the Navy had, there's no doubt about it. All these small Army posts, Governor's Island, for instance, were next door to them. They understood the press. They were a little less formal and you didn't feel the sense of the almighty power of the captain of the ship, where he was god on board ship. You didn't have that same feeling. They could be tough and you could disagree with them sometimes and you did, but they had already, when I started covering them, the beginnings of public affairs officers in the Army. They had one in Washington. The Navy had some but they didn't do a great deal in Washington. I think the Navy also made the mistake later on - I think it's a mistake now - of getting a lot of press specialists and a lot of newspapermen to take over jobs in public relations. The Army has pretty generally stuck to the idea of having a good Army officer run public relations and then get their specialists under him. I think that's the way it ought to be done.

I'd much rather have a good naval officer who doesn't know anything about the press but who is willing to learn to take over the job than I would have a second-rate newspaperman. In peacetime you're going to have a second-rate newspaperman. Even in wartime you may have second-rate newspapermen. I'm coming to that later. I think in any case that the press wants to know the facts and the background from a public affairs officer, and the average newspaperman can't tell them the facts about the Navy. He doesn't know enough, specially in those days.

I remember talking about this with "Count" Austin years ago when he was public affairs officer of the Navy, and I remember talking with "Judge" Eller when he was, and a great many others - Page Smith. They all, without knowing a damned thing about it - became good P.A.O's. When Count first came into office, we had a couple of tangles, but Count changed, he changed his mind. There was no problem as long as the officer was a top-notch officer. If he was a second-grade officer he was no good at the job as he wasn't at any other.

Q: This, then, does explain the silent Navy attitude about publicity?

Mr. B.: Yes, in part, it did. The Navy was apart from the people, there's not much doubt about it. It did live - that famous quoatation of Stimson's was partially true, you know, the one that he made in this biography that Bundy wrote for him. It's not completely true, but partially true. It had its advantages and disadvantages, but the Navy was sort of ingrown in many ways, isolated, and insulated from public feeling to a great extent.

Q: And also emphasized so much the classified nature of information?

Mr. B.: Too much so.

Q: Did the Army do this?

Mr. B.: Only in certain things, not to anywhere near the same extent. Of course, the Army didn't have too much to classify! There wasn't much that wasn't known. Neither did the Navy, for that matter.

Q: Pre World War II the Navy didn't have much either?

Mr. B.: No, not too much, but they had some things like radar which we developed ahead of the British really, although the British claim we hadn't.

I should have said along the way that I'd been going intermittently to Washington during these years to try to get stories down there and to make acquaintances, see people. I guess the first Secretary of the Navy at that time that I knew pretty well was Claude Swanson, and then I went on from there.

Q: How efficient was he as Secretary of the Navy?

Mr. B.: He was good as a political contact. That was his chief value.

Q: He'd been a senator?

Mr. B.: Yes. That was his chief value. He wasn't any good as an administrator or an innovator or anything of that sort. But he was good as a political contact and he could often get things done on the Hill which somebody else couldn't have done.

Then I got to know Josephus Daniels later on, who was then still living and running his papers in North Carolina. I remember seeing him on a couple of occasions. He was attracted by some of my reports on the Navy which he still read.

I remember seeing him on one occasion in some Washington hotel room, I think, where he had his shoes off and socks half off! He was a delightful fellow to listen to. He was awfully definite in his views, but he was a great delight to listen to.

Q: You vindicated your wisdom in making frequent trips to Washington and making contacts there. Do you want to say something about the value of this to a reporter at that time who was interested in the military?

Mr. B.: Well, contacts are always the key to a reporter's trade. In fact, to know anything - of course. Many of these trips and ideas I had to sell to the Times because the idea of making periodic trips from New York to Washington immediately created problems. First, you had to spend money to do it. Second, there might be some jealousy on the part of the Washington Bureau of the Times that here's an outsider coming down to cover some of their domain.

Q: Yes, you had the great figure down there, did you not?

Mr. B.: The first head of the Washington Bureau when I was working was Richard Houlihan, and Arthur Krock later on. I'd gotten to know Arthur Krock in New York slightly. I should say that I wrote some editorials. Old Dr. Finley, who was the editorial head of the Times at first, then Charles Merz was appointed when Arthur Sulzberger started to come up into ascendancy. From 1937 on part of my duties were to write for any department of the paper editorials, Sunday book reviews, news analysis, anything else, all for the same salary. I was the first person on the Times - the only one at that time - who had that requirement.

Q: An ecletic reporter!

Mr. B.: My salary was increased as a result, but not very much. I wrote a great many editorials on military affairs well, I guess when I retired I was the oldest member of the editorial board - I mean the one who'd been there longer than any of the rest of them. I suppose that from the early thirties on I wrote a great number of the military editorials, most of them as a matter of fact, including the series which the Times produced with Charlie Merz before World War II, which were intended to try to get us prepared for the war. Of course, they were not signed. They were a series of very long editorials, three or four of them, in which we advocated things that the Navy and the Army and the Air Corps needed.

Q: This was a bulwark to President Roosevelt's program, then?

Mr. B.: Yes, although Roosevelt really didn't take action on some of these things, as Buell brings out, especially on the size of the Navy, till very late indeed.

The contacts in Washington that I made were invaluable later. First of all, I learned to know the ropes. I didn't make as many contacts on Capitol Hill. I didn't pay much attention to that, frankly. I paid attention more to the strictly military end of it, not to the appropriations or or legislative end, although I got to know a few people up there, including old Dewey Short of the Armed Services Committee and, of course, Vinson, and a few of the senators. But I didn't regularly attend the committee's hearings or debates or anything of that sort. I left that entirely to the Washington Bureau.

After a time I came to be accepted by the Washington Bureau and Arthur Krock welcomed me. We got along well. I didn't get in their hair and so forth.

Q: This was a specialty that they weren't following?

Mr. B.: Well, they hadn't developed it. They had a man who covered the military, two of them, as a matter of fact – one of them was Wood and the other one was someone else. He had occasional stories but usually they were done more or less from the legislative or appropriations point of view. The technical tactical, and strategic they hadn't done very much with.

Some of the stories I wrote got the Navy's back up quite a lot. I remember one series. There was quite a lot of bitterness between the Board of Inspection and Survey and the Bureau of Engineering. Admiral Bowen, the father of the present Admiral Bowen – it was the beginning of high-pressure steam and Bowen was pushing that.

They were having a lot of trouble with tubes bursting steam leaks and various other things. I wrote several stories about this and Bowen was quite incensed, I remember. I got most of the stories from the Board of Inspection and Survey, which inspected these ships. Then Bowen started to open up and explain his point.

Q: This was a detraction for his efforts?

Mr. B.: Yes, he thought so. Fundamentally, of course, he was right in pushing the high-pressure, high-temperature steam. I think he was a little ahead of the art because the technology hadn't developed really enough for the welds and piping, for instance, to stand some of this.

I don't know whether there's anything else in those years.

Q: How much time were you spending in Washington in this period?

Mr. B.: That's almost impossible to say. It was intermittent. I spent a lot of time traveling because I would not only go to Washington but, as time went on, I went around to nearly all the important Army and Air Force maneuvers and I made a point of visiting the principal military, naval, and air bases in the country where there'd be background, like the Air War College later and Fort Benning. I tried to get to nearly every one of the important centers of tactical thought about once every two years. I couldn't possibly do it once every year unless it was just overnight.

At Fort Knox, the armored school, when the Army did its first (in those days supposedly long march with armored forces), the old Seventh Mechanized Brigade, I went with them from Fort Knox to Fort Oglethorpe in Georgia. This was in the days when Patton was a brigadier general. He was along on the march and played polo at Fort Oglethorpe. Then again when they had maneuvers in upstate New York at what is now Fort Drum - it was Plattsburg in those days, I covered those and I remember writing about them. This one particular incident stuck in my mind because we had all the military attaches at Fort Drum and the Army was going to exhibit some of its new tanks, of which it had only a handful. I remember that it finally ended that out of the five or six tanks it had they all got out of commission. One of them bellied up on a stump, another one broke down, and something happened to the others. Finally, there was only one that passed in front of the military attaches, who were certainly not impressed, least of all the Germans.

We were woefully unprepared in those days. This

culminated, and I've never forgotten that, in 1939, just about the time of the German invasion of Poland, with a large maneuver in upstate New York, again at Plattsburg, and the Seventh Mechanized Brigade, which was our biggest armored force composed of half-tracks and tanks and personnel carriers, participated. I remember the last days of August up there. One after another these military attaches left the maneuver precipitately, the German last of all as a crisis came in Europe. Finally there were very few left.

Then, just as the maneuver ended, the Seventh Mechanized Brigade was scheduled to take what was then a very long mechanized march from Plattsburg down to the World's Fair of Tomorrow, which was opening in New York, called The World of Tomorrow. They went by way of West Point and I accompanied them. We got into New York in September, early September, clanking down the streets and out to Flushing Meadow, to this ironically named World of Tomorrow just at the time the Germans were really going into their blitzkrieg in Poland.

We thought we had a very impressive armored force and discovered we didn't!

Q: Did you find that you had any particular liking for the Army over the Navy as you did this, or were you completely — ?

Mr. B.: I always loved the sea and still do. Of course, when you have old ties you obviously are tied to those, but I had a tremendous number of very good friends in the Army and they were highly respected men whom I grew up with more or less. This was the great advantage I had. I grew up with a lot of these younger officers before they came up to high rank. That really is the only way to cover the military. I did that both in the Navy and the Army and the Air Force.

For instance, I got to know, as I said, then Colonel Dalton. He ended up as a major general, and there were a great many others. I knew General Drum very well who was in World War I and much older than I was. Of course, he's the one that Roosevelt is said to have said, "Drum, Drum, he's always beating his own drum," and he was. Drum wanted the job that Eisenhower had but never got it. Drum turned down the Stilwell job in China. He was a great egotist in some ways. It's just as well that he didn't get either job, I think, although he was a bright man. He'd won his fame as a staff officer in World War I really, on Pershing's staff.

Q: I guess what I wanted to ask was did you find that your stories on the Army were generated more easily than those on the Navy?

Mr. B.: I think there were fewer obstacles usually. You immediately encountered a communications problem with the Navy if you were at sea. If you were at sea there was a communications problem of considerable importance. That wasn't true if you were on land or writing from Washington, but the problem of Navy communications for the press has never been completely resolved even today, I think. It's much better today if they want to expedite it, but certainly up until the time I retired you could still encounter considerable communication problems in a Navy ship at sea. They have so many other higher priorities. Often the press has, by regulations, to go to the nearest commercial shore station, at least that's what he's supposed to do, and then be relayed on land wire, cable or by radio, and sometimes you get garbled.

Of course, we're far ahead of the British Navy and I was coming to that when we got into the Omaha beachhead business, which was a scandal. But the communications problem with the Navy, from the point of view of the press, was a major one. Today it is very much better than it was originally, partly due to better communications, but you're still subject to garbles, you're still subject sometimes to delays, which are not deliberate delays. Of course, you're also subject to censorship when you write from a

Navy ship, not precensorship usually, unless it's something that's very glaring, but you simply sign this pledge not to reveal classified information.

Q: From the point of view of the Editors of the papers, were they perhaps more interested in stories about the Army than they were about the Navy, keeping in mind their readers?

Mr. B.: No, I don't think so. I think they played that impartially, depending on the importance of the story. I had many front-page stories about the Navy, exclusive stories, and many about the Army.

The *Times* in those days was playing up the military and they would put things on the front page and give space to them that other papers didn't give. It was not infrequent that I would write two or three columns in one day about a maneuver or about something the Navy had done. For instance, the Russians were trying to get the design of our battleships, you remember, in the early thirties, and I wrote a series of stories on this. Then we had a whole series of stories, about ships we'd given to South America. The *Times*, I think, played these quite impartially, depending on what they judged to be the newsworthy interest. I wish they'd give the same amount of space today! Of course, the *Times* has changed in this period. It must be said they now have a lot of things in the paper that they didn't have in those days - a women's page, for instance; they had none of that then.

Q: What was their attitude in the thirties toward countries in Latin America run by dictators?

Mr. B.: I would find that hard to say because I don't remember the editorials we ran on this. The editorials expressed the editorial position of the paper. I think we were against dictators, generally speaking, but I don't think that we made a terrible point about anything in Latin America. I think that such relationships as we had with the Latin-American countries and they've developed in a different way since then because we didn't have those formidable service missions that they've got down there in many of these countries now. We had a few officers but not many. We had a few officers coming to the United States and we had some American ships being sold to Latin America, but developed methodology was really a product of World War II.

You see, before World War II most of the armies of the world would want to send their officers to be trained to the Ecole de Guerre, to the French Staff College, to to France. Here was the best army in the world, supposedly.

Relatively few would think of sending them to Leavenworth. To a lesser extent, this was true of the British Navy. A lot of them liked to send their navy people to Britain.

Q: To Dartmouth?

Mr. B.: Not to Dartmouth because that's a midshipmen's school. We had had associations with Latin America. Of course, a number of Latin-American naval officers, not many, but some, graduated from the Naval Academy, and some Japanese naval officers. So, I would think the relationships with South America were sort of in the doldrums. They were not considered of high importance.

The *Times* has changed completely from the thirties. Editorial policy of the *Times* in the thirties could be described in two words to be against sin, to be against Hitler, and nothing else, really. Their editorials were bland, often quite well written, on a great many different subjects, but we didn't take any very strong stands. And that was a deliberate policy of Adolph Ochs. He didn't believe that a paper could take a strong editorial stand and still preserve objective news columns. He thought that the tail would wag the dog, and I think that has happened. Often, the editorials that we wrote in those days were so bland that they irritated some of the staff.

But, on the other hand, when you look back at it, the Times was a far more objective paper in its news columns than it is today.

Of course, after Adolph Ochs died, Sulzberger took over as the top man, his tenure, and his own self-confidence, perhaps not quite certain at that early period. After Adolph Ochs died and Sulzberger took over, the editorial policy started to change a little. Sulzberger picked his men. Charlie Merz was his man, and Merz had more of a point of view. His point of view was toward the liberal; he'd once been a liberal, he'd changed his mind to some extent and his attitude, but he'd been quite liberal when he was on the World, and he shifted a little bit toward the center, toward the right. I wouldn't say the Times' editorial policy in those days was liberal, but I would have called it independent, more or less. There were some things on which we took stands but it wasn't couched in anywhere near the strong language that the editorials are couched in today. It wasn't as sweeping. We tried to present both points of view. If we took a stand in an editorial, we'd say this, but on the other hand, that, and then at the end we'd say we feel that this overbalances that. That gave way altogether later on back in the late fifties and early sixties. But there's no doubt that in those days the news pages were the be all and the all-important thing. The editorials were of secondary importance, although there was an opportunity for good writing in the editorials which I think is not often presented today. Today the editorials are more intellectually, perhaps stimulating but not usually particularly distinguished for their writing.

Q: I wanted to ask you if you had any coverage of the arms limitation treaties in the early thirties?

Mr. B.: Yes, I wrote about the London Conference. I didn't cover it personally.

Q: You didn't go?

Mr. B.: No. I think this, however, was in the form of analytical articles or Sunday articles. In those days the Times used to carry articles of semi-opinion and analysis of considerable length on what we would call today the op-ed page of the Times. It was an entirely different type of page than it is now. There was never really any such thing as the op-ed page, but on Sundays in what is now the Review of the Week section they would carry fairly lengthy articles of analysis.

I found one here dealing with the Mt. Shasta episode,

which I wrote in 1932, and I assume that I wrote some although I don't remember offhand about the London Conference. I know, in fact, that I wrote about it at one time or another, but just when I don't know. I know I wrote about the great controversy between the 6-inch gun cruiser and the 8-inch gun cruiser advocates, the deficiencies of the latter, and so forth.

One of the interesting things that developed as war came closer, at least it was interesting to me, I attempted when I was in this country - (I'm coming back to my European trip later) - to make contact with some of the foreign military attaches in Washington deliberately and particularly cultivated the German and the Japanese. In those days, the Japanese had quite a little Japanese colony in New York, the old Nippon Club. I've forgotten where it was but somewhere in the Sixties, I think. And there was a Japanese naval office in New York. It was supposed to be a procurement office, I think, in New York. I met this officer and the Japanese consul general and various others. I was quite conscious - they, I think, had made the initial contact and I didn't turn it down, but I was quite conscious that they were trying to get whatever I knew whenever I came back from fleet maneuvers. In fact,

I told the Navy about this, and I was at the same time very anxious to get anything out of them. So it was sort of a duel of wits that never got anywhere really. But one of the amusing things that happened during this period.

I went up to lunch at the Nippon Club a couple of times with this naval officer and one or two of his associates and, partially as a result, the Japanese consul general asked Helen and me to come in to dinner. We lived out in Chappaqua, in Westchester County, so when we came in for late dinner we usually had to spend the night in town or something of the sort.

In any case, we started in to dinner with our evening clothes ready to spend the night in town and we suddenly discovered, as we were on the train, I read some account in the *Times* of a dinner the consul general had given the night before and that was the night we were supposed to have been there! We'd gotten the dates completely mixed up. You see, this consul general had been very friendly before that. This was the worst offense we could have given the Japanese, because they considered it a deliberate slight, and it took us a very long time indeed to convince him that this wasn't deliberate and to win our way back to his graces.

When we did, it became embarrassing, a little embarrassing,

because shortly before 1939 he commenced to send quite expensive gifts, a very beautiful vase, which I had to send back. I did it on my own and just told him that I couldn't accept these things.

Q: Did the Times have a policy of any sort about that?

Mr. B.: They didn't have any policy at the time, but a policy gradually developed; I think I was the first one who sent any of these things back. There used to be a great business of sending Christmas gifts to newspapermen; not only from the foreigners, but I mean the movie department would get a lot from the movie companies, liquor and so on. I never got much of those. I got a few, but I invariably sent back any gift.

One of the first of these was the vase. This created further friction with the Japanese.

Q: How would you sent it back? With what sort of note?

Mr. B.: I wrote as polite a note as I could and said it was just not our custom and I just could not accept this, that the Times would not want me to, and so on, and I think I sent him a slight, inconsequential gift.

In any case, I did meet some of the Japanese, including the attache in Washington, and I met the German military attache, von Botticher, who was a very advanced thinker as far as military affairs were concerned and a very good man.

I was just trying to find here before I go to von Botticher this old invitation from the Imperial Japanese Navy, Inspector's Office, 1 Madison Avenue, New York City, for the visit of a Japanese squadron to New York. Vice Admiral Zengo Yoshida and his squadron came on a visit. The Awati was not a very modern ship, needless to say, and this was in 1936, but it was already obvious Japan was building up. This was after the Japanese were abandoning the naval agreements. I don't think they denounced it till 1937, if I'm not mistaken.

Q: They circumvented it, however.

Mr. B.: Yes. There were a lot of rumors and reports already about them building these over-sized ships. The Awati was one of the older ships that they had. We went out to the squadron in the Hudson and ate these uncooked fish and various other things! They were all very cordial. But there was even at that time a very noticeable reserve on the part of both the Americans who dealt with the Navy and the Japanese who dealt with their Navy. I don't think the average Japanese officer expected war with the United States but the two were wary and that's the only way it could be described.

In Washington, as I said, I came to know von Botticher, the German attache, who had a number of his family, one or two of his daughters, I think were married to Americans and were living in this country. He was more or less Americanized. He'd been here for some time and was here through all the early phases of the war. He was a pretty good source of information. He was not originally a Nazi, at least to my knowledge he wasn't. He was fairly frank, particularly when the Germans were winning. He could get information which it was difficult to get in any other way. Sometimes after the war started, particularly after the invasion of Poland, I asked him details and he got some stuff from Germany. I came to know and rather admire him.

I suppose, going out of sequence a little, I ought to state here that later on when he went back to Germany on a visit he met Hitler for the first time. He'd never met Hitler before, and Hitler turned on his charm. Von Botticher told me about this later. Von Botticher came back glowing, he never had met the man before and apparently Hitler had him on his right hand at dinner and talked to him. Hitler had a tremendous amount of charm if he wanted to exert it. From then on I think von Botticher's usefulness declined, at least to me. He was still very friendly, but he was trying to convince Americans that Hitler was all right, which was a little hard to do!

In any case, this poor man - and I say "poor man" advisedly because he was far more objective than most Germans. He was not a Nazi and he was a decent person. He went back to Germany after we entered the war. He was a lieutenant general, I guess. After we came into the war, there was a period, of course, of internment and finally in Germany he ended up in an insane asylum. He was torn so badly by what he discovered of the Nazi excesses and by the fact that his daughters were American and half his heart was here. The poor chap died, I believe, in a mental institution. But he was a very interesting man, a very useful source. Of course, he also tried to propagandize. I remember he showed me in the German Embassy in Washington after the Polish campaigns a famous propaganda picture which was shown all over the world called "The Campaign of the Eighteen Days," the campaign in Poland. That was one which the Germans used to show the power of the blitzkrieg and how they overwhelmed the Poles in a short time.

Q: Mighty frightening propaganda!

Mr. B.: Yes.

Well, to backtrack a little, in 1937 I went to Europe.

Q: Before you go, there's one more question that occurs to me. What was your relationship with the Naval Intelligence Office in New York in those days?

Mr. B.: It wasn't so much in New York. I used to stop by the Naval Intelligence Office in Washington quite frequently when I was down there. I knew most of the other officers. I knew Captain Puleston and various others at various times, and I would sometimes get some very good information from them. Naval Intelligence in those times used to publish a little fact sheet about the navies of the world and I used to get those regularly.

I dropped down to the Third Naval District headquarters fairly frequently and saw some of the intelligence people there, but they had a very much narrower view. They didn't get the whole picture, as they did in Washington.

Q: Did you know Paul Foster when he was there?

Mr. B.: Oh, yes, I knew Paul Foster.

Q: When he was there?

Mr. B.: I didn't know him when he was there, no.

Q: And what he accomplished when he was there?

Mr. B.: No, I didn't. What did he accomplish?

Q: The raid on the Japanese office. That became knowledge.

Mr. B.: Oh, yes. I knew Paul Foster very well later, but I didn't know him really at that time. When was that now?

Q: Around '37, I think, or something like that.

Mr. B.: I may have been in Europe then. I was in Europe for a considerable period.

Q: I'll let you go to Europe now!

Mr. B.: I started in England and tried to see as much as I could in a finite period of the armies, navies, and air forces and meet as many of the military leaders as I could.

Q: Were there any appointments made in advance for you or did you have to do this on your own?

Mr. B.: In some cases I tried to make appointments in advance. I usually sent cables ahead to the Times' offices in these areas, but in other cases I often had to wait until I got there and could be specific. In the case of London, and I've never forgotten this, Ferdie Kuhn was then The New York Times correspondent, and after I got there I was talking to Ferdie about people to see and he said, "Oh, don't bother with Churchill, he's just a nut."

Churchill was then a maverick M.P.

Q: He was the Cassandra of the Parliament.

Mr. B.: He was, and unfortunately, I took Ferdie's advice and didn't meet Churchill till many years later.

But I went to a number of British bases and to see a little of the British Navy, not much. It was chiefly an overall view from the point of view of London.

Q: Did you discover anything about the British radar picture?

Mr. B.: No. That was very tightly held. I'd known a little about our radar experiments, but very little, and I didn't know just how advanced our own U.S. Navy was. We had radar on ships, as you know.

Q: Did you ultimately know Watson-Watt?

Mr. B.: No, I never met Watson-Watt.

In France I saw most of the then leaders, including General Gamelin of the French armed forces. I've never forgotten that Gamelin told me in French, "My soul is at peace," when I asked him about the preparations of France for war, which was an ironic statement.

Q: What did he mean by that?

Mr. B.: I said, "Are you satisfied with the French preparations for war?" and he said, "My soul is at peace," which means yes! He had perfect confidence. Well, everyone was saying that. The U.S. military attache, who had a high reputation, I can't think of his name, in Paris at the time, a brigadier general, (Fuller, I think) was saying that the French Army was the best in the world, there wasn't any question about it. They all had that impression, nearly everyone did. Our own people believed it - believed in French theory, believed in the French Army. I remember being shaken - I talked with this military attache and I talked with people in Paris, then I went to the French Naval Academy at Brest and the Army was having a maneuver up in the Champagne area on the old World War I battlefields. I went up there to see this, and I remember not being impressed at all by the smartness of the poilu. The soldiers dragged along and they didn't look like they had much morale, they didn't salute, and they didn't look sharp in their uniforms, very haphazard.

I came back to Paris and I told this attache this. I said, "they didn't look good to me." He said:

"Oh, don't pay any attention to that. The French poilu always looks like that but he always rises to the occasion."

It shows just how wrong you can be. Unfortunately, I took his advice and I did not report my feelings. I wasn't confident enough of my own ability at the time. It is true that a lot of armies look ragged in peacetime and rise to high occasions. But there was something rotten at the core with France and the French. I thought some of the rottenness was in Leon Blum's government. They had nationalized the French aircraft factories and there was a reduction in the output of those. I went to some of those and was not at all impressed by that.

Now, there's a great attempt to say Leon Blum had nothing to do with the decline and fall of France, but I think he did. I think France was completely divided between the Left and the Right. Politicians were corrupt in their heyday and the Army was infected. It's pretty clear in retrospect, I think, but it wasn't equally clear then and unfortunately I did not report my impression.

Q: What were your impressions in Britain?

Mr. B.: At that time, in 1937, there was a very small Army, and one that had experience chiefly in colonial wars. They didn't have too many tanks, just as we didn't. It was a very small Army. They had very good field pieces, good artillery. I was impressed with that. The thin red line was very thin indeed, but it was professional, I think.

That also was beginning to be the time when you had the Liddell Hart-Leslie Hore-Belisha controversy. There was a great deal of difference of opinion about what the British Army should be and should do.

From France I went on to Germany, this was Nazi Germany, of course, where the *Times* was already very unpopular because we'd written strong editorials against Hitler . . .

Q: And the Jewish question.

Mr. B.: Yes, the beginning of the persecution of the Jews; well, it was more than the beginning but the bulk of the concentrations camps had not been developed, I guess, at that time but they were beginning to be.

The *Times* was regarded with some suspicion. It was the first time I'd been in an absolutist and authoritarian country with a dictator, so I was very careful in what I did also about what notes I took. As a result of the *Times*' attitude I really got no firsthand information in Germany at all.

Q: Were you shadowed in any way?

Mr. B.: I can't answer that. I assumed that my baggage would be searched in the hotel. I think it was, largely because things seemed to be in somewhat different positions than they were when I left the room. I wasn't conscious of being shadowed. On the other hand, I'm quite sure the Germans knew most of my movements. It wasn't that kind of surveillance, if there was surveillance. It wasn't oppressive. You could go many places with no feeling that you were being watched. In fact, I did go to a great many places.

When I went to Europe in '37 I went over by sea. Helen came with me as far as London, then she left and came back. I went over on the same ship with Percy Black, who was our Assistant Military Attache in Berlin and a very good one. Truman Smith, at that time, who acquired considerable fame later, was the Military Attache in Berlin. He was the one who dealt with the visit of Lindberg, the controversial visit of Lindberg, and who was a great defender of Lindberg. Truman Smith lived over here in Connecticut, or he did until he died. His wife is still there. He was a very thorough student of German military preparations. I got quite a lot of information from him and, of course, I applied to see various things, all of which were turned down.

I asked to see the head of the general staff and as

an indication of the German displeasure with the _Times_ they said no, he was unavailable, but I could see a lower-ranking man, General Keitel. Keitel was not then the top man, and I did get to see General Keitel. He was a red-faced Prussian, or he looked like a Prussian, who did not seem to me to have much brains. It was a futile interview, as I was sure it would be, but many of these things served as impressions and were useful in that respect.

Keitel struck me at the time, and I didn't have any particular perspicacity about it, as a political officer pure and simple and not as a combat officer - an entirely different type from von Botticher in Washington who was a real combat soldier, although he was a attache.

From there I went on into Poland, which was a refreshing change in many ways because even though Poland was a sort of medieval atmosphere it had a sense of greater freedom than Germany. The people on the farms still lived as kind of serfs, but they weren't serfs. They had their own independence. They were tough, stout people. Warsaw itself was a city largely of dirt streets. There were some paved streets, but a correspondent there I knew lived way back on a dirt street.

I saw the famous Polish cavalry, including Pilsudski's own regiment, demonstrate on horseback their prowess with the sabre and the lance, and these troikas, the three horse drawn carriages with machine guns mounted on them firing at the gallop. That was a good education in what happened later because these people were magnificent horsemen, some of the best in the world. They had very few tanks. I saw some of the Polish planes and was not very impressed. They had a small aircraft industry of their own.

Normally, I would have gone from Poland into Russia but my visa had not arrived! I had waited for a long time and I more or less had given up the idea of going to Russia so I went on down to Austria and stopped there for a little while. I got what I could in Austria, which was still an independent country. It wasn't yet under Germany.

Q: Did you see Schuschnigg or anybody like that?

Mr. B.: No, I didn't. I saw some of the military.

Q: While you were in Germany did you see anything of the naval establishment?

Mr. B.: No. They wouldn't let me see any of the naval business at all. I saw that later, but I didn't see it until after World War II. I got it all second-hand, really, the Navy and the Army and the Air Force.

Then I went to Italy where I found another different

type of autocracy, much looser than the German.

Q: A Latin type!

Mr. B.: Yes. It was there but it was much looser. It was a much more pleasant place, in a way, to be, even though you were sure they also watched you in a discreet way.

I remember a great parade that Mussolini reviewed past the Coliseum, and on the walls of the Coliseum a map of his imperial glory, a map that he had had put up there showing the extent of the old Roman Empire and then the extent of the modern Mussolini Empire and how he was expanding it all the time by comparison. I watched the bersagliere in their plumed hats doubletiming past the reviewing stand, tanks, and so forth.

I got, from our correspondent principally, but also from the attaches and other places quite a good picture. There I met Tommy White, subsequent chief of staff of the Air Force, who was then our military attache in Italy - our air attache, he was the Number 2 man. In fact, in all these countries I met the military and air attaches and got to know some of them quite well. Tommy was a lifelong friend. I knew him later on very well when he was chief of staff and at other times.

When I was in Italy I suddenly got a Russian visa, so

I backtracked all the way back to Poland.

Q: How long had this been pending?

Mr. B.: Three months, I guess, or longer. I applied in Washington long before. But this time, in 1937, was just the time of the purge trials, the great purge trials, when Tukhachevski was purged.

I went by train from Warsaw to Moscow and it was a very interesting experience. You changed the gauge, of course, when we got to the Polish frontier. You had to get out of your sleeping car and go into another one.

Q: Was this the narrow gauge?

Mr. B.: The Russians' is a broad gauge compared with the European gauge. And they went through your bags with a fine-tooth comb. As I said, when I was in Germany I was particularly careful about notes I took. What I would do, I made it a habit when I was talking to somebody to memorize the salient facts as well as I could and then, when I got a moment to myself back at the hotel or elsewhere, I would write them down to keep them in my memory. When I got arrangements whereby I could type very brief notes, I sent them back by the diplomatic pouch or by our military attaches addressed to me in New York so I wouldn't have any incriminating evidence on me! I didn't trust the Germans at all. I did exactly the same thing in Moscow.

Of the three countries the Moscow impression was the most palpable. It was terrible. Germany was next, and Italy the least. In Russia it was black night. You could feel it as soon as you got there. I was met at the railroad station by Harold Denny, our correspondent who had married Ambassador Bullitt's niece. Harold was obviously very, very nervous and worried. He immediately, as I think I told you before, greeted me with saying, "For God's sake, keep your mouth shut. They know you were in the Navy and a Naval Reserve officer. My secretary's disappeared and my driver's disappeared and I don't know what will happen next."

He was very upset and nervous. He'd been there too long, out of communication.

I remember sitting in the middle of his apartment at night, a rather bare room, not very well furnished, he and his wife and another American, talking in whispers to make sure that what we were saying was not recorded. He was sure that everything he said was recorded, and I think he was quite right because this was par for the course in Moscow.

Faymonville, I think, was our attache in Moscow at the

time. He gained some fame in World War II.

Of course, I applied for a lot of things, none of which were granted. I talked to Faymonville and got a very good insight from him. I found that he was far more cautious in his assessment of the Soviet Army and their capabilities than, for instance, our attache in France had been about the French Army. Faymonville thought that maybe they could fight. He wasn't impressed with some of the things they did, but he thought that they had capabilities. This was before the Finnish winter war when their reputation was so much hurt.

Faymonville had a cocktail party for me to which he invited a good many of the Russian military. I met some of them there, but none of them who came to Faymonville's gained fame in World War II.

Q: Did they bring their wives with them?

Mr. B.: As I remember, this was a bachelor party, but I can't be sure of it. In any case, I got nothing firsthand in Moscow. What was particularly valuable was the atmosphere. The stuff that I got from the military attaches, which you didn't duplicate in Washington because you got the personel talks with them. You asked them questions, which you couldn't ask in Washington because they weren't there. I found that this was really valuable later on. It served as a great backlog for the future.

Q: It was really a learning trip, wasn't it?

Mr. B.: Oh, yes, I learned a lot on this trip.

Then I left Russia. I was never so glad to get out of a place, and I've felt that way since then when I was there. It's oppressive, it's somber, the people didn't smile, they were scared and frightened. That after a time communicates itself to you. You always had to watch what you were doing or saying. I wouldn't have thought of taking photographs. I didn't attempt to in those days. I wouldn't have talked politics. I kept my mouth shut as far as possible, except I think once in the middle of Harold Denny's apartment very quietly. I remember Denny being terribly perturbed because this young American who was visiting there at the same time I was and had come to him through the Embassy - I think he was a cousin of his wife's - was a small arms nut and he was talking about the Russians' small arms. Denny thought, gosh, this is a sure way to get arrested and sent off.

The smallest thing, you see, would perturb people.

Well, we came out of Russia. They went through your suitcase at the Polish frontier with a fine-tooth comb. I'd got no notes that they could focus on because I'd sent them back, nothing they could really object to.

Q: Who was ambassador then? Standley?

Mr. B.: No, no, Standley didn't get to be ambassador that soon. That was later.

And then I returned to the United States very considerably I hope, a wiser man.

I should have mentioned I also went to Prague. I went to Czechoslovakia and saw the famous Prague works at Brno, where they made the tanks and other things. I got a feel of the Czech situation to some extent. At that time, it was beginning to heat up.

I wrote a series of reports for the *Times* which subsequently was published by Knopf. It was the first book I'd done and it was called *The Caissons Roll*. It's a very amateur book. It was the first one I'd tried. It was newspaper republication and that really it not usually good as a book. You have to do a complete rewrite. But it was topical at the time and served a purpose.

Q: What reception did the dispatches get in the press?

Mr. B.: I think pretty good. I don't have the letters I got on this. They're down at Yale, I guess, but I think they got a good reception. The *Times* seemed pleased with them. There was worry, of course, because they were all pretty pessimistic.

Q: Was there any resultant contact with government officials in Washington?

Mr. B.: Oh, yes, I talked to everybody in Washington when I came back. I usually came back from these trips overseas and I would talk to Army intelligence, Navy intelligence.

Q: You were debriefed?

Mr. B.: Well, most of the things I got, of course, I put in the paper and I simply hadn't anything else.

Q: Did you undertake any special mission for any of the intelligence people?

Mr. B.: Oh, no, I wouldn't do that. You can't do that. You can't mix these things.

Remember, I spoke at our last meeting about the Navy feeling that they had a hold on me as an officer in the Reserve, even though it was voluntary. That didn't jibe with a newspaperman's mission, and in addition to that it might be embarrassing if I went to Russia as a naval intelligence Reserve officer. It would be very embarrassing to me, perhaps, and not altogether healthy. So I would never mix - I wouldn't do that for the CIA for anything. I wouldn't mix newspaper work and intelligence work. It just isn't right or doing justice to either one. Now, that doesn't mean that I wouldn't help the country in any way I could with any information, but I wouldn't do any mission for them at all. I don't believe that jibes with the two objectives.

I should have said earlier that during this period - I spoke of knowing Admiral Pratt. I knew Admiral Standley quite well, got to know him very well when he was CNO and, later, Admiral Stark, and Admiral Leahy. I knew Admiral Leahy very well. Leahy, of course, became really what amounted to a kind of chief of staff to the President. He didn't function as that. He was the President's naval advisor, but he was an invaluable source during World War II. I used to go in and see him in the White House very frequently when I visited Washington.

Standley I had known well when he was in the Navy and CNO, so he was still useful as a newspaper source as ambassador later on.

I can't think of any other really pertinent information on that period, so we come up almost to the start of World War II.

Q: The fact that you came back from these various European countries and wrote articles on the military situation and the attitudes, did this produce any closer contacts with members of the Congress? Were they curious about this sort of thing?

Mr. B.: Some of them were very definitely so. I did a lot of speaking. The first talk I made, I think, was after I came from the fleet maneuvers in 1932, to the Naval Academy Graduates Association in New York. From then on I did more and more speaking. Any talks, of course, to the military or for the Naval Academy Graduates or anything like that there was no fee, but I also became associated later with a lecture bureau and I went out around the country, most of them, however, not until after World War II.

I spoke, as I recollect, to some congressional group in Washington a couple of times.

Q: What about the war colleges?

Mr. B.: I spoke there later.

Q: Not after this trip?

Mr. B.: I can't remember whether it was after this particular trip or not - I don't think so, I didn't do too much speaking at that time. I was getting so immersed in preparations for the war that I don't think I did too much speaking. I did later.

Q: When you came back, do you recall your own personal attitude toward the conflict that was coming? What did you think?

Mr. B.: I was absolutely sure there was going to be war. I didn't have any doubts about it after being in Europe. The question was when, and I didn't know when. You had on the one hand the belief that Hitler would wait until, say, 1942, when his programs were over, and the belief on the other hand, by those who knew him, that he was in too much of a hurry, he wouldn't wait, he'd make an excuse. But I thought it was an inevitable conflict.

Q: Did you see us being involved in this conflict?

Mr. B.: Less certainly. I thought it very likely and I thought we ought to prepare, but I didn't see it as a certainty. As a matter of fact, I was quite opposed to our getting in, especially after Hitler invaded Russia, unless it was absolutely vital; of course, we came in the back door. We came in through the Pacific. I thought that the two greatest tyrannies in Europe might knock each other off, which I thought was all to the good. I never believed that we should let England go under, but by the time Hitler invaded Russia I thought that this was all the more reason for us not to fight for either side and substitute one tyranny for the other. But that, of course, really had no logic after Pearl Harbor.

I think that probably terminates the prewar period.

Q: Just a few years prior to the outbreak of World War II, it is apparent that President Roosevelt was intent upon building up our Navy and preparing in some sense for future conflict, but he was having great difficulty with the Congress in getting outright appropriations for the Navy in particular.

Mr. B.: I don't recollect the details of this, but my impression was that the Vinson-Trammel Act - when was that, 1937?

Q: I think so.

Mr. B.: For a two-ocean Navy was approved rather overwhelmingly. Of course, it was an authorization act which is not an appropriation act and there's a lot of difference between the two, as you well know. On the other hand, money for shipbuilding seemed to start to be forthcoming about that time. It was money for personnel that was not forthcoming. You recollect that even up to the start of World War II, the ships were manned only about 80 percent - sometimes 60 percent, and they were having difficulties getting enough trained people for new ships that were coming in. The battleship Washington, successor to the one I helped to sink in the Texas, was doing her commissioning trials in New York sometime in this period. I've forgotten when it was. I went out to see her with another group of reporters. Her problems were, I think, personnel more than anything else. She had a lot of green people aboard.

I saw Roosevelt once or twice during the prewar period. He from time to time would see reporters who were interested in specific subjects. They'd have ten or fifteen minutes with him. He could be charming when he wanted to be and nasty when he wanted to be. Usually when he was seeing reporters he tried to be charming. I remember coming into the Oval Office and sitting in the chair beside him, seeing this uptilted cigarette-holder which he always used. He would talk about the Navy and its needs. I don't remember anything particularly outstanding being said.

Actually, the value of things like this to me are more important as background and as some insight into the character of the people than as news. They couldn't be used as spot news in many cases, anyway. They could have been used as background. But they rarely said anything that was of any tremendous, earth-shaking importance. However, you did meet these people as contacts, and many of them that I met in those early days subsequently became quite important and famous in World War II. It was invaluable to have known them and then to be able to keep up the contacts.

So, in this sense, the foresight of Arthur Sulzberger and General Adler was, I think, well repaid.

By the time World War II started I had learned enough about the military so that I had a little more confidence in what I could say and do.

I should say the only other thing I remember here. We started - I've forgotten when this did start - some sort of parachute training in the United States on a very modest basis. They originally used some of these parachute jump towers in New Jersey and then they moved down to Fort Benning later on. I think I'm anticipating myself because I'm pretty sure this was after the war had progressed for some time. It was probably after the invasion of Crete.

Q: Were you cognizant of any new vehicles coming on stream that later could be used for amphibious operations? Was this an area that drew your interest?

Mr. B.: Oh, it drew my interest, but there were very few at that time.

Q: The Marines were working in that field.

Mr. B.: Yes, but they hadn't developed anything that was up to the point of really being used, as far as I remember. It depends on what period you're talking about.

Q: The late thirties.

Mr. B.: If you're talking of up to the outbreak of war, I had not seen personally any amphibious vehicle that I recollect that presaged what did develop later.

Q: In a general sense, when you came back from Europe with the conviction that conflict was inevitable, whether we got into it or not was questionable, did you look upon your role as a reporter and as a newspaper commentator as a means of educating the general public about this developing conflict?

Mr. B.: Number 1, I think this brings up the whole question of what a military analyst should be. My concept of the term at that time was one that was very, very broad indeed, he had to be a whole lot of things to all people. Mark you, I said that I did everything for the price of one. I wrote editorials. That means an opinion. The opinion, though, had to be approved by the paper. I wrote analyses, and this was the stickiest area because into that I put my own opinion and sometimes the paper didn't like it. I had to fight for the right to do that. I said, look - this came up very frequently - look, if you don't believe I'm right in something like this, you'd better fire me and get another military analyst, because as long as I'm writing as a military analyst, I've got to write what I think is so.

Then, I wrote straight news stories, which are supposed to be quite objective, and I tried to keep them that way without in any way taking a side. Then, I wrote background Sunday pieces, which had room for certain analysis, and I wrote book reviews which, of course, are the reflection of the views of the reviewer.

I did all those things and when you ask was I trying to educate, yes, I suppose I was. But if you're talking about straight factual education, the point I was making before about paratroopers came most to mind. I, by this time, had accumulated, by the time the war was really active and we were about to get into it, a great deal of background knowledge. Some of it I gleaned down at the Parachute School at Fort Benning, which I visited frequently and went up in in the planes with the men as they jumped and I watched. I didn't jump myself but I saw them do it and knew what kind of equipment they carried and what we believed to be possible.

I also studied as much as I could of the German methods, much of which I'd gotten from intelligence sources, from our own people.

So, when a thing like the invasion of Crete occurred, I was able to write background information articles for the Times describing the organization of our own paratroopers, the kind of weapons and equipment they carried down with them, how they landed and so forth, most of which was accurate. Of course, I didn't have the detail that we have nowadays, but we had a lot of this information. The Times was the only paper that had that.

You say did I educate. I think in that sense I educated.

I tried to take, in this great debate between the America Firsters, the neutralists, and the interventioners, a completely objective role, as far as I was concerned, and to keep my own feelings out of it. But I was opposed and so stated outside the Times to our entry after the Germans invaded Russia, on the basis that it was to our own interest not to substitute one tyranny for another. Of course, as I say, that was entirely academic after Pearl Harbor and the Pacific situation which, of course, might have happened at any time. In other words, I felt that I would like to see us stay out of it but I didn't believe it was going to be possible.

Q: I was thinking, as you talked, of that whole effort made by people like George Sylvester Vierick, who tried to convince the Americans . . .

Mr. B.: But that was German.

Q: That was German propaganda and you knew the situation as it was in Germany to a large extent. Did this provoke you to be more emphatic in getting your viewpoint across?

Mr. B.: No. I think he was speaking largely in political terms and I didn't write too much about political things in those days. It was more or less strictly military things. Of course, when Lindberg made some of his assessments I had some ideas about those. I've forgotten whether I wrote directly about those or not. I admired Lindberg and still do and I think he had a lot of ideas that were quite right, but I think on the other hand he became too biased in his own mind and made some very bad strategic judgments.

Q: In that same period, what about the destroyer deal that we made with Britain? Did this draw forth anything? Did you comment on that?

Mr. B.: I wrote about it, I know. I've written so much, you know, that it is almost impossible for me to remember the details - literally hundreds of thousands of words. In the war period I think I wrote every day for about four to five years and sometimes as many as three to five articles a day. So that certainly when the destroyers-for-bases deal was announced I undoubtedly wrote about the bases we were getting and about the destroyers and so forth, but what I said now I haven't the vaguest idea.

Q: I recall that that arrangement drew forth a lot of isolationist sentiment in certain parts of the United States.

Mr. B.: Oh, yes.

Q: Was there any reaction to some of your own articles in this area?

Mr. B.: Oh, yes. We were subjected all during the war but particularly before we got into it and when the great debate was on to a tremendous amount of letter writing, sometimes definite letter-writing campaigns.

For instance, before Germany invaded Russia and long before we got into the war, when the Communists were taking the line that Germany was all right, when they had the deal after the Polish campaign, any indication at all that maybe Russia wasn't all right or that the United States ought to get into the war or that certain things were not just as they thought would evoke a storm of letters - I mean to me personally or to the editor about my article. And since we tried to answer each of the letter-writers, we soon found out that some of these left-wing letter-writing campaigns were just that. They were not spontaneous. Fictitious addresses were used because we'd get them back from the Post Office saying "no such address," or they used fictitious names. Sometimes the same trite phrases were used again and again which were typically Communist phrases.

That changed, of course, after Russia was invaded. Then, anything that you said against the valorous Russians would be leaped upon immediately. For instance, I once called the Soviet Army as it started the war as kind of an armed mob or horde, as it was in those days, in describing this army of foot soldiers as it drove cattle before it and conscripted villagers to dig fortifications and that sort of thing. In fact, it remained that way throughout a large part of the war, except for the crack divisions which became guards divisions.

We got all sorts of letter-writing campaigns over nearly anything. You'd be surprised how sensitive readers were in those days and how even the slightest thing would stir them up.

We also got lots of letters of commendation. Usually, we found that if the people liked a piece they wrote to you and if they didn't they wrote to the editor.

Q: Hoping to undermine you!

Mr. B.: We had attempts to undermine us very definitely. Very fortunately, I had the bosses backing me up - perhaps in the next transcript we'll come to that. Both from high sources and low there were many attempts made to neutralize my opinion or shut me up - from the Air Force, from General Marshall!

Q: How did they go about this?

Mr. B.: We'll come to that next time, perhaps. I believe next time we might be able to get rid of all my recollections about the war. I don't know. I hope so. I don't want to keep you forever!

This was a very stormy period and particularly the period when the great debate in America was going on and before the German invasion of Russia. Then you had America Firsters supported by the Communists, you see, very strongly. They didn't want that support, but they got it. So you had a mixture of opinion ranging from extremely conservative to far left, both with the avowed purpose of keeping America out of the war. That changed abruptly when Germany went into Russia. Then you had terrific pressure from the leftists the other way. And, of course, right along you had considerable pressure from the interventionists.

One of the things that came up early in the year was the need for conscription and here I had a number of exchanges with General Adler. He was highly in favor of this. He thought that we ought to get started ahead of time. I wasn't so sure but I was, at that time, not so much against it. I was against it as a permanent thing after World War II was over.

General Adler was a very interested Reservist. He spent a great deal of his time trying to help prepare the nation for war and this was a great help, as far as I was concerned, in everything I wrote.

I think, looking back on that period of the undeclared war between the invasion of Poland in 1939 and Pearl Harbor (and it came to an actual shooting war, as you recollect but without any declaration), looking back at it, I'm quite sure the American people did not realize to what extent we were involved in the Atlantic before we ever went to war. The realization came very slowly if they did know it, because often the announcements of events were either not made or were made long afterwards, delayed, and sometimes lost over other stories or something of the sort.

Q: Don't you think that the Neutrality Patrol, the title itself, was a beguiling sort of thing?

Mr. B.: It was. It was intended to be beguiling to American public opinion but it was actually, of course, a thinly disguised euphemism for hostilities.

That period between Poland and our entry into the war was a very busy one, not only for all the armed services and most of the people who were interested in defense, but it was extremely busy for me because I was trying to keep track of what was going on in the war itself in Europe, trying to write about that with all the sources that I could get, both open and those which were not normally available, like von Botticher and others that I talked to. At the same time I was trying to cover our preparations for war. I did a lot of traveling in this country. I went to all of the larger maneuvers and a good many of the areas such as Fort Benning, where preparations were going on.

As I think I said before, I attended both the Tennessee maneuvers, which General Ben Lear presided over when some of the National Guard had been called into service, and the famous Louisiana maneuvers where Eisenhower made his reputation with General Krueger and General Ben Lear.

Q: Also, were you interested in the training and the speed-up in the training of pilots for the Navy?

Mr. B.: Yes. I visited Pensacola and naval aviation training stations. The Navy had no large fleet maneuvers that I know of in just that period. They were so busy with the Atlantic. I don't think they had after 1939 a large fleet maneuver until we got into war. They had small ones, but I didn't attend those, as I recollect. 1939 was the last time.

Q: Am I right in thinking that the enlistments for the Navy produced a very able group of men at that period?

Mr. B.: Yes, and I think from the Depression, throughout the Depression, you got a very choice group, many of them college graduates or with one or two years of college who had not been able to find jobs on the outside. The Navy was more selective than the Army and you had a very good quality of personnel, without any doubt. And you had your choice, to a great extent, of officers, too, because, as you recall, a lot of Annapolis graduates were not commissioned in the early parts of the thirties. My own class was allowed to resign on graduation if they wanted to. That was in between the Naval Disarmament Conferences. So I think the Navy did have quite a good group. There were still a lot of carryovers from the past in the Navy who were pretty iron-bound. Some of the senior officers were pretty rigid in their thinking, but I think the more active younger, more professional officers were coming to the fore, without a doubt, and, as shown at the start of World War II, most of them quickly came to the fore.

Q: In that time and thinking about what you just said, were you cognizant of what was going on within War Plans in the Navy? Did you have any special contacts there?

Mr. B.: No, not really. They were very, very secretive about this. Of course, I had known right along from general knowledge and talks with Captain Puleston and others what the Navy's general plans were in case of a Pacific war and what they envisaged, the old business of fighting their way, but not by the stages we took, fighting their way out to the Philippines to hold Manila Bay until the fleet could get there. We did not envisage the extensive use of air power to the same extent that it was actually used. We did not envisage a step-by-step, island-by-island campaign.

We had changed that even before World War II started, before we were in it, our concepts had changed, but just a relatively short time before. This is one reason I think our war plans were really all mixed up, because the Army had one set of plans for the Philippines, MacArthur had another and the Navy had still a third. The Navy never believed at that period that Manila Bay could be held, and they did not believe at that period that you could get there in any foreseeable time, quick time period, which would relieve the islands. On the other hand, I don't think they ever expected the Japanese fleet to score the successes they did score. In fact, I know they didn't. And the woeful performance of our submarines in the Asiatic Fleet was never expected.

I remember very vividly writing one of the early articles after we were in the war saying nobody in the Navy could ever have anticipated that the Japanese could have landed in the Philippines without losing a single major combat ship, which was true. We thought that that concentration of submarines, the biggest in the world, and what General Marshall had said was the biggest concentration of B-24s in the world, would be a good defense, maybe not hold them off but at least inflict heavy casualties.

Q: For one thing we didn't count on defective torpedoes, did we?

Mr. B.: No. Well, of course, that was another story altogether. And some defective commanders, quite a few of them.

I suppose I should really perhaps conclude this session with the actual start of World War II as far as we were concerned.

Perhaps I should just jump back one moment because there was one period here where I found myself considerably at odds with some of our policies.

Remember before we got into the war the British were trying to order more and more arms and planes from the United States, and the policy of the administration was to let them have this, even at our own expense. I didn't think that was too good an idea, particularly in view of the situation that then existed in England, and I wrote one or two pieces which showed that we were doing much the same thing as we did recently in the case of Israel, stripping some of our operating forces in order to send the material overseas. I wrote quite a few factual pieces describing what war reserves we had and what was happening to them. We gave a tremendous amount to Britain in that summer of 1940 - that year of 1940-41.

Then we started turning over B-24s of which we had very few. Our Air Corps was quite concerned about this, and the British were pressing us hard to get them. I remember writing one piece which elicited a response from Commander, Coastal Command, Royal Air Force, Air Marshal Slessor. He wrote a letter to me, I think, and also made some sort of a public statement. I think he was on a purchasing mission to the United States, and he stressed the importance of these planes to Britain. I still wasn't convinced but Roosevelt continued to give them the planes.

Q: Were you somewhat apprehensive that Britain could hold out? Was this one of the factors?

Mr. B.: I thought it was completely uncertain at that time, and I still think in retrospect that if the Germans had been determined to gain local air superiority over the southeast of England and had confined it to that, that they could have made a successful landing. I think they dispersed their efforts so much and shifted from one objective to another that they couldn't succeed. Hitler's heart was never really in the invasion. It was improvised, as we know now, and impromptu. But we didn't know that then and neither did the British.

I think that probably was one of the outstanding conflicts that occurred then. I had the feeling that we were in a situation where we ought to consider our own interests first and foremost, that this was a world of complete change. Don't misunderstand me. I wasn't an isolationist but I felt very strongly that we had to be able to defend ourselves in the Western Hemisphere. By that I included South America and Greenland, and we didn't have anywhere enough to do it. Then, after the invasion of Russia, I felt very strongly that we would be intervening on the side of one or the other of the tyrannies and that they'd probably end up with one or the other supreme (as, indeed happened) instead of letting them exhaust each other. There was no reason to expend good America blood for that purpose.

I tried not to let any of this affect my analysis. I tried to be as objective as I could. I gave both points of view when I analyzed, then I would come up with some conclusion, often. But most of my stuff was just pretty straightforward and factual. I think it was because I tried to be unbiased that I got a certain reputation, because people came to depend on that more than on some of the more violent things that were being said all the time by others.

Q: What other policies were you in disagreement with? You said there were several, and you mentioned one, the stripping of ourselves in order to supply Britain.

Mr. B.: I'm just trying to remember now. There were one or two others.

Q: I suppose the shipbuilding program, the small craft?

Mr. B.: The shipbuilding program at this time was creating bottlenecks in all the American shipyards. There weren't enough skilled people to go around, and we were trying to build for Britain as well as ourselves. Logjams were developing everywhere.

In addition to that, I seem to remember that there was the question of industrial mobilization or mobilization in general in Washington. Bernard Baruch was very strongly on one side. He believed in his old industrial mobilization plan, which was somewhat dated. It was based upon a concept that was somewhat out of date. But he was fighting a vigorous battle to get this enacted, to get Roosevelt to carry out exactly his plan. I don't remember the details of this now but every once in a while he would call me up after I had an article on the subject and either object to or appraise the article in question.

Actually, mobilization in Washington came to be such a political exercise, even throughout the war, until it was finally settled, a struggle for power between the War Resources Board and some of the other war agencies, that it didn't follow necessarily a logical or rational pattern. Baruch's plan was logical and rational but it didn't allow much for personalities or for politics and some of it was dated in its lack of emphasis on certain types of raw materials which were more plentiful when it was drawn up.

I remember being involved in that to a certain extent. The scope of what I was writing about grew broader and broader because I discovered, as I think the *Times* did and nearly everyone else, that modern war meant everything. It dawned on me gradually that this was the meaning of total war. It was everything, psychology, and everything else. I didn't have too much time to devote or too much space to devote to things that were not primarily military but I often did touch on these other aspects in frequent articles.

At the time of Pearl Harbor — I'm trying to remember what I knew about it beforehand. I knew nothing about Pearl Harbor, of course, nobody did, but I knew something about the war warning message. I hadn't read it but I knew something about it. I think all of us were pretty tense. I had heard of but had not attended an off-the-record press interview that General Marshall gave in Washington about three weeks before Pearl Harbor. Marshall gave this interview to permanently based Washington correspondents, not all of them, but to about eight or ten, including Time magazine and one or two others, with the purpose of preparing them really for the shock of war. He thought that was was coming and he wanted in an oblique way to get the press ready for it, and he had this interview which was completely off the record and wasn't reflected even in background stories at the time. It wasn't for publication at all. I heard about it from some of my friends, including Bob Sherrod, who attended. You know Bob Sherrod, probably.

Later - I think it was during the war or just after the war, I got transcripts of their notes from two of them and they were very nearly identical. I remember that Marshall made some egregious errors of judgment. He was talking about the defensibility of the Philippines. He was also worried the Japanese might strike a little too soon. He was telling about the plans for getting large reinforcements to the Philippines but, he said, they were already heavily defended with the biggest concentration of B-24s anywhere in the world. And he said if the Japanese attacked the Philippines they'd lose a lot of ships and he said, of course, we will hit the paper cities of Japan with B-24 bombing raids and set them all on fire.

It was pointed out to him by one of the correspondents there who knew more about the B-24 than he did that they didn't have the range to reach Japan from the Philippines and return to base. That model of the B-24 didn't. Marshall said they could fly above the altitude of any Japanese antiaircraft guns, and, he said, rather naively, "Oh, well, they will continue on to Vladivostok in shuttle bombing." And, of course, we had no agreement with the Russians whatever and were scarcely speaking to the Russians at that time.

I remember this very vividly because after the war was over and I was writing this short book called Great Mistakes of the War, and was doing some research into the early phases - I have it in the book that's coming out next year, too - I wrote to Marshall to ask him if these transcripts were accurate and it's a measure of the size of the man that he wrote back (he made some other statements which were similarly way off base about the merchant marine and various other things - he obviously didn't have a knowledge of the Navy as General Kruger had, for instance, or of the details of the Air Force); after the war and said he didn't have his papers at hand or the transcript of the press conference but to the best of his knowledge and belief these transcripts were correct. It takes a rather large man to admit his arrors in the light of history four or five years afterwards. So that struck me about Marshall. I don't think Forrest Pogue - the Marshall biographer ever used that particular incident. I don't know why he didn't. It seemed to me it was quite interesting and revelatory because Marshall was not at that time the up-to-date great strategic brain or technological thinker that people imagined he was by any means. Neither were a good many of our people, of course, but this press conference revealed a great over-appreciation of the effects of air power which had been sold to him, I'm convinced, by the Army Air Corps to whom he gave their head. You remember, he brought Arnold in to sit on his right hand, and Arnold was a great salesman. He was also a very good air force general.

But you had around the top then Arnold's bright boys who were selected by Arnold himself, people like Harold George, who subsequently came to be a general, Tommy White, who subsequently became the chief of air staff - Tommy was in air intelligence then, and Possum Hansel, who ran the early days of the attacks on Tokyo and Japan and had an air division, I think, in Europe, the great planner, and Olive and various other people who subsequently came to top rank in the Air Force. They were absolutely sold on more or less the Douhet theory of air power, that air power could win the war by itself. They were also absolutely convinced that we had to have a separate air force even at that time, before we got in the war. They were also convinced that they must sell this to the American people.

I remember vividly several occasions in Washington, one a dinner which I was asked to attend with Possum Hansel, Harold George, and various others at which they were obviously trying to propagandize me, sell me on this idea. I was receptive to new ideas, but I wasn't convinced. Later, as I recall it, just before we got into the war or just afterwards we were building up an air intelligence service and they offered me a commission in the Air Force if i'd come into intelligence. Well, it smelled a little bit to me because I thought they were trying to really propagandize. I'd got to be good friends with Possum Hansel and Tommy White and I told them both that, that I felt I could do better by doing an objective job outside than representing any one service.

In any case, I think Marshall was imbued with the early views that were really epitomized by de Seversky, victory through air power. Seversky was a very persuasive talker.

Q: Apparently so.

Mr. B.: I got to know him quite well and we used to argue and debate a lot. As a matter of fact, the Times was greatly influenced by him for a while, as was the Readers Digest, and for a time the Times ran some of de Seversky's syndicated pieces, much to my dislike, because I felt that they were way oversimplified and later on the war proved they were. He was talking about a few pilots and a few planes, just like Douhet did, coming over a city and just reducing it to rubble and scaring the people to death and the war's over.

In any case, I remember hearing something about this Marshall interview about three weeks before Pearl Harbor and being surprised and a little appalled, but also hoping he was right and that these B-24s could do some sort of a job that would deter the Japanese. As it turned out, they didn't deter them at all. They knew exactly how many we had and what they could do and where they were and so on.

When Pearl Harbor came I was at home in Chappaqua on Sunday morning. I remember hearing the news, I guess on the radio. I don't know how I happened to have the radio on. Maybe somebody called up. And being absolutely appalled, then going into the office on Sunday and trying to make heads and tails out of it, writing something. What I wrote the next day I don't know, but I know that I wrote, within three or four weeks, one piece called, "This Is a War We Could Lose," which appalled a lot of Americans and shook them because, you know, we had always regarded the Japanese as these curious little people who didn't know how to fly and all the myths about them.

Q: That should have been dissipated with Pearl Harbor, however!

Mr. B.: Well, you see, the news of the complete catastrophe at Pearl Harbor leaked out very slowly and many people thought it was a fluke and blamed it entirely on Japanese treachery and surprise. I don't think they were prepared to accept fully the strength of the Japanese until later on when they had repeated victories that showed just how dangerous they were.

Shortly after that I went to Washington, I guess in that first week of Pearl Harbor. We got a man out to Pearl Harbor - Foster Hailey - as fast as we could. He sent a message to the *Times* describing roughly the damage that occurred, which the Navy objected to greatly because it said it evaded censorship as, indeed, it did. I don't think we printed it all. We printed rumors or something of that sort. But I went to Washington and got some of the bad picture. This must have been the week after Pearl Harbor, after the imaginary air raid on New York which occurred on a Tuesday, as I remember. Pearl Harbor was Sunday. On Tuesday an air raid alarm by 200 planes on New York City planes that were supposed to be 200 miles away was sounded. You've heard that story. Actually, some people went up to the roof to try to spot them. The Army insisted it was true; it was a crisis of poor communications, and early war jitters.

The first week in Washington I guess I talked to Forrestal and to everyone else I could. I'd gotten to know Forrestal fairly well and Struve Hensel was there with him. I guess Di Gates had been in there. I don't know whether he was still there then or not. I don't remember particularly what they told me but I do remember the denouement.

At that time the Army's Munitions Building was right next to the Old Navy on Constitution Avenue where Navy headquarters were then. The CNO was there and everyone else was there. I remember going through that passageway from the Navy Building to the Munitions Building - there was a little arcade that went from one to the other. I left the Navy building and started to go in the Army building and a couple of Army MPs stopped me and asked me for my pass. I said, "I haven't got any pass yet. I've just come here." So they said, "Well, you can't come in." I shrugged and went back and there the doors were guarded by a couple of Marines and they wouldn't let me in the Navy Building! I was marooned in there until I could finally convince one or the other. It was one of these early war panic situations. Nobody knew what was going on and no one knew what passes were required.

It was funny in retrospect.

Interview No. 4 with Mr. Hanson W. Baldwin

Place: His residence in Roxbury, Connecticut

Date: Monday morning, 16 June 1975

Subject: Biography

By: John T. Mason, Jr.

Q: Well, Sir, it's mighty nice to be with you again this morning.

Mr. B.: Thank you. It's nice to be here, Dr. Mason.
    The interview with Admiral Pratt that you inquired about took place down in Panama. I saw him at other times but this particular interview . . .

Q: And it was in the mid-thirties sometime?

Mr. B.: Yes, it was during a fleet maneuver, and I think the old <u>Saratoga</u> and <u>Lexington</u> had participated, as I remember, on the Pacific side. One of them had just bombed the locks of the canal very successfully. So the question of what air power could do, particularly naval air power, was uppermost certainly in the minds of the people who participated in the maneuver, all of the naval officers, and, to those who were interested in military affairs in other minds, too. I think you have to bear in mind that during the early thirties and mid-thirties there was very little interest in military and naval affairs.

The Navy, after all, was only about 90,000 men and 7,000 officers and there maneuvers were generally ignored by the public, except for the few papers that actually paid any attention to them, The New York Times was a shining exception. I was the only one from an individual paper that I remember, who was sent to fleet maneuvers to cover them, and the Times would usually put my reports on the front page. Later, Waldo Drake and the Los Angeles Times provided some coverage.

So you could say that the public wasn't violently participating in any controversy pro or con, but all people who followed aviation and followed the Navy were quite interested. In fact, I'd get many letters after I wrote about the fleet maneuvers from naval officers and from others commenting on this point or that.

So it was quite obvious after the participation of the Saratoga and the Lexington in one of the first bombing attacks on the canal which was deemed successful that I should ask Admiral Pratt, who came down there as an observer at the time - he was, as I remember it, CNO, so this must have been the early thirties; that I should ask him about the role of the battleship. I wrote a piece about his reply which is indexed in the Times somewhere and, as I recall it from memory, he hastily reassured me and said that the battleship was still the capital ship of the navies. I think I asked him that direct question. The definition of the capital ship had just become prominent because of the Washington and London naval treaties and I said, "Has the battleship been replaced by the aircraft carrier?"

He was very definite in his opinions and he said no. Well, of course, many of the younger air officers and pilots didn't agree with him, although the real thrust of naval aviation was just coming to the fore then. They weren't in high enough rank, they didn't have high enough officers back of them except for Admiral Moffett, of course; let me see, when did he die, in 1932?

Q: 1932, I believe it was.

Mr. B.: I think he'd been killed just before my interview. I'm not certain of these dates. That's a thing that would have to be checked.

They didn't have anyone on a par with Admiral Pratt who could stand up to him and say this isn't so, nor is that the way it's done in the Navy! So, in that sense, there wasn't controversy, but to say that the battleship admirals believed in the carrier right along and that the carrier would replace the battleship would be, to my mind, nonsense. A lot of them didn't believe this. Some of the more foreseeing ones foresaw the important role of aviation.

Q: Like Admiral Reeves?

Mr. B.: Yes, Admiral Reeves and I think later, after they were indoctrinated, as Buell said in his book, Admiral Spruance, who was a battleship admiral originally, saw the value of the carriers. Anyone who had an adaptable and flexible mind quickly came to see that the carriers were important, but not all of them had adaptable and flexible minds. It was very hard for a man like Admiral Pratt who'd spent his whole life with battleships to change his opinion quickly. Nor could he have been effective as CNO if he'd tried to revolutionize the Navy overnight and go to carriers because he'd have had so much opposition from his own people.

My opinion is that there were real battleship admirals just as today there are real bomber generals. There were those people who wouldn't be swayed until just the last moment of proof. Even just prior to World War II, you remember, we produced a 1.1-inch gun out of the Bureau of Ordnance, the hose gun, so-called, which was destined to shoot down all aircraft that came near it. It was a terrible flop and was replaced by the Oerlikon. This was Admiral Furlong's baby and I had many a debate with him about it. But many admirals believed that a plane just couldn't approach a battleship with safety with this kind of armament and they freely said so.

As the years went on leading up to World War II what had been primarily a Navy debate did broaden into more of a public controversy because the public became more interested in military and naval affairs, particularly as the war approached and as new armament came in and planes showed what they could do.

Q: New types of planes?

Mr. B.: Yes, exactly. Certainly, at the last; not at the last, but in the years immediately before World War II, the old question of dive bombers against the battleship, against the capital ship, how vulnerable a ship was to bombing, all that was raging. It had raged ever since the Billy Mitchell business, which created terrific controversy, as you know. And it was to the great credit, I think, of Admiral Moffett and the Navy that they came out of the Billy Mitchell business with a naval air arm keyed to the Navy instead of a divisive split as the Army had. I still think that "unification" resulted in triplification rather than unification. If I were going back to go through it again, I would say that we have almost inevitably increased the defense budget unnecessarily at just the wrong time because actually air power in the form of the manned bomber was being replaced by missiles just as we did this.

I think that really would dispose of that particular controversy, if you agree?

Q: Yes, indeed. Do you want to talk about the Bureau of Engineering?

Mr. B.: Oh, there's just an incident that I thought about and I don't think I mentioned before.

Sometime before World War II and I do not remember the dates, it depends on when Admiral Bowen was Chief of the Bureau, the father of the present Admiral Bowen. Incidentally, is he retired, the one who was the head of Defense Intelligence?

Q: I'm not sure.

Mr. B.: The junior Bowen was a young officer but he was a vice admiral and I have met him. His father was a crusty old sea dog and very jealous of his prerogatives, but Admiral Bowen was a good engineer. He introduced high-temperature, high-pressure steam into Navy installations, as I remember 600 pounds pressure and 1,000° of heat. It was very new and required much stronger piping and joints and welds. They had a lot of trouble with this. The welds didn't hold in the piping and the joints leaked and I think they had one or two accidents. The Navy then had a Board of Inspection and Survey which was headed by another admiral whose name I've forgotten, but who was either senior to or just about the same time as Admiral Bowen. This Board of Inspection and Survey was supposed to inspect all new ships and also old ones periodically and report on their deficiencies, what was needed, and how well they performed, and so forth.

For sometime there was a considerable feud going on between the Board and Admiral Bowen about this high-pressure, high-temperature steam. I had a friend on the board who, with, I think, with the knowledge of his admiral and with his approval, would tell me a great many things about what had happened to some of these installations. I would check them out and write about them. Admiral Bowen would get furious. Then I would go to Admiral Bowen and get his side. I tried to report the thing fairly.

Looking back, I guess it was because of the personality of Admiral Bowen (he was very crusty and not a very personable guy) that I really didn't entirely believe him then, but in retrospect, he was absolutely sound in his desire to get a new marine engineering plant into the Navy. He may have been a little ahead of his time because the state of the art wasn't quite up to containing this new beast that they had harnessed with these terrifically high temperatures. As I remember it, there were a number of accidents, some men were scalded to death and things of that sort.

It was a short-lived but rather active controversy. It went on for about a year, as I recall it, sometime in the thirties. Then it died off as preparations for war broadened or I think they eased off on the temperatures and the pressures for a little while until the state of the art caught up, and then they went to even higher temperatures and pressures.

Fundamentally, there was truth on both sides, but Admiral Bowen had vision about the necessity for a new engineering plant.

Q: He wasn't a Rickover in the sense that he couldn't prevent some accidents from happening?

Mr. B.: No, not in those days. I think Rickover has been very,

very cautious and careful. He's never allowed the designs to get ahead of the state of the art.

Q: Admiral Hustvedt told me that you were on board the North Carolina; I guess that was in 1941, when she was having her gun-firing trials off Newfoundland, that you were one of the correspondents on board. And he said that Admiral Andrews, who had the Third Naval District at that time, attempted to apply censorship to what the correspondents would write about the performance of the North Carolina. Do you recall that?

Mr. B.: Oh, yes, I remember the North Carolina trip. Actually, I think I have a photograph down in the basement of her firing her guns, and I vaguely recall the censorship. My recollection is that the North Carolina was never off Newfoundland. He may be right, but she went to sea from the New York Navy Yard in Brooklyn and went out, I thought, off the Philadelphia capes and fired out there. I remember that Walter Winchell was aboard, much to my disgust, and there was a very objectionable Hearst man, I think, who was trying to get photographs and he didn't know anything about big guns or about the concussion and some of the sailors played a very dirty trick on him, on this photographer, and told him to stand too close to the turrets when they were firing and the concussion knocked him over and almost broke his ear drum and broke the camera!

Yes, I remember the trip very well and I remember Admiral Hustvedt. This was before we were in the war.

Q: Oh, yes.

Mr. B.: I do remember that there was a hassle about censorship. Of course, that was not new. It happened all the time. I told you, I think, when I was down at fleet maneuvers in Panama the last time and they wanted to censor the golf scores! I don't remember how the North Carolina incident turned out. I knew Admiral Andrews quite well, and I think we got the thing through without much problem. We weren't trying to reveal screts. We were trying to tell what actually went on. If we'd known a little more and revealed more secrets we might have done the Navy some good, because you remember the design of the North Carolina class was defective, and one of them almost was sunk down off Guadalcanal.

Q: Yes, that was the Washington, was it not?

Mr. B.: Yes, and she was struck by a Japanese shell once and there wasn't enough armor in the right places. In any case, I think we did write about some of the damage done by the concussion of these guns when they had full load, and there was a good bit of damage done to the ship, especially to the light plating and to some of the officers' quarters.

I don't think many in the Navy had ever realized what a terrific bang these things made when they were fulled loaded for full range, you know, long range. It's really frightening when you're on the same ship to have a 16-inch gun go off at full load and high elevation, because you get an awful whamp in the stomach and ears and everywhere else!

Q: I haven't had that experience.

Mr. B.: I don't recall the details of that particular censorship business, though. I wish I did. I'm sorry. I think it came out all right. I don't recall that there was any controversy.

Q: Earlier, you talked about the news conference with General Marshall over in Washington prior to the Japanese attack on Pearl Harbor. You did not attend but it was attended by correspondents who were there on the ground locally.

Mr. B.: In Washington, yes.

Q: And that raises a question about your specialty as military analyst for the Times, you were somewhat eclectic in your interests and areas. How did this jibe with the Times' system of having bureaus with their own staffs and being jealous of the prerogatives of the bureau?

Mr. B.: Well, you have to have some tact about this, of course, and you have to work with people. I did that and, I think when I first started coming down to Washington very frequently; and

I started this long before the war in the days when Richard Oulahan was Chief of the Washington Bureau, long before Arthur Krock, and there was a man named Lewis Wood who had loved the Navy and had worked with it for a long time, way back in World War I and before that . . .

Q: Any relation to the present Lew Wood?

Mr. B.: No. He was a very nice chap and we got along well and he didn't object. In fact, he was always complimentary. You see, in those days no one was covering the Navy or the Army as a full-time beat. They were too small and too unimportant, and the people in the Washington Bureau would be assigned if the Secretary of the Navy was going to have a press conference or something very important was happening. Then, they would go for a one-shot story, but nothing more than that. I was the only one who was doing this full-time and who had developed contacts in the Navy and the Army and Air Force. So there wasn't as much of that jealousy as you'd think. Lew Wood was not covering the Army and Navy. He was doing something with Congress at the time.

Q: Which was the main topic of interest in Washington.

Mr. B.: Yes. So there wasn't too much of it. There were occasions when there was some, particularly in some parts and

and with certain personalities, but not a great deal of it. If you were discreet and tried to stay out of the hair of the local correspondents and deferred to them to some extent, then I think you got along pretty well. I didn't notice any particular jealousy. As a matter of fact, I used to come down there so often that toward the last, when I retired, as a matter of fact, the Washington Bureau gave me a lunch.

Q: You were sort of an extension of the Washington Bureau as a specialist?

Mr. B.: Yes.

Q: You also said last time; mentioned the attack on Pearl Harbor and the fact that the _Times_ did have a man out there?

Mr. B.: They got a man out there. They did not have a man at the scene at the time, except for the local correspondent, the stringer, as we called him, who, I think, worked for the _Honolulu Star Bulletin_ or something like that.

Q: Oh, I see, it was a secondary assignment?

Mr. B.: Well, yes, he was just a stringer, not a full-time correspondent for the _Times_. But we did get a man out there very rapidly after the attack. He got there well before the investigating committee which was there, I think, within three or four days after the attack. He was a former Associated Press correspondent and he apparently got back some information to the office about the damage done. They were his own figures but they were the first intimation of the extensive nature of the damage, which I don't think we printed but it came for the office benefit. Then, of course, heavy censorship was put into effect and nothing else got through.

Q: That's an interesting point, that you didn't print the data you got. This was self-applied censorship, was it?

Mr. B.: Well, I have to refresh my memory about this. It's possible we did print it in a vague form. There were so many rumors at that time and so many were false from so many different sources. I think you will find if you go back and look at the first three, four or five days after Pearl Harbor, that a whole collection of reports, many of them wildly different in estimates from many different sources all over the world, not only from Pearl but from Washington, from London, from Japan, and so on.

Q: All of them charged with emotion, too, I imagine?

Mr. B.: Oh, yes. It was a typical beginning of a war. I don't know whether some of the reports from this correspondent were printed in that form or not. I don't think they were because I think his were more accurate than the rest. I don't believe they were.

We did use self-censorship quite a lot during the war. I used it time and time again. As a matter of fact, I wish we had a little more restraint today in some of the things that are being published than we do have.

Q: Does this reflect a change in philosophy?

Mr. B.: Oh, yes, the press today has changed considerably.
Well, shall I go on with World War II?

Q: Yes. You were going to say something about the efforts to restrain your writing and reporting.

Mr. B.: I think I can take those up better by individual examples as we go on through the war.

Q: All right, Sir.

Mr. B.: I don't know whether I've covered Pearl Harbor completely.

Q: No, I don't believe you did.

Mr. B.: I think I said before I was as surprised as anyone. I was home in Westchester on that famous Sunday and hurried in to the office. Then we had these series of alarms about air raids starting on Monday and Tuesday, which were all false, of course, but very specific and vouched for by the Army each time; 250 planes on their way to New York and so forth, part of the usual fountain of panic and hysteria that always accompanies the start of a war.

My memory of that December is somewhat vague. So much was happening so rapidly and in so many places that I found it very difficult to keep up. I was starting to write every day and sometimes two or three articles a day, and I was trying to keep up with the progress of the war in Europe at the same time that we'd stumbled into a new war in Asia.

Q: How did you go about organizing yourself for this task?

Mr. B.: Well, we had fairly complete files which, of course, grew as the war grew, which were the results of all the preceding years, and I gathered up everything I could in the way of data and statistics about the military powers of the world and also maps. When I'd been to Europe before I neglected to say that I deliberately bought as many maps, military maps where possible, as I could and brought them back to the Times. Some I gave to the Times' map department, some I kept myself and I set up a big map board in the office. I had a great big map board made and I tried to keep track of battle lines and so forth.

Q: You had a war room yourself!

Mr. B.: Yes, and I had a very good assistant who has since retired from the Times. I guess I hired him just after the war started. And I had a couple of other people who were assigned to me then. At one time, I had about four or five people.

Q: All of them with military backgrounds?

Mr. B.: No. Very few of them had any military background, except one. They learned the hard way. Most of them did the sort of clerical and routine tasks. There wasn't anyone to really help out on collecting information, unless it was a telephone call. We made contacts always with the public information officers.

Q: You didn't actually have a deputy, then?

Mr. B.: I had one man, George Barrett, who subsequently became a reporter on the Times, and he would fill in until he later went into the Army. I think he would fill in on the calls to Governor's Island, where the Army headquarters were, and to the Third Naval District, and what not. He got to know the people by name and when there was a release he could get any routine information or something, so he would take care of all that.

Later, a man was assigned to me who was specifically; just about that time, just before the war; assigned to keep track of the draft and of the National Guard and of the morale of our forces. He visited a number of war camps; he had had some military experience. He'd been in the Army in World War I. He was a rather erratic sort of individual and very emotional, but he wrote as a result of this a long memorandum which was subsequently sent to General Marshall by the *Times*. The morale at that time, just before we entered the war, was pretty low. A number of the National Guard had been mobilized. They had been very restive and scrawled signs up on their barracks, "Ohio over the hill in October" and that sort of thing.

Some of this led, I think, to greater attention on the part of the Army to not only discipline but to the little things of morale, including food and barracks and giving them more training. Then when war came, of course, that all was dispelled.

Q: Prior to the war, was this a reflection still of the isolationist thinking?

Mr. B.: Partially that, but partially the fact that Americans, I guess, just don't like discipline. The National Guard was mobilized, as you recall, about a year before the war, and they found they were sitting around twiddling their thumbs in too many cases. They weren't doing much.

Q: And they'd given up good jobs!

Mr. B.: Yes. So I think it was that to a great extent.

Q: It must have been important for you to be in Washington quite frequently at this point, because that was the focal point for whatever information there was?

Mr. B.: Yes, I went down there with increasing frequency whenever I was in this country. Of course, I started going overseas after a while, but the first month of the war I think I was in Washington only once and then only briefly. Things were in too much of a tailspin to find people who could talk to you in Washington. That was the great problem. They were all frantic; nobody knew what was going on. They were all trying to pick up the pieces and there was just no organization and virtually no one; if you remember Admiral Stark was still there. Admiral King had not completely taken over the whole show. The people who subsequently developed as spokesmen like Admiral Horne and Admiral Edwards hadn't arrived. Although I could get in to see Forrestal and some of the civilians, the people in high authority, or even the friends I knew and people I knew well, were so busy that you just didn't want to take too much of their time. There was a real sense of frantic worry, and I remember I reflected this in a piece I did in early January, saying this is a war we can lose. That seemed to shock a lot of Americans. They hadn't really taken that in before because you'd gotten a lot of these soporific communications from the Philippines, which were going down the drain, and Americans still thought, well, as soon as we get the Navy organized again and as soon as we get something started from Australia we'll take over and it'll be a short war. They were thinking in those terms, and I tried to disabuse them of that.

The thing I remember next most vividly is the fall of the Philippines and the; to me and I think the Navy, shocking fact that the Philippines fell without a single major Japanese ship being sunk by the American Navy or by any bomber. I didn't expect the bombers to sink them, but no major Japanese ship was lost, as you know, in the capture of the Philippines. I think no Navy man before the war would have said that was possible. We had the greatest concentration of submarines in the world there but they didn't do a thing. The bombers displayed all their vaunted prowess and General Marshall's optimistic estimates didn't do a thing. The Philippines fell just about as had originally been thought long before the war and as some Navy people felt even when the war started. But it was not the official estimate, it was not the belief into which a lot of people had talked themselves. It wasn't the belief of many of them that it would fall that quickly.

Q: The abandonment of Manila as a base, was this a factor in it?

Mr. B.: No, I don't think so. We couldn't have held Manila.

It was impossible.

Q: But the submarines were dispersed as a result of that, weren't they?

Mr. B.: You mean the loss of the Cavite base and the loss of the Sea Lion, I guess it was, the first submarine. I think that had something to do with it, but this was not the really basic factor. The submarines were dispersed anyway by orders and not replaced in many cases. They should have had more of them around Lingayen Gulf and they should have had more of them in the actual places where the Japanese invaded. In many cases, they missed the invasion altogether. But, remember, they did make contacts and the torpedoes didn't work or the skippers were timid. I think there was one thing after another. They really achieved nothing, except, I think, the sinking of one merchant ship at Lingayen which was not a very important ship, anyway.

Of course, the loss of Manila didn't help the way it was done because MacArthur didn't tell the Navy about this until the last minute, so a lot of Navy stores were left there which would have been useful, quite useful, and a lot went up in smoke. But even greater damage than that was done by the Japanese raid on Cavite, where the torpedo warhead storage was ignited. That was a real handicap. As it developed, it wasn't as much of a handicap as people thought because the torpedoes didn't work anyway! Whether their detonators didn't work or they ran deep or what not.

I think this was a shock. I reflected this shock and it irritated some in the Navy. But, on the other hand, I had written just after Pearl Harbor that the job of defending Hawaii was primarily the Army's. A naval base, to be secure, had to be defensible and attacks against it were supposed to be primarily the Army's job, which was the doctrine at the time. The Navy was not supposed to be defending its own bases, particularly those overseas, and the Army was responsible for that. Many Navy people were looking for a crutch at the time, particularly those who were emotionally involved and most of them were. I think most of them liked that particular article.

Sometime after that I had the painful experience and I don't know whether I mentioned this before of having to interview the younger son; one of the younger sons, of Admiral Kimmel, who was then a student at Princeton. This boy called me up and said he'd like to see me. He told me who he was and I said, well, sure. So he came up from Princeton and it was really a pitiful thing. He said:

"Do you really think my father is as guilty as everybody says he is?"

This must have been in early January or late December, maybe a little later than January. Yes, I think the report for the Roberts Committee came out in late December or early January.

Q: January, I believe.

Mr. B.: I think it was right after this report came out. I tried to be as kind and gentle as possible. I felt so sorry for this youngster. He was a very nice-looking boy. I explained again what I had said in my article that the job of defending the base was primarily the Army's, that I knew very little about the details - and I did at that time - of the attack or what went on before the attack. But I said also, "I think there's been a national state of mind that it can't happen here and that we reflected this."

I couldn't offer him very much solace, but I did the best I could. It was a painful interview, that's all I remember about it really, and I remember the boy's opening remark: "Do you think my father's as guilty as everybody says he is?" That's an awful thing for a youngster to have to face.

Q: May I interrupt the train of your thought by asking, prior to that and prior to the Japanese attack on Pearl Harbor and sometime before that, there had been a Royal Air Force attack on the Italian fleet.

Mr. B.: Yes, at Taranto.

Q: Had you read anything into that, at the time? I know some of the people in Washington did.

Mr. B.: I wrote something about that and I would hesitate to say what it was now. I know I wrote something about it. I think I said this was an indication of the increasing power of the air arm, but I just don't remember. I wrote so many thousands of articles that what my reaction was at that time, I don't know.

It's very difficult, as you know, to disentagle what you know now from what you knew then, and your feelings now as to your feelings then. Sometimes you tend to rationalize and say, oh, yes, I knew all about that and I thought this. I don't want to do that. I'm not at all sure that I was perspicacious, but I don't know. The only way you could tell that would be to read what I wrote. Many of the things were abysmally wrong, I'm sure, and others didn't show any foresight at all. Some may have shown a little. Basically, of course, your great problem was writing on the basis of limited information, very limited, not only hidden by censorship but above all, by the all-important details and by the fog of war which often was almost impenetrable because you'd get so many different accounts, varying accounts. It would be almost impossible to sift out the truth from the false.

Later on in the war, when I went overseas myself and saw the people doing the fighting or when I got to a person like Admiral Horne, I could ask him about a past action and he would tell me. I'd get the facts and I knew they were the facts. But at that time that source hadn't opened up yet. So, whether I had really learned one of the lessons of Taranto; there was a difference here in a sense, though not from Pearl Harbor, that was another point that was made the most of by the battleship admirals. They said, oh, well; I remember their saying this about Taranto and also about Pearl Harbor; these ships were in port, they were anchored, they were only half-manned, they weren't underway. Then they got the additional shock of the Prince of Wales off Malaysia, as you remember. She was a battleship fully underway, maneuvering and all that, and antiaircraft guns firing.

So, there was still a controversy, even after Taranto and even immediately after Pearl Harbor. A lot of people discounted this as a surprise attack, which it was, and as unprotected ships in harbor, and it couldn't be done again on the open seas. So the full efficacy of air power wasn't appreciated even then and I don't think until later.

As I remember, and I'm skipping around here because it's the only way I can do, I went out to the Pacific in August . . .

Q: Of 1942?

Mr. B.: September of 1942, yes. I prepared the way as well as I could in Washington. I've forgotten whom I saw there but I talked to various people, including Forrestal.

Q: This was after Midway?

Mr. B.: Yes, it was after Midway. We'd won Midway and we had just gotten into Guadalcanal the month before, on 30 August I think it was, in Guadalcanal and I started out to the Pacific about the middle of August or the end of August.

Q: What kind of a commission did you have when you went to the Pacific, what kind of a roving commission?

Mr. B.: The *Times* left it largely up to me. I said I wanted to get down to the South Pacific to see what was going on and I wanted to get to Pearl. I couldn't do anything else except play it by ear from there.

I went to Pearl first and spent some time there.

Q: I wondered if you enjoyed the kind of status that Morison had?

Mr. B.: You mean from the Navy?

Q: Yes.

Mr. B.: Oh, no. Well, I was a correspondent, that's all, fully a correspondent. They couldn't have done that in any case. It wouldn't have been fair to the rest.

What I was going to say is that when I came to Midway, and I don't know whether I mentioned this previously, Waldo Drake was the Public Information Officer. Had I mentioned that?

Q: I don't think you had, no.

Mr. B.: He was a commander, I guess, in the Naval Reserve and he'd been with the <u>Los Angeles Times</u> and I'd run into him at fleet maneuvers and various other places before. He was a rather smooth guy, very smooth in some ways, sort of sycophantic to superiors. He'd rage and rant about Navy censorship in peacetime at these maneuvers and the stupidity of the Navy, but he would never take it up to the top. He'd never fight against it, he'd never go to see the admiral, which I would do. He'd always let me lead the way or someone else lead the way.

Waldo was a very curious guy and most of the press didn't like him too much. He was all out for Waldo and, because he was smooth and sort of devious, he wasn't too well liked.

Q: He was Nimitz' top press man.

Mr. B.: He turned up as Nimitz' top public relations officer, after Nimitz succeeded to command. Part of this was, I guess, that he must have met Nimitz maybe at a fleet maneuver or something of the sort.

Q: I think it was earlier, through the NROTC, when Nimitz was at the University, you know; earlier, much earlier.

Mr. B.: Down at what university?

Q: Berkeley.

Mr. B.: That may well be.

Q: I think that's where they first met.

Mr. B.: That may be. Waldo had quite a reputation around the Los Angeles area because he had been with the <u>Los Angeles Times</u> for a long time covering the Navy and aviation and so forth.

In any case, when I got to Pearl, the other correspondents who were there were really down on Drake. They didn't like him at all, and it developed that he kept a black book of correspondents, a lot like Arthur Sylvester who was MacNamara's man. This black book was very much hated. Drake really had a sort of a (I should say it in this day of women's lib) feminine trait, but it was almost that of pettiness and a kind of retributive dislike if somebody crossed him. A number of correspondents that they'd had out there had serious confrontations with Drake, but Waldo was in solid with Nimitz because; one of the reasons was he always played up to him, the other reason was he was a very good tennis player. He played tennis with Nimitz quite a lot. He stuck in that job until finally Forrestal got a man named "Min" Miller, a classmate of mine, out there to take over.

Through thick and thin Waldo stayed there despite the dislike of the press, and Forrestal had sense enough to know that he was doing the Navy a lot of damage. He was antagonizing so many people and playing favorites and needlessly withholding stories and things of that sort. Finally, Forrestal gave "Min" Miller orders to go out ostensibly as an assistant to Waldo, but actually to supplant him and to do it without antagonizing Nimitz, which was the hell of an assignment! And he did it. They did it by virtue of kicking Waldo upstairs. They made him a captain and sent him back to the West Coast and eventually to Washington.

Q: He had a young assistant named Jim Bassett, too. Did you run into him?

Mr. B.: Yes, oh, yes, I knew Jim Bassett. He was with the Los Angeles Times. He was a different kettle of fish, though, altogether, and the press could get along with him.

Waldo, of course, did not do anything to me. He was catering up to me, first of all because he knew I knew the Navy thoroughly and because I was with the Times and had a little reputation.

In any case, I spent some time in Pearl and I saw Nimitz and various members of his staff. I saw the damage that had been done and some of the salvage, which was still going on, talked about the war, filed a couple of innocuous pieces, then said I wanted to get down to the South Pacific. It developed that Admiral Fitch was going down there to take over command of Air, South Pacific, so I got in a patrol plane with him and flew down, first to Palmyra Island, which was a beautiful little tropical atoll with some Marines holding it. Everybody was scared to death that the Japs were going to come at any time.

Q: It had been bombed had it not?

Mr. B.: Then we came to Canton Island. We stayed there overnight. We never flew at night. That, too, was lightly held. I think in this case by the Army, with a few Navy people there. There was a big freighter up on a reef that had been there since the first days of the war, rusting away and run aground. There were almost nightly alarms but nothing happened. They knew the Japs were close by. It was before we'd really gotten into the mandated islands. We were still fighting for a toehold in Guadalcanal and hadn't gotten any farther than that.

Then we got down to the Fijis, and I saw the Johns Hopkins medical unit and an old friend of mine, a doctor from Baltimore, who was with that unit. Then we went on to New Caledonia and Ghormley's headquarters and flagship were in the harbor. Emmet O'Beirne, Frank O'Beirne's younger brother, was, as I remember, either operations officer or air officer on Ghormley's staff; I've forgotten which one. It was quite apparent when you came into the harbor that things were all wrong. It was just clogged with shipping, a lot of it just lying there. I knew this before I went down because I neglected to say Admiral Good went down on the same flight. He was sent down by Nimitz to see why it was taking so long to unload in Caledonia and to get the logistics straightened out. That was his special task on this trip.

He was a very delightful chap, Good, with a good sense of humor.

I went in to see Ghormley. I stayed there a couple of nights, I guess.

Q: Had you known him in London?

Mr. B.: No. I'd met him briefly, I think in Washington before the war, just very briefly.

He was really completely defeatist. He was almost despairing. He was heavily overworked and he said, "this is a shoestring operation, we haven't got enough of anything. We're just hanging on by our teeth." He was very frank about this. The impression it made on me was very negative, of course. It had to be because here was a time when you needed tough, hard, almost ruthless men. He was a miscast, in my opinion. He should never have been in that job. He was a superb planner and he should have been kept as a planner, but I don't think he was a good operator. I think the magnitude of his task, the fact that this was rushed by Admiral King, as you know, the whole operation, and there weren't enough ships, there wasn't enough of anything.

Q: He was the ruthless driver in the picture!

Mr. B.: Yes, overwhelming. I talked to Emmet O'Beirne about my impressions afterwards and I said:

"Look, he's almost defeatist," and he said, "I'm afraid so."

The staff didn't share these impressions entirely, but they were becoming infected. So the whole thing was very unpleasant.

I then flew up to Espiritu Santo where the gloom thickened because this was really a primitive operation. We had both Air Force and Marine planes and some Navy planes based there. It's a very nice little harbor.

Q: Were the Seabees there?

Mr. B.: They'd built the airstrip, I think, and then I think most of them had moved on to Guadalcanal or somewhere, I don't know.

Q: To Tulagi, wasn't it?

Mr. B.: Yes. There was a ship in the harbor that had been torpedoed. It wasn't a man of war. It was a merchantman. I've forgotten what it was, a transport. She was sort of half on the bottom. There were a lot of injured and wounded people being treated in the hospital. We stayed there overnight, got an impression, and then Admiral Fitch was going up the next morning to Guadalcanal, so I tagged along on his coattails, otherwise you didn't know when you'd get in there. It was hard to get in at that time.

Q: How many dispatches were you sending off?

Mr. B.: I wasn't sending daily. First, you had to fight through censorship and that was quite a task, especially in the South Pacific. I don't think I wrote anything from there. I was coming to that in just a minute.

We got into, as I recall it, a C-47 flown by the Marines, in fact by a classmate of mine, a man named Hudnall, who was a Marine major, I guess, then. These old goony birds were flying to Guadalcanal dodging Zero raids. They always would come down low as they came in to Guadalcanal, quite low to skim over the wavetops so that the Zeros couldn't attack them so easily. I remember looking out of the window as we came in, just before we arrived there, about half an hour I guess, and a couple of aircraft appeared high up. We didn't know whether they were Zeroes or our own. We spent rather a nervous few minutes, but they turned out to be ours.

We landed at Henderson Field which was commanded by another classmate of mine named Fitch, who was in the Marines, an aviator. It was one of the roughest fields I'd ever seen, with a strange control tower, this old makeshift tower, wooden, what did they call that? They had a name for it, a Japanese architectural name.

Q: A pagoda?

Mr. B.: A pagoda. They called it the Pagoda. It was a muddy

field, rough, and people were all distributed around it in the foxholes and the pup tents. It had been raining an awful lot.

I went along with Admiral Fitch over to General Vandergrift's headquarters. It developed that just the night before the Japs had made this raid which had penetrated into the headquarters area and the headquarters staff had repelled it. One of the headquarters men had been killed, I think, and two or three Japs were killed within sight of Vandergrift's tent. And I discovered to my great surprise, as indeed I think to the whole American public's, that we were just holding onto Henderson Field by the skin of our teeth. We didn't have any other foothold on the island. We just had this little narrow enclave.

Q: And the Japs were in the ramparts, were they not?

Mr. B.: The Japs were all around the whole place, the entire rest of the island, and I had had the impression from the communiques and all the publicity, as indeed everyone had; I hadn't even had this impression dispelled at Pearl Harbor except that people had told me we didn't hold the whole island and the Japs were still fighting hard; that we held most of the island and were fairly secure. Well, this was far from the case.

I went down after Admiral Fitch had done some of his talking; I had dinner, I guess, or lunch, with General Vandergrift. I talked to him frankly and asked him if he was going to hold because by this time I'd talked to a lot of other people and they were all pretty jittery and many of them were nervous. There was a nightly bombardment or bombing and that gets you jittery, and in addition to that there were these continuous attacks and they'd been fighting and holding on by their teeth, getting intermittent supply and not very certain supply, and had had a lot of casualties. So there wasn't anything like the feeling that Ghormley reflected of complete defeatism but there was a sense of jitteriness.

So I asked General Vandergrift whether he was going to be able to hold Henderson Field and hold the island and he said, "Hell, yes." It was an entirely different attitude than Ghormley had. I remember that reply very vividly because I quoted it, and Vandergrift quoted it later in a book.

Then Admiral Fitch was going back that very next day to Espiritu Santo where he was going to set up his command and take over the air in the South Pacific. He thought it was very essential he get things moving, particularly the logistic planes, immediately. They were flying in drums of gasoline. We had drums of gasoline on the C-47, I forgot to say, aviation gas; it wasn't aviation gas then but it was the gasoline they used for those propeller-driven planes. It wasn't the avgas you have today. We were filled up with that and with ammunition. They were flying these things in because they didn't get enough from ships, so we were a fiery coffin!

So I faced the choice of either taking my chances and

staying on there for about two weeks or going on back and fighting this thing through censorship. I knew I wouldn't get anywhere in filing anything from Guadalcanal. General Vandergrift wasn't empowered to really get anything through and I thought I had a hell of a story because I'd learned while I was there and in Pearl and in Espiritu and in New Caledonia about the details of the first Savo Battle. I knew about that. One of my informants described it to me as sitting ducks, our ships were sitting ducks, and I learned about the torpedoing of the Washington and the torpedoing of one of our carriers. I learned we had only one capital ship and one carrier left in the South Pacific that were capable of mobility, and a lot of other details. So I knew I had a hell of a story and I would have to fight this through top censorship to get it out. I wouldn't be able to get it out in Guadalcanal or Espiritu, perhaps not even in Pearl, but I would try it in Pearl.

I was faced with the likelihood of having to stay there for a couple of weeks because transportation was very intermittent and they would not take up space on these aircraft that were going out to Espiritu with correspondents if they had wounded to go out or other things of that sort, rightly, of course. So Admiral Fitch's plane was the one I took. I went out again the next day. I only stayed there overnight.

Q: What was Fitch's attitude at that point? Of course, he hadn't been involved.

Mr. B.: As I remember, he remained calm and cheerful. He realized the magnitude of the task he had and was itching to get to work. He was sent down there by Nimitz specifically to organize this thing and get the logistics, air logistics particularly, working. I think he had a positive attitude despite all. He knew, of course, a lot more than I did because he'd been privy to it at Pearl, but I think he was astounded, too, by what he saw in New Caledonia.

I flew back to Pearl as fast as I could. I don't remember how I came back or who it was with. Maybe with Admiral Good. Fitch, of course, stayed in the South Pacific. I think I did go back with Admiral Good and I exchanged a lot of notes with him on the way because he had a lot of things he had to put into effect at Pearl. As I remember, he was on Nimitz' staff as a kind of J-4, logistics. I think he was charged with logistics in some way. He may not have been the senior officer on that but he was one of them at that time.

When I got to Pearl I got a few things through, the preliminary story which, however, did not really tell the situation at Guadalcanal.

Q: Did you have to fight to get that?

Mr. B.: Yes, and I encountered some of the dumbest censors I ever encountered. One in particular I remember, who had been a submarine captain and relieved of his job, and without any experience just made a censor. He was one of the submarine captains who failed in the early part of the war.

Q: Did they have a set of strictures they were working with?

Mr. B.: They were supposed to have but I was going to cite this example. I used what really, I guess, was an obsolete phrase that was used widely in World War I to describe anti-aircraft guns, I said ack-ack guns, which was widely used then and this man thought I was writing in code and he sent it back. Then, number two, I said something about some casualty on Guadalcanal. I described Frank Goettge's death, although I don't think I mentioned him by name. He had been killed just before I got there. I knew Frank Goettge from old days. I played football against him, I think I told you, when he was on the Marine Corps team. He was leading a patrol on Guadalcanal and was ambushed and he and his patrol were wiped out, but I said something about "shot in the head," and he struck out "in the head." I couldn't get the logic to this, the reason for it, and I had quite a discussion, not to say quarrel. He was one of the dumbest men I ever met, really. He should never have been in command of a submarine. I took it up with others, too, but I knew I was not going to get too much. I talked to people in Pearl and they said, "Look, you'd better take this back to Washington. Our hands are tied. We can't release this."

So I immediately flew back to the West Coast as fast as I could after filing a couple of stories. I've forgotten what

I filed but I know . . .

Q: They were stories that you yourself had censored?

Mr. B.: No, no, I sent them through censorship. Oh, no, I wouldn't try to evade censorship.

Q: No, but I mean you had toned them down.

Mr. B.: Oh, yes, I hadn't written the full story.

I no sooner got back to New York than I told the *Times* I had the hell of a story and I told them what it was but I'd have to fight it through censorship in Washington. So I went down there. I wrote the stories first and took them down there; a series of stories, which the *Times* wanted. I told about the Battle of Savo in general terms, without mentioning ships' names, how many cruisers we lost, and how ships were sitting ducks. I told about the situation on Guadalcanal and likened it to our holding La Guardia Field on Long Island and that's about all.

I finally got these with some very minor changes through censorship in Washington, I guess with the help of Elmer Davis, who was in the Office of War Information, although I'm not sure he had much to do with them.

They created a sensation when they came out, as a matter of fact, and it was for that I got the Pulitzer Prize later.

Then, on top of that, at the end of November, and these articles came out in October, I guess, at the end of October, Ghormley was relieved by Halsey. That was announced, and people falsely credited me with that relief and I didn't particularly like that idea, first because I liked Ghormley although I knew he was not the man for the job.

Q: How did you deal with that situation in your dispatch?

Mr. B.: Ghormley?

Q: Yes.

Mr. B.: I didn't mention his name. I gave the atmosphere as well as I could in the South Pacific at the time, said there was only one battleship and one carrier left. I fudged this very carefully because I realized it was very important that the Japs not know exactly how damaged we were, but by the time these articles came out we'd gotten another couple of ships down there and things were somewhat better.

Partially as a result of these articles appearing in October, I got an invitation from General Wedemeyer, who was then, I think, a brigadier general or a colonel, and who was known in those days as a planner. He was General Embick's son-in-law. General Embick was a well-known Army general, prewar general, who was quite well known for his planning. He was a thinking general and was sort of right wing in his political thinking. Wedemeyer was decidedly so. In any case, Wedemeyer was then serving on what I believe was a joint strategic survey committee of the Joint Chiefs of Staff. The Joint Chiefs of Staff had no legal justification, as you know. They were just set up by Roosevelt and they occupied the Public Health Building across from the Navy Building on Constitution Avenue.

Wedemeyer got in touch with me; I'd known him before the war, and I knew vaguely he was doing something connected with planning, and he asked me very secretly to come down to Washington and appear before this committee and talk about the South Pacific. He said it's so secret I don't want you even to tell the Times about it.

So I did. I went to Washington and, of course, combined it with some work for the Times. I went over to this solemn conclave. As you recall, the Joint Chiefs were then Admiral Leahy and Admiral King and, yes, by then, Stark had gone to London, General Marshall and General Arnold. General Arnold wouldn't have been a member unless Marshall had reorganized the Army and set up the Air Corps as virtually a separate organization. The Joint Chiefs had done their own organizing. Leahy really was not a chairman. He didn't act as an operator, an executive. He viewed his role as an assistant to the President. So he sat there and he did open the meetings and so forth. I didn't actually attend their meetings; this is what he told me later; that he did not try to dominate the discussions. He would interject the President's views or, if he felt something was completely off course, he would try to reflect this. But as far as the planning was concerned, it was more, I think, a product of Marshall and King and Arnold, with Leahy interjecting. He didn't hesitate to say if he didn't like it but he wouldn't try to dominate the discussion.

Under their direction they set up a number of committees, quite a few committees, and I think the name of the committee I attended was the Joint Strategic Survey Committee. I didn't keep records on this or, if I did, I've given them to Yale.

I came into this room in the Public Health Building with a very long table and I should think there were about twenty-five or thirty officers from all the services around the table, including Wedemeyer who was, I guess, the senior from the Army. There were quite a few Army officers, some from the Army Air Corps, and quite a few Navy officers, most of them in the rank of colonel. Wedemeyer was either a brigadier general or just about to be promoted, but I think he was probably one of the senior ones. And they started asking me questions about the South Pacific. Wedemeyer asked me to tell them what I'd seen.

I spoke much more frankly, of course, than I was able to do in the pieces I'd written. I described how the Washington had been torpedoed and almost blown up and how there was only one battleship and one carrier at that time left in the South Pacific. We were just hanging on by our teeth and so forth. When I said this about the ship damages and about the cruisers that had been lost at Savo, and I gave them the names of the cruisers in this secret meeting . . .

Q: At Savo Island?

Mr. B.: Yes, and in some of the subsequent actions. A Navy captain stood up, violently angry, and said, "I object to that. I object to that. This is top secret information. Admiral King has given the strictest orders that no one is to know about this." Nobody said a word, not even Wedemeyer. I was astonished, completely astonished. I couldn't believe my ears. I said:

"Well, of course, I understand it's top secret information. I haven't published this, the names of these ships or the exact losses or details and I don't expect to. I was asked to come down here in top secrecy and not even tell my paper about it, and I've done so."

This captain continued to protest. Wedemeyer interjected then and said:

"Well, I suggest you just tell us about the importance of air power in the South Pacific and the influence it's had on the war."

So he diverted it to that, which I then proceeded to do at some length. The captain sat down, still choleric. The questioning went on and I suppose took about an hour or an hour and a half. I left, and about three to four days later Drew Pearson had a column in which he said that the Navy had been holding out on the other services and that when I came to testify it was the first time that many of these officers had heard of the losses at Savo Island . . .

Q: And he mentioned you by name?

Mr. B.: Yes, and the first they knew of the fact that we had only so few ships left in the South Pacific. He mentioned several others by name, I think. Brown, Captain Brown then, later Vice Admiral Brown - it was Brown who was the very choleric captain.

As a result of that column I got an equally choleric letter from "Cat" Brown accusing me of leaking this episode to Drew Pearson. I got very angry at that point! I let Brown have one in return because the last person I liked was Drew Pearson and I never leaked anything to him. Like Jack Anderson. I despise that kind of journalism and I wasn't going to leak anything like this, anyway. So I told him he'd better put his own house in order and he'd better find what officers on the committee had leaked this because I had nothing to do with it.

Well, it ended up; "Cat" is like that, you know, he's very volatile, or was very volatile, he apologized and we became good friends. I kept that friendship with him until he was in the Sixth Fleet later on. But this was a curious side effect of my visit to the South Pacific, and it was true that Admiral King had held out this information. I don't know whether Wedemeyer knew these facts or not. That's one thing I've never discovered and I'd like to ask him now whether he knew that these ships had been sunk. But the officers of lesser rank in the Army and the Air Corps, had no idea of what had happened at Guadalcanal or Savo in that August or September, no idea at all. And here it was by this time along about November and these same officers were supposed to be planning! That, I think, is a hell of a way to run a war.

Admiral King was obviously, and this brings up the point that I guess led to these interviews, on a hot seat because he had been pressing for Guadalcanal right along. He had been the one who said go in, even on a shoestring, and these repercussions, these losses, this naval ineptitude, would not sit well with the American people and wouldn't increase his fame or fortune. So that may have been one reason why he wanted to withhold this. Of course, there was an obvious reason in the case of the ships' strengths that were left in the South Pacific. He didn't want to tell the enemy about it, although I think they knew most of these things because they had air reconnaissance over the whole area and they had the larger part of Guadalcanal and all the other islands in the Solomons. You couldn't very well disguise where our ships were, and they knew what was in Espiritu Santo and so forth.

However, you were on the safe side if you didn't tell them that we were down to one battleship and one carrier, and that wasn't done till long after the event. But King's motivation on this I'll never completely understand and Brown's violent reaction, except I think probably Brown was instinctively afraid of what Admiral King's reaction would be if he heard about this.

Q: Was there any reaction from King as far as you were concerned?

Mr. B.: No.

Q: When Drew Pearson came out with this?

Mr. B.: No, none directly, except this letter from "Cat" Brown, which may have reflected something he'd gotten.

Q: Was he on King's staff?

Mr. B.: He was, I think. At least, he was on the Joint Chiefs of Staff. Whether he was on King's personal staff, I don't know, but he was the senior naval officer on this committee at the time.

Q: What was the reaction of The New York Times when you had gone down to testify but not . . .

Mr. B.: I told them about it afterwards. I told them later why I went down to Washington and that I had been asked not to mention it. In those days, I could go directly to the publisher, and I told the publisher some things I told no one else on the Times at any time because I found, as you always do, that if you tell something to too many people it starts to get spread around and leaks. I wouldn't even tell the managing editor some of the things. The publisher, I knew, would keep it absolutely quiet and he did. So we had a personal confidential relationship which was very useful.

Q: How were you able to cover the European theatre, which was very active?

Mr. B.: Let me go on with this just a minute because there's an aftermath to this.

Partially as a result of these articles that I'd written, which revealed things to the American public for the first time, I got another call from Elmer Davis, who was the Head of the Office of War Information at the time. He wanted me to help try to crack the hard nut of the Navy, as he called it. He said he couldn't get anything out of Admiral King, it was quite impossible, and he felt it was essential to the American public that the Navy tell more of its story, and he found that it was a hard-crusted service, and could I help. So I talked to Elmer Davis for some time.

By then I'd established; and this must have been done in the spring and summer of 1942, relations with Admiral Horne and lesser ones with Admiral Edwards. I don't know when Horne actually took that job, but when Stark gave up, Horne really was CNO then, as I understand it. Horne was a very personable, likeable chap, and I think that he had Forrestal's ear. I know that Forrestal encouraged him to talk to some of the press. I don't remember who the other newspapermen were he saw. I never saw them with him, but he would talk to me every time I came to Washington and often on very short notice, and he was very frank both retroactively and prospectively. He would tell me about future operations that were planned, of course trusting me not to say anything about them which I never did until after the event. He would tell me the details as they then happened of past naval battles, which I'd never have gotten otherwise. For instance, I remember later the "charge" of the small boys at the Battle of Leyte Gulf, which saved some of the jeep carriers, had never been described and he gave me a vivid description of this, and I ran it on the front page of the *Times*. It was a heroic story. Of course, the details weren't all in, you didn't have it all, but you knew that these ships had done it. Some of the ships couldn't be mentioned by name, but you could tell the story.

He was invaluable and the Navy owes a tremendous debt to Admiral Horne for what he did for the Navy during the war. If it had not been for him and to a lesser extent for Admiral Edwards, who was also very personable and approachable but who was much more immersed in the details of King's staff work, and for Jim Forrestal, the Navy really would have been behind the eight ball, because there was no one in Washington who was reflecting either the Navy's problems or seeing that the Navy got any credit for what it did, or telling the story in any way, shape, or form.

Admiral Horne's light has always, I think, been hidden

under a bushel. He ought to have been given more credit for judgment, moral courage; because he didn't have any fear of Admiral King apparently or of what he was doing, and he never had a confidence violated by any of the people he saw, and I think he saw only about three or four others besides myself. I don't know who they were. He was extremely competent and had a very pleasant personality, and he understood the importance of public relations.

It is true that at the start of the war Admiral Hepburn was in public relations. He didn't know anything about it, but he learned and he tried his best, and they gradually improved.

But, as a result of Elmer Davis' query, I got him in touch with Admiral Horne. I told Admiral Horne what Elmer Davis had said to me, that they were having a hell of a time, and that I thought it was very important to the Navy and to the country that Davis have a pipeline into someone in the professional Navy, rather than just Jim Forrestal, who could really fill him in. Davis did make contact with Admiral Horne and, to a lesser extent, with Admiral Edwards, and from there on things were better. They were not perfect but they were better.

So, really concluding this particular part of the war and the particular part of this episode, and trying to answer in a sense some of the questions this professor asked me about Admiral King and the results of Guadalcanal upon his career, I would think that King well knew that after some of the early disasters in Guadalcanal he was on the spot. But, to give him credit, I think he was a bulldog, tenacious type and he was determined to see that he won through. He had to see that more or less. If we lost, he probably would have lost his job, although I'm not sure about that. And I think the relief of Ghormley, although I can't be sure of this either, was the doing of both him and Nimitz, and I'm sure it was decided on long before my articles appeared, not long before, but some time before they appeared, and that the timing was a coincidence.

Q: I want to ask how Nimitz fit into the picture. Admiral King was applying pressure to get things going in the South Pacific, and how did Admiral Nimitz fit into that picture? Was he of the same mind? Did he want to get things going, or was he a little more cautious?

Mr. B.: I can't answer that. I would think that Admiral Nimitz initially would have been more cautious, but once the die had been cast and we'd decided to go into Guadalcanal he felt it was absolutely essential to go along with King that it be held and we extent our foothold.

I would think what you said a moment ago that he, Admiral Nimitz, was responsible for Ghormley's relief is true, but I would also think that he had been getting harassing cables from Washington because King could see from there that things were not working and that things weren't right. King had his own channels of communication, of reporting, anyway. People would come back from the South Pacific and tell him about things. After all, he knew about Savo and he kept that quiet, he knew about the Washington and the carriers. He knew about the drought of shipping, maybe not the details but the general picture of stagnation in Noumea.

So I would think that Nimitz was, well, not being heckled because I think King had confidence in Nimitz and believed, as far as possible, in allowing him to run his own show, but I would think that he wouldn't hesitate to query or suggest. And I imagine you'd find in the cables somewhere something about Ghormley from King, but I'm not sure. But I am quite sure in my own mind that Admiral Good's report after his trip had a good bit to do with Ghormley's relief, because really Good was sent down there on a trouble-shooting expedition. That's what he was doing. He was to find out what the situation was at firsthand, particularly about logistics, and to come back and report, and that's what he did. He did it in a very short time. They knew time was precious. That's one reason he came back as fast as he could. It took a little time then because this was September; I don't remember when Ghormley was actually relieved.

Q: He was relieved on the 18th of October.

Mr. B.: I was going to say it was probably toward the middle or end of September when we got back to Pearl, somewhere in that area, and it would take a little while for the reports to be absorbed, to decide who was going to relieve him. Halsey had been in the hospital, you remember, with dermatitis and he was probably just coming out of the hospital. They'd made the decision to relieve him before this. Do you mean it was announced on the 18th?

Q: That was in the chronology of the war. That is the date, so I imagine that was the date it was announced.

Mr. B.: Yes. My recollection was that it was announced some time toward the end of October, but I don't remember the details. I'm sure it was decided upon before it was announced, that's all I was getting at. Therefore, there wasn't too much of a time lapse after the return of Good to Pearl and the decision.

Q: You must have been helpful to Admiral Good. You rode back with him and discussed the whole situation and gave your impressions and, as a trained person, this must have been helpful.

Mr. B.: He was much more trained that I was! He was much more helpful to me. I was still pretty inexperienced, but we exchanged impressions and he was very frank. A very likeable personality. I never really saw him again; I saw him but I was never shipmate with him again.

Q: Well, I started to ask you how you were managing to cover the European theatre at the same time, simultaneously with all the other.

Mr. B.: When I went on overseas trips I made no attempt to do a worldwide coverage. It would have been impossible. I then concentrated on writing about the theatre in which I was. My job really was two or three fold. When I was back in the States, and I was here most of the time, I would try to write about the war as a whole, maybe one theatre one day and one the next, and so forth, depending on what was happening.

When I was overseas I would write more reportorial pieces rather than analysis pieces, although there was some analysis in some of them, about that particular theatre. And I made periodic trips like this one to the Pacific and one later to North Africa and to England.

Q: Yes, Torch came in November of 1942.

Mr. B.: I didn't go to Torch but I went to North Africa in 1943, just after Kasserine Pass, and went all over the area and actually, as often happens, I wrote far better pieces from there and far more detailed than I did from the South Pacific. I got the Pulitzer Prize for the wrong series! Pulitzer Prizes are like any other newspaper prize, too, geared to topical opinion and the sensational. That's that problem. It's the dramatic and the sensational, and these series from the South

Pacific came as a thunderclap to the American people. That's the only reason I got the prize really.

Q: But, in a sense, this helped to alert us to a greater effort, did it not?

Mr. B.: Yes, I think it did good but I'm talking as an example of reporting. I think I'd done much more thorough and comprehensive jobs. I did one about North Africa. I did coin a phrase, and I didn't coin it because it was old, in North Africa which stuck like the "sitting ducks" in Guadalcanal; that was I said the America GI was thinking of mom and apple pie. And he was. Then I also used a quotation of General Alexander, the British general, later marshal. He said to me:

"You know, your chaps don't wear the old school tie." I knew what he meant by that. He meant that they hadn't been trained in the British concept of noblesse oblige. They didn't look out for their men. He was talking about the younger officers, and this was true not of the West Pointer but it was true of a lot of the Reserve officers. They'd come through the National Guard, they'd just come into the service and we had many of these in North Africa. They wouldn't see that their men got fed first or properly, that sort of thing. They just didn't know it and they didn't have that British old school tie aspect of looking out for the underdog first.

Q: Did you have much knowledge of Torch before the enterprise actually was launched? Were you in on the Norfolk planning and that sort of thing?

Mr. B.: Oh, no, I wasn't in on the Norfolk planning at all. In fact, I didn't get to Norfolk in that period. But I talked to Admiral Horne, I think, in general about it. I'm trying to separate my knowledge of what I now know and what I knew then. I find it almost impossible, but I'm sure I knew something about it.

Q: There, again, you must have run into Admiral King's penchant for secrecy because he was awfully tight-fisted about this?

Mr. B.: This is where Admiral Horne, I think, showed so much moral courage and really paid such a compliment to me and I think the others in whom he confided, because regardless of that penchant for secrecy he would tell you about forthcoming operations. The only other one who would talk about those in any way was Admiral Leahy. I used to see Admiral Leahy when I went to Washington, too. He wouldn't talk in any detail but he would talk in general terms. For instance, Admiral Leahy was very opposed to the planned invasion of Japan, the foot invasion, and I talked to him about that before the event a number of times. I asked him if he really reflected this in the Joint Chiefs of Staff discussions and he said no, "I don't take that to be my role. I have registered my opinion but I'm really the President's representative and what the President has decided on I can't oppose."

And I said, "Well, do you ever tell the President about this?" and he said, "Sometimes." He wasn't very positive on this, you see. But I saw Admiral Leahy in the White House when I'd come to Washington and I would see Admiral Horne. I'm sure Admiral Horne spoke of Torch ahead of time but I doubt that it was in any great detail.

Intermittently, when I was back in the States between these trips, I would go around, too, in addition to writing analysis pieces, to some of the Army and military places and Navy. I remember at various times meeting General Patton, I think at Fort Oglethorpe, Fort Knox and then again later in some maneuvers when he had taken over one of the armored divisions. He was then wearing his "Green Hornet" uniform, as some of the press called it, and his pearl-handled revolvers. He was quite a dynamic figure.

And it was interesting that I ran into him again in North Africa. Patton had just come up to the front to take command after Kasserine Pass when we'd taken a hell of a knock, you know. He was out in the desert at his headquarters. This was one of the few times in the war when we experienced lack of air superiority and it was quite often disconcerting to see these German Messerschmidts come swooping down as you went up to headquarters at the front. The Germans didn't have any real air superiority because they didn't have enough planes, but they had enough to make it hot and heavy for us at times and to harass us. You always were looking up to the sky to be ready to duck, and I remember several occasions when we had to hop out of a jeep in a hurry and hide alongside of the road. Patton, at this time when I came to see him, was very down and I got another side of him at this time because I'd never seen him in this mood before. His son-in-law was Johnny Waters, General Waters, who had command; his last duty was as a full general in command of the Army, Pacific, and Johnny Waters now lives in Maryland, just outside Washington.

Johnny and I were schoolmates at the Boys' Latin School in Baltimore. He was about four or five classes behind me. Johnny went to West Point and subsequently rose up the ladder. In this early fighting in North Africa, just before I'd come there, I guess, in the aftermath of Kasserine Pass, Johnny's outfit had been overrun by the Germans and Johnny had disappeared. Patton didn't know whether he'd been killed or captured or what had happened at the time I saw him. Patton was a very emotional guy and he was, I'm sure, thinking of his daughter and worrying about it. There were tears in his eyes when he talked about Johnny and I saw an entirely different side to the man than I'd seen before.

In any case, on the African trip; as I remember it was in March and April 1943, I went all along the front. I would try to see the entire front, not just the American, and I saw a lot of various commanders involved. I went also along that very small portion of the front held by the Free French. This was before we'd made junction with the Eighth Army. There was a division between Montgomery and the rest of us. The French had a lot of picturesque troops there, including the Goums, the Algerian native levies who loved the knife they used on unsuspecting Germans and who lived in a really primitive way, lying on straw when they were wounded, throwing their dirty bandages outside the tents, and eating virtually raw meat. The French were light years behind in what we considered sanitation. The British, in turn, were behind us. I remember going up to the British portion of the front and their headquarters was in an abandoned railroad station. I went in there and spent the night very uncomfortably, wrapped in some blankets, sleeping on the floor, I guess, with a British officer. Early in the morning, in this British voice, he said:

"Don't mind me. Every morning, I strip down and take a cold bath," and he proceeded to take a cold bath.

I learned after I'd spent the night in this flea-infested place that they had all sorts of diseases there, cholera and everything else, which didn't fill me with confidence. The British never paid much attention to this sort of thing. It's curious. They just took it in their stride. I guess they'd been just so used to diseases over the world.

Q: They were colonials!

Mr. B.: And their medical and health provisions were really

far behind ours. The field hospitals and everything else were very, very uncomfortable compared to the Americans. Maybe we pampered our people too much.

In any case, I flew down over the gap in the desert around the southern end to see General Montgomery, who was then quite a famous figure. An insufferable bore, in some ways.

This was just after the battle for the Mareth Line. That line, as you remember, was the last German defense line before the Eighth Army, which had been pushing from El Alamein along the coast and had come into Tunisia in an attempt to link up with the American and Allied forces joined the front under Eisenhower. Eisenhower, of course, had his headquarters in Algiers at this time. The Mareth Line was a very closely fought battle. The Eighth Army almost lost it and only won it at the last moment. I knew this and I went down to talk about that and to meet Monty.

I felt it was always a part of my job on these trips to try to meet the leaders so I could describe them as necessary later and also to try to get their feeling. It was a very unpleasant day because a kind of a sandstorm, which they call the Khamsin, was blowing and nothing is as unpleasant as a sandstorm in a desert. This wasn't a violent one, fortunately, but it wasn't very nice.

I finally got to Monty's caravan, as he called it, where he had a picture of Rommel in his office. The old boy deigned to see me and I started on the wrong foot by asking him about his tactics. He said:

"My tactics? I won't divulge my tactics to anyone." He went on from there and talked about "my" men and "my" army and "my" this; the big I, everything was the big I. He personalized everything and he showed this arrogant egocentrism which was characteristic of him. It came out later, of course, in his dealings with Churchill and with Ike. I got a little out of him but I got a good bit more out of talking to his staff officers, who were frank in saying at the time of the Mareth Line battle that they thought the "flap" (retreat) was on again.

Then I flew back to Algiers. Usually on these trips I'd write one or two or three spot news stories, and then I'd sit down and try to analyze the whole situation in the theatre and write several long pieces about this, and I'd file those either from Algiers or London or whatnot. They had to go through censorship but they were analytical rather than spot news.

I got back to Algiers and I hadn't seen Eisenhower and he was in that old former castle up on the hill. I knew General Bedell Smith, his chief of staff. I'd known him before and I came in to see him, and Bedell Smith said:

"I'll get you in to see him as soon as I can. He's in a foul mood today."

Bedell, of course, was a man who was plagued by ulcers and sometimes his moods were awful, he snapped off his words. Poor guy, he eventually had much of his stomach removed. How he got through the war, I don't know. Sheer guts, I think, because he really had bleeding ulcers and he had to watch his diet all the time.

Anyway, I got in to see Eisenhower finally and I started talking about the general situation, which didn't appear to be so favorable then. The Americans had taken this awful knock at Kasserine Pass, and General Alexander had been named to head the field forces on the American side, which lots of people thought was a slap at Ike, and Monty was shooting his mouth off on the other side. I brought up the name of Monty and Eisenhower burst out with, "Goddamit, I can deal with anybody except that son of a bitch!" Ike found him very difficult to get along with, but it's a credit to Ike that he did get along with him. He controlled his emotions, he controlled his temper (until; sometimes he blew up in private), and he did get along with Monty, yet he could be very positive when he wanted to be. "Ike" and "Monty" came to be good friends later and a mutual respect developed. At that time the going was tough.

Ike was under fire because of Kasserine, the general poor initial showing of some of the American troops and the Darlan contretemps. Some friction with the British was developing, which had been exacerbated by the Casablanca conference in January where the Americans felt they were out-maneuvered and out-staffed by the British, and a British reputation for "slickness" and "guile" was spreading in the American forces.

After the war Eisenhower told me that he had to fire, or rather ask for the relief of, one British officer on his staff (this was just after I was in North Africa). A recent book has said this officer was relieved because he had depended too much upon ULTRA, the British equivalent of MAGIC, and had failed to forecast Kasserine. But this does not jibe with what Eisenhower told me later. He said this officer, presumably the Intelligence Officer (named as such in the book, "Bodyguard of Lies" but unnamed in Eisenhower's conversation with me), objected so strenuously to the Allied attack upon and occupation of the little island of Pantelleria that he had to be relieved. Pantelleria is a rocky islet which occupies a choke point in the Sicilian Narrows, and it was described in those days as a fortress. It was heavily garrisoned and armed, but in the event, its Italian garrison had no stomach for a fight. After some heavy preliminary air bombardment, it surrendered without any amphibious assault. The British officer had forecast a diaster for us if we tried to launch an amphibious attack upon it.

In any case Eisenhower's position at this time was delicate, and the Anglo-American differences about war startegy, whether to attack what Churchill called the "soft underbelly" of the continent, or to assault across the English Channel, were almost at their peak. It was about this time that Eisenhower said, a remark he later confirmed to me, in essence that, "He was the best damned lieutenant-colonel in the U.S. Army." Lieutenant-Colonel was his permanent rank, and he knew he was under fire and there was talk about his relief; he meant that if the President and his superiors didn't have confidence in the way he was running things they had better relieve him.

Ike and Monty were just getting to know each other and Monty was pushing just as hard as he could to see how far he could get with his boss, which he did later in France and in the final campaigns to the utmost extreme, till it became a political issue almost. It was a question of whether it was Eisenhower or Monty, and Churchill later told Monty, "You know it isn't going to be Eisenhower."

So they finally came to that extreme.

I then went on up to England.

Q: Before you tell me about that phase of it, what about the naval aspects in North Africa?

Mr. B.: Oh, yes. Wherever possible, I visited warships in port. It was a curious military force in North Africa because we had the Free French and all these odd bits and pieces of land armies, and we had a couple of Free French ships in Algerian harbors, we had the British, and we had the Americans. There were a lot of odd bits and pieces.

I saw Admiral Hewitt, as I remember, aboard his flagship and I got as much of the naval picture as I could, but the Navy at that time, except for the business of patrol planes and antisubmarine warfare, was more or less inactive. I mean there was no big operation on. We were still fighting the land battle in North Africa. The burden of getting supplies to the Eighth Army, of course, was the British Navy's, not ours. We were simply supplying, chiefly through Casablanca and through ports farther to the West where there wasn't such a submarine menace, but also we were bringing ships in to Algiers, convoys in to Algiers, too.

There was a feeling and I should have mentioned this, I guess, on the part of the Navy; that part of the Navy that had participated in the original landings in North Africa, that we should have initially moved much farther to the East, instead of just confining our landing to the Algiers area. We should have moved almost as far as Tunisia.

Q: Bizerte?

Mr. B.: Perhaps, certainly near there. The Navy had felt that it could do it, especially in retrospect, looking back at it. I don't know whether I got this from Admiral Hewitt or from someone else who was there, but I got that point of view from a considerable number of U.S. Navy people. They thought they would have avoided a lot of land fighting and a lot of problems that had since developed, if we had established a logistics supply base and an actual landing much farther to the East in the Mediterranean than we had done.

Q: Did you meet that other colorful naval character, Sullivan, who was clearing ports?

Mr. B.: Oh, yes, I met Sullivan in a couple of places around the world.

Baldwin #4 - 379

Q: But in North Africa?

Mr. B.: In North Africa I met him and we talked about what he was doing. He was a colorful character, very colorful. I met so many people on these trips that you know I've really forgotten who I met, and it would take a long bit of research to check it because I was very careful about keeping notes. I didn't try to keep too many notes because the security problem was one thing and the other point was that I absorbed so much so rapidly. I'd keep enough notes to be able to write an analysis and a story, but then they had served their purpose and I'd destroy them or file them away. I would have done better if I'd kept a diary with full names and so forth, but I really don't know how I would have done it. I just was so busy every minute.

Yes, I met Sullivan. I saw some of the work he was doing. I met, of course, General Bradley, who was over there at the time and was just assuming a top position. Fredendall had just been relieved, I think, and rightly so, by Patton. I met General Ryder, who commanded the 34th Division and several other people particularly in the Army who were later to come to fame in the European campaign.

I tried to get as broad a picture as I could of all operations. I visited the Army Air Corps based ashore, saw what they were doing, but again the details now elude me.

Q: Did you also deal with the Free French? Did you see de Gaulle?

Mr. B.: de Gaulle wasn't in North Africa. He was in London. I saw him in London.

As I say, I went from North Africa up to England. That was an interesting flight.

Q: The Bay of Biscay!

Mr. B.: Yes. I'm trying to remember how I got from North Africa to . . .

Q: Spain?

Mr. B.: No, I didn't go to Spain, that was neutral for us. I may have gone to Gibraltar, but I don't think so. Isn't that funny? I don't know. I may actually have gone up by PanAm. PanAm was flying circuitous routes across the Atlantic, down through Africa and Portugal from England, then back to the United States. I came back to the United States that way. I know that.

In any case, I got to England. At that time everything in England was chiefly our bombing forces and I concentrated on the Eighth Air Force, but I did meet de Gaulle, who was then a figure in London. He was a cold, figure who assumed an almost majestic pose and wasn't about to unbend. This was part of his role, but in part it was also dictated by the reactions he had gotten from the British and from his own countrymen to some extent, from the Free French movement. He was dubbed a traitor on one end by the Petain government, and on the other hand the British treated him with great reserve. You remember Churchill's famous remark, "The greatest cross I have to bear is the cross of Lorraine.

De Gaulle was a cold figure with a great bit of ego like Monty. He personfied himself as the salvation of France. He always wanted people to realize that he represented France and therefore there couldn't be any slighting of him because he represented France. I think this is the impression he tried to give consciously. In any case, his personality was something like that. So meeting with him was a rather chilly business. You didn't feel any rapprochement and it was very difficult to get him to talk, especially through an interpreter. My French wasn't good enough to really conduct a conversation. He would answer in monosyllables and wouldn't encourage further questions! So I just formed an impression of him and that's all.

But I did meet in England Jimmy Doolittle, who commanded the Eighth Air Force, and most of the Air Force leaders. I'd known some of them before. Oh, and this brings me back to a previous point I guess I should have mentioned.

Possum Hansel, General Hansel, who's retired now and living down, I think, in Hilton Head or somewhere like that, and Larry Kuter, who's a retired Air Force general, and various others, who were young Turks of the Air Force in those days. They were Hap Arnold's boys, and I'd come to know Hap Arnold . . .

Q: Freddie Smith, also?

Mr. B.: Yes, although I never knew him, really. He was a little more senior in rank. And General White, whom I'd known in Rome, I think I said in my last interview I'd met him in Rome. But I'd met many of these people in Washington and had gotten to know Hap Arnold very well. In fact, every time I'd see Hap Arnold during the war he'd always say, "Well, how is the war going?!" He was a very cheerful Irishman, a very likeable fellow, and he picked some good men.

Many of these people I had known in the Air Force were in England. What I was about to say, and I'm going back retrospectively now, was that when the war started, or just before it started, I can't be sure of the timing, General White, I think, was heading Air Force intelligence or starting to develop Air Force intelligence. Possum Hansel was in it and a man named Olive and Larry Kuter, I think, and some others. They had been talking to me for a long time to try and convince me that air power alone could win the war. They'd talk about strategic bombing. And they offered me a commission in the Air Force, come into air intelligence, and we'll give you; I don't know what, a major's commission, or something like that, they said. They put a good bit of pressure on me and I said no, thank you, after I'd talked at long length to the Navy and various other people about coming into the services, and I finally decided not to do it. We were all on a good and friendly basis despite this and I met some of these people in England again and I got a good bit of information from them about our Air Force operations and about the fact that the bomber was not completely queen of the air. They were having a lot of difficulty with the German fighters and had about decided that they were going to have to escort the bombers on day time raids, which they did with the P-45 later on.

I talked to the British Navy and to our Navy, got some insight into the seriousness of the submarine campaign which was not then as bad as it had been in some ways, but it was getting worse again because the wolf packs were gathering. I covered the old business of the dichotomy between the Royal Navy and the Coastal Command. Jack Slessor was then the British head of the Coastal Command, as I remember, and I got to be quite friendly with Slessor of the Royal Air Force.

Then, I eventually flew back to the United States by this circuitous route that the old PanAmerican clippers used.

Q: One more question. What was the U.S. naval picture there?

Mr. B.: It was minor at the time. This was before the all-out effort was concentrated in the Mediterranean.

Q: Stark was there?

Mr. B.: Oh, yes, I talked to Stark. As I remember I did, I'm not sure.

Q: What was the value of his function, his office, there?

Mr. B.: It was primarily liaison at the highest level. He became very intimate with the British. Because of his past CNO status he had a high ranking there. He knew the whole picture and, to some extent, he could get things done. Also, he had a pipeline to Roosevelt. He could go to Roosevelt if he wanted anything. I don't think he ever did without King's knowledge, but I don't know that. Roosevelt thought quite highly of Stark, although I think he felt that King was the right man in the right place at the right time.

It was a coordinating liaison job more than anything else.

Q: I've often been curious about it because it was superimposed upon the NA's job and we had some mighty good men in that job.

Mr. B.: Yes. Well, they were under him but the operating forces weren't, of course. He really didn't have an operational function. The operational function was either exercised down in the Mediterranean and later, when we came up, it was exercised nominally for the invasion of Normandy through the British admiralty, which had the senior command. I think every naval commander including Kirk and others would always visit Admiral Stark in London and take his counsel and ask his help and so forth. But actually, he didn't command them, as I understand it. He never had an operational command in that sense.

The chief things I got about the Navy were I think techniques and tactics, particularly ASW and countermining, and what kind of ships were needed. I heard a lot about landing craft from both sides and how they were going to be needed in great volume for subsequent operations in North Africa and also on the continent.

There was a great deal of discussion of the utility of planes like the B-24, which were being flown in the Bay of Biscay patrol against submarines.

There was also talk about building jeep carriers as ASW forces.

That's about it, as I remember.

Q: How interested had you become in amphibious warfare?

Mr. B.: Again, I'm relying on memory. It was looming larger already because of the Pacific, of course, and my visit to Guadalcanal. I knew about the amphibious tractors we were preparing, building in the States. I'd become interested in it. As I say, I heard a lot about landing craft in England but I don't remember the details. I'm sorry. I just don't remember what my thoughts were at the time about it. I knew we would have to have it in order to get back into the continent.

Q: Were you on that side of the Atlantic when the Casablanca

Conference came?

Mr. B.: No, I was back. As I say, we flew back by a circuitous route in a PanAmerican clipper. We stayed at Lisbon overnight and then we flew down to Dakar and stayed there overnight. Then we flew over to the hump of Brazil. One of the passengers aboard was former Governor Lehman of New York, who'd been assigned as some sort of semiofficial aide to the Red Cross mission in London.

We had a very rough crossing. These were the small clippers. They didn't take very many passengers. In those days there were not many passengers going, anyway. They put baggage in overhead racks which, of course, isn't allowed now unless the racks close up. In those days they didn't close. We got into the middle of the Atlantic and ran into a violent thunderstorm and the whole clipper bounced up and down and the baggage fell out of the overhead rack on Lehman's head. I thought he was a very good sport. It didn't hurt him very much.

Q: What was the condition in Dakar when you were there? Had the French capitulated?

Mr. B.: Wait a minute. Did I say Dakar? My memory as to where we landed is extremely hazy.

Q: Yes.

Mr. B.: We didn't land at Dakar. No, the French had not capitulated. This came later. We landed south of there. What is the name of the place, a primitive market town? I'd have to refresh my memory, I really don't remember. I know we made four or five stops on the way back, including one at Trinidad, and before that Brazil, and then came on up to the United States.

Q: You were very lucky to have only one-night stops, say, in Lisbon and other places. Other men had to stay a week or something!

Mr. B.: I know.

Q: Was this the power of the Times?

Mr. B.: No, oh, no. It was just the weather. Oh, you mean getting aboard?

Q: Yes.

Mr. B.: I don't know, I got that in London somehow and the press did have a priority not over the military or other important missions, but they had priority over others. And I wasn't bumped. I was warned that I might be bumped on the flight, but I wasn't.

Q: Were you interested, were you involved in the Alaskan campaign, which began early in 1943, I guess?

Mr. B.: By remote control. I never got out there. I had been to Alaska several times before the war and I knew the terrain pretty well. But I wrote about it. I also said it was very clear that the Japs wouldn't get anywhere there because any army of ground soldiers that invaded Alaska (I often used to use a phrase which is not original with me) would never reach the United States. They would remain in Alaska as skeletons, starve to death, or maybe one or two emaciated victims would get down through all that thick tundra and forest. It was a diversion. I'm sure I didn't realize then how successful a diversion it was because it tied down more than 250,000 American personnel, which was absurd. When you go out on the Aleutian chain now, as I did quite a few years after the war, I guess about ten or fifteen years ago, and see the wreckage of what we built there in places like Adak, the elaborate officers' clubs and quonset huts still there but sinking into the tundra, the docks which have been destroyed by earthquakes and storms and all this elaborate installation, it is apparent it was a very successful diversion on the part of the Japanese at the cost of a few thousand men. We put an awful lot of strength up there.

Q: There must have been quite a contrast between what we did in places like that, installations and so forth, and what our Allies were able to do?

Mr. B.: You mean the spartan nature of their efforts?

Q: Yes.

Mr. B.: Yes. I mentioned that already as far as the French and British were concerned in North Africa and I saw that even more vividly in Normandy later. It's particularly noticeable when it comes to medical treatment, field hospitals, and things of that sort.

Q: Was there any feeling evident on their part because we had more?

Mr. B.: I don't think so. We gave them, of course, as much as they wanted. Their whole system is different. It's keyed to a different social system, keyed to a different concept. For instance, the Goums, if you had tried to cook their meat for them there would have been a rumpus because they were issued raw meat by the French and that's the way they wanted it. They didn't eat it raw all the time but they had their own particularly religious tabus about how it should be cooked. And this was true of a lot of British Indian troops. So some of the spartan nature was keyed to the nature of the society from which the troops were drawn.

In the case of England or of metropolitan France, their men were just not used to the creature comforts that we got. The normal bed in a British field hospital was a stretcher, for instance, and they stayed on the hard stretcher while they were in a field hospital. Sometimes, later on, they were on the deck with nothing else, and ours, of course, were usually cots of one sort or another. The difference was most pronounced often in the sanitation. There again their standards were different from ours, particularly the French. The British had somewhat higher standards of sanitation, and the British doctors were excellent and undoubtedly saved a lot of lives.

Their system is different, too. Their clearing system of wounded is entirely different than ours. Everything, even aboard ship, is keyed to a different life style. The Americans used to like to get on British ships because they had a wine mess! Or get on French ships for the same reason. The British were amazed we didn't have a wine mess. They thought we were very backward. Sometimes it was a good thing, sometimes it wasn't. Actually, given the American temperament, I'm convinced Josephus Daniels was right, but it's often very awkward when you don't have a wine mess and cannot offer a visiting dignitary a glass of wine or a drink.

Q: Actually, as the war developed in the Pacific, we did have what amounted to a wine mess, did we not, under the guise of medical . . .

Mr. B.: Medicinal liquor, yes, particularly for some of the pilots who came back from difficult missions. Then I guess a lot of the officers just violated the regulations and kept liquor aboard. Many of them did, I'm sure. They did that even in peacetime to some extent before World War II. But most of them didn't. Most of them were conscientious about it.

Q: Well, you came back to the States after this trip?

Mr. B.: Yes, and I believe that I spent all the rest of 1943 and the first part of 1944 in the United States, with trips around to various bases in this country.

Q: For training purposes and that sort of thing? Did you go to Jacksonville, for instance?

Mr. B.: Yes, I was in Jacksonville and Pensacola and Corpus Christi, Norfolk, and various other places, Army as well as Navy. But I wasn't continuously on the road. I was trying to do what my primary job was, which was an analysis of the war day by day, an analysis of what was going on, the background explanation of what such and such an operation meant. If there was a parachute operation, I would try to describe the parachute troops, what equipment they carried, and the weapons, and their organization, and things of that sort that weren't generally known to the public. If there were communiques from both sides about a battle in Russia, I would try to interpret what this meant, whether it was victory or defeat, and sometimes it was pretty difficult to determine because both the Russians and the Germans lied and both of them were very tight-mouthed in any case. But you could generally tell the trend after a time, some knowledge of terrain, very good war maps, and a knowledge of the military organizations concerned were of great value.

There was a lot going on obviously in both 1943 and 1944, both in the Pacific and in Russia and all over the world, so there was never a dearth of something to write about.

Q: Were you syndicated?

Mr. B.: No, there was no syndication in those days by the *Times*. They did not allow anything to be syndicated. That gradually changed. I did appear on radio several times, and that was the result of an internal battle. The *Times* had refused to allow any of its people to appear on radio. At one time they didn't want them to write outside the paper and I just said I was going to write outside. I obviously owed first loyalty to the *Times* and anything I got went to them first, but there were other things that I expected to write and I did.

The radio business really came up several times and finally, I guess it was on this last trip to England where I had been urged to conduct a short radio program about the course of the war, that it came to a head. I had discussed this with the publisher. He wasn't very enthusiastic. I also discussed it with the managing editor, and he was firmly against it. I think this offer came to me while I was in England. In any case, I remember writing back to the publisher and just telling him that I expected to do it, and I never got a negative and never got any other kind of answer.

Q: What was back of the attitude?

Mr. B.: It was a curious attitude at the time in those days. They thought you were, the Times property; it was an exclusive paper. Everything that they ran, everything that they produced was theirs and their reporters were theirs, too. They didn't encourage outside writing. Well, I made the point constantly that outside writing increased the value of the man to the Times, he became better known. The Times was not a national paper, though it aspired to that. And, in my own case, one of the things that helped me a great deal in becoming a military analyst was the writing I'd done for military magazines, and then for outside magazines. I had written for Life and The Saturday Evening Post and I had written for the old Infantry Journal, now Army and occasionally for the Naval Institute a long time ago. Then, other than magazines, I had made a lot of talks. I felt all this had helped a great deal to lend authenticity and to get my name known, as indeed it did. Then I had published two or three books at that time. All of that helped.

So the *Times* finally came around to this point of view. It took a long time for them to do it. It ultimately ended up in that I actually had for a short time, a very brief TV program. I was the first one on the *Times* to have that. When the Korean War was on I did a brief weekly news commentary on the course of the war. Now the *Times*, of course, has come full cycle. They encourage their people to get into TV and radio and anything else.

Q: I wondered if the point wasn't made at any time that the *Times* deemed your services quite valuable and your material of great interest, then did they not have some obligation to have it more widespread?

Mr. B.: I made this point repeatedly. At that time they did not have the *Times* syndicate as it is now. They now have a very extensive syndicate now, about 282 papers. It depends on what those papers buy as to how much syndicated material they get. They may get only the news columns, they may get the columnists and the editorials, and they may get the Sunday features, they may get only part of it. But in those days this was very limited. They had only something like 60 or 70 papers and it extended only, as I remember, to news articles and to nothing else beyond that. They felt that other types of articles were the property of the *Times* exclusively. Some of my news articles were syndicated and would appear in other papers, but if I wrote an analytical piece it wasn't, or if I wrote a Sunday piece it wasn't. So that was the distinction then made.

In any case, I found plenty to write about. I know I wrote about the invasion of the Marshalls, but later on as an aside to this, and this is out of order, when Howling Mad Smith got into the famous controversy in the Marianas with the Army general also named Smith, I wrote quite a lot about this problem, partly because I had known the general commanding the Army, Pacific, Lieutenant General Robert C. Richardson. He was one of those who most resented the fact that Howling Mad Smith had relieved the Army general named Smith and he said it couldn't be done, that no Marine Corps general, no one except the Army could do this itself. He carried the cudgels. He was a fiesty little guy and he had a lot of moral courage. He carried a little weight with Marshall and the people in Washington and the 27th Division had a lot of New York political connections so he made quite an issue out of it.

I had known some of the background of this because the Army unit involved was from New York State, it was a National Guard outfit originally. Also I'd met Howling Mad and I knew how vocal he could become! This became temporarily quite a cause celebre. I wrote quite a lot about that at the times, pro and con, and got, incidentally, some indignant letters from Irishmen in New York, including former Mayor O'Brien, who was mayor only for a short time, because I had criticized the effectiveness and the morale of one of the National Guard regiments in this division, which was an Irish regiment, really, one of the famous fighting regiments in New York. Really, the tenor of these letters and there were quite a few from New York Irishmen was to me amazing, because in the middle of the war there was only one thing they were interested in, up the Irish, you know. It didn't matter how ineffective or inefficient anybody was, if you didn't say they were wonderful, that was it!

I wrote quite frequently during this period, particularly in the early part of January, and we knew, of course, that the invasion of Europe was scheduled later in that year. I had kept in touch with all the possible areas where they might invade, I'd studied my maps and looked at various places, and I'd written some what might be termed unofficial forecasts, they weren't forecasts but estimates of where the best places to land might be. I hadn't gotten any information from Admiral Horne or anyone ahead of time. I did later, but when I'd written these pieces I hadn't.

Q: What sort of care did you exercise not to help the enemy by suggesting the likely spots?

Mr. B.: Well, I think anybody can look at a map. That brings up the other point, of course. I sometimes was accused of helping the enemy because I was perhaps quite accurate in my analysis or accurate in my estimate of what might then transpire. But my point was and it still is, and I think most of my friends agreed with me and came to agree with me more later on that we would have been crediting the enemy with being very dumb indeed if they couldn't have done the same thing, with a thousand men on the general staff, that I was trying to do as one man looking at war maps and studying terrain. This is all that I did. For instance: the invasion of Norway when the Germans seized Norway by airborne and sea invasion, I had one of those old pilots' guides. I had gotten a whole set of those before the war which tell about all the harbors of the world, their depths and their capacities, and so forth. I had gotten them as up to date as possible. I got into this sometime before because I knew I wanted more data about obscure ports. I studied these and found out that the Germans had seized every port that was capable of handling a ship of any size in Norway. What were left were a lot of two-bit little things which the British would have a terrible time in using. So I simply pointed this out in a piece that I did and said the British probably couldn't stay there because they couldn't sustain their logistics. That happened to be right.

In the same way I studied the Atlantic coast and the likely place for invasion. I pointed out they'd get much less resistance if they landed somewhere far away from England, but on the other hand, they'd be far away from the center of Germany and they would not be able to provide the air cover that they could provide from England. I did this for ports and rivers and so forth. Some people thought it was perhaps too accurate, but I was always very careful and always thought about whether

I'd be giving away any real information to the enemy. I never did this under any circumstances unless I felt it was going to do a hell of a lot more harm than good and I can tell you of one or two specific instances.

I'll come to those later. There were two instances really.

Q: They being what, so you won't forget them?

Mr. B.: One was U.S. tanks, the other was replacement depots in Italy.

I should interject here that along the way and before we come to the invasion of Normandy, after I would write as objective pieces as I could and sometimes pieces which were critical of American actions or American lack of actions, the foreign propagandists would pick these up. Tokyo Rose picked up some of my things and read off paragraphs. Sometimes they were read off accurately but taken out of context, just the paragraphs they wanted, and sometimes they were distorted. This infuriated some of my friends in the Navy, but not too many of them. Most of them knew this was purely propaganda and it stimulated them to see the whole thing I had written because a lot of them agreed with some of the comments I was making.

But I did have some few officers who seemed to me to be rather shortsighted officers, making strenuous objections to some of my analyses and I'd get an occasional letter or two saying, "What are you playing into the hands of the enemy for?"

Well, I bent over backwards to avoid playing into the hands of the enemy, but I invariably answered them and said that you can't write anything if you're just going to parrot the communiques and I have always tried to write something that was constructive.

I recall that one of the criticisms that irritated some people concerned our intelligence estimates of Japanese strengths in various Pacific islands. After the conquests of some of these islands, it was shown that our estimates were way off the mark; in many cases much too low, and I believe I pointed this out in those few cases where the facts became available.

Q: What about Lord Haw Haw? Did he pick up your stories?

Mr. B.: I don't know. I never heard him, you see. I doubt it. He was so centered on England. He was trying constantly to tear down their morale.

On the other hand, I got criticized very frequently by our gallant allies, the Russians, because they didn't like many of the things I wrote. I remember one thing that created a tempest in a teapot here as well as, I guess, in Russia. I called the Russian Army an "armed horde," which it was. I mean in those days they used to drive herds of cattle before them, and they confiscated all the civilian vehicles, carts and wagons, and drive those, and get armies of peasants to dig their fortifications. At the start of the war it was just that, it was really an armed horde, except for a few crack units.

Q: And they'd detonate the mines?

Mr. B.: Yes.

The phrase "armed horde" created a lot of flak from fellow-travelers in this country. "How can you call our gallant allies 'armed hordes'?"! "They're great and fine and so forth."

Q: But there was no official reaction?

Mr. B.: Oh, no, not officially from Russia. You'd get some comments from the Russian papers sometimes, which is official, as far as Russia goes.

As the time came for the invasion of Europe, I was determined to get to that, so I arranged to go back to England in a jeep carrier which we'd built in this country and turned over to the British. She was commissioned but not operational and was carrying back a deck cargo of airplanes and also stuff down below, as many airplanes as they could carry. They couldn't fly because they were just packed wingtip-to-wingtip.

Q: Was that an ex-Liberty ship?

Mr. B.: No, no, this was one that was specially built on a merchant ship hull by, I think, Kaiser. This ship was going to England about a month before the invasion, or something like that, so I took passage in New York aboard her. Believe it or not, I've forgotten her name. The only regular officers aboard were the captain and the executive officer, who had been called back from retirement, I think. All the rest were Reserve officers, the Wavy Navy, as they called it, or were merchant marine officers. It was a strange ship in wartime. This ship was traveling alone, unescorted and not in convoy. She wasn't a high-speed ship. Jeep carriers weren't. They could make 20 knots or so but not much more. And she wasn't operational, so she had no aircraft to protect her. She was absolutely green, the whole crew and all the rest. A strange thing in wartime, just this time, she had a lot of British women and children on board going back to London, going back to England, after the blitz. They had been evacuated to this country. So we didn't make for a very formidable fighting force, and what amazed me with my long respect for the Royal Navy was the lack of discipline and the abandon on this ship. Possibly we come back to the female influence, possibly the obvious let down in discipline was due to the presence of some of the women aboard who were freely flirting with some of the officers and vice versa, and to the fact that the ship had a wine mess.

I remember we were in the midst of the worst submarine zone one night and we were down in the mess before dinner and the officer who was about to take the deck had six straight scotches. In the Royal Navy, of course, in a well-disciplined ship, they keep very strict tabs on this because the officer signs a chit each time, and if he starts drinking too much of that they take away his privileges or do something to him. This ship hadn't shaken down. As I say, there were only two regular officers aboard. The captain didn't notice what was going on, I guess, and the exec wasn't really a good exec. It didn't fill me with any ease at all to know this man was going to have the responsibility of the deck and of the ship. Well, by luck and by God and because the submarine menace really had been pretty well worn down by then in that area, we got there.

I think we landed in Liverpool and I went around various parts of England to see some of our forces before the invasion. I went down to Bristol where General Bradley then had his headquarters, and then went on up to London and waited there after getting all the British accreditation, which you had to do, as well as our own for D-Day. We knew or we assumed, we were pretty sure it was going to be sometime around the 1st of June, but we didn't have any exact date. There were various kinds of accreditation, those who were accredited to the navies, the various navies, those who were accredited to the Army and the Air Force, and we were all strictly kept apart like sheep and goats.

I remember that after some effort and some discussion, particularly with John Mason Brown, who was, as you know, with Admiral Kirk, I had gotten assigned to the Augusta, which was one of the things I very much wanted. I wanted to get the whole ringside picture, if I could. I was accredited to the Navy and I guess I was the only full-time correspondent of a daily paper, I think, aboard the Augusta. There was a photographer,

I know there was, and I believe a radio man aboard. I think there were only three of us, three or four, and John Mason Brown, of course, and General Bradley had his headquarters on the ship, which was the flagship of U.S. Navy forces under Admiral Kirk.

While we were waiting we suddenly got this word from press headquarters. In those days The New York Times' headquarters was in the Savoy Hotel. It had been bombed out of its old office which was farther down on Fleet Street, so we were all in the Savoy Hotel. I got a call one afternoon to report with all equipment, which meant the helmet and your clothes, whatever you were going to carry with you, cameras, at the Admiralty next morning. A great crew of us, including, I guess, all those who were accredited to both navies, the British and the American, appeared there with all this gear which was, of course, certain to attract attention. They were right out in the street near that bomb shelter that they had built for Churchill, right by the Admiralty Arch, and we waited there fairly prominently for some minutes, then were ushered into cars and got on a train. We hadn't been told where we were going along the south coast. Then the escort officers broke down and told us that this was just a trial run. We were out to try to fool the Germans and the known German spies and it was part of a deception technique for D-Day, and the press had been roped into the various deceptive measures.

We were taken down to this little port of Fowey in Cornwall that happened to be right near the estate of Daphne du Maurier, whose husband, General Browning, was head of the

British paratroopers. He was not there, but we stopped in Fowey, which was a very picturesque port in those days, a little Cornish fishing village. In the morning I visited some of our landing craft. We had a lot of LCIs there. I don't think there were any LSTs, certainly not as we know them now. They were all relatively small craft, but a lot of LCIs. There were no craft that could- well, they could get up on the beach but they weren't really adapted for beaching like the LST is.

We visited them and I found one or two officers I was looking for and then in the afternoon we were all taken up to Daphne du Maurier's house, you know, the writer?

Q: Yes.

Mr. B.: And we spent the afternoon there looking at her estate, which is just like some of the places she describes in her books, very mysterious and half of it closed off and a lot of tall grass around! A delightful host. Her children were there and her mother. She's a very delightful person. I'll always remember her. Then we got on the train and went back to London and waited for the real D-Day!

Q: How did the press react to being used for deception?

Mr. B.: I think we were all fairly cheerful although we were sort of on tenterhooks like everybody else and we were anxious to get the thing started.

We finally went down on the real D-Day; I guess it was two nights ahead of time, yes, it must have been because the day was postponed once.

Q: Did you assemble quite as ostentatiously?

Mr. B.: Not in as large groups. I think the groups were separated at that time. Those who were going to one port went together. We were going to Plymouth. The Augusta was in Plymouth, so I went with all those who were assigned to ships in Plymouth, which was a fairly sizeable group but not too big. The others went on some other trains in some other direction.

We boarded the Augusta after some brief delay. I remember I think it was late at night. I think, too, that this time we assembled outside the Admiralty in the evening. I think it was either after dark or just before dark. It wasn't quite as conspicuous as before.

We were aboard the Augusta and all set for next day, and in the morning we woke up to find that the D-Day announcement had more or less leaked, at least we thought it had because the radio had carried some word about a big storm in the bay and about a postponement in plans and another bulletin said invasion imminent. It got everyone aboard the Augusta rather jittery and sore, and the few newspapermen who were aboard were rather irate. Whether one of our colleagues had leaked this we didn't know or whether anyone had done it. Later on, I think, it came out that all this came from:-not from England at all and not from any correspondents involved but presumably from a misreading of something in the United States or from German radio. I don't know. It didn't do any harm in the event but at the time it seemed ominous, an ominous start to the proceedings, particularly since we had all been briefed very thoroughly after we got aboard the Augusta. A few of us had even read, or were reading, the plans, the detailed plans, not only for the landings but also for what was to transpire after that. General Bradley had told me, I don't know whether he told everybody, that he expected thousands of casualties and the airborne troops were sort of sacrificial troops and so on. So we were all fairly jittery. We didn't know what was going to transpire.

Incidentally, in the plans, which I never see mentioned now, Patton and his Third Army were supposed to land in Brittany, not where he actually came across later, into Normandy. I didn't even see that mentioned in Morison. But Patton was shifted, not at the last minute, but shifted, I guess, just after the first few days when our beachhead was obviously being hemmed in. Originally, Patton's Third Army was supposed to be landed at Lorient and, I think, St. Nazaire.

In any case we proceeded after the one day postponement on schedule to France. On the actual invasion night I was up all night, I'm sure. I may have had an hour's sleep at the beginning of the night just as we were pulling out of Plymouth. It was a pretty fresh sea and we were bobbing a little. The small craft, you could see as you passed them, were making fairly heavy weather of it. It was choppy in the Channel and there was a fairly brisk wind, and there was not very good visibility. You couldn't see very far, but it was a very impressive sight to see this great flotilla, or what you could see of it as you passed it. You couldn't see very far but you could see ship after ship, as you passed.

Q: What was the spirit on board the Augusta?

Mr. B.: I think it was good. It was determined. Nobody knew what to expect. As I said, there was a slight sense of, I wouldn't say dread, but of worry, as there was bound to be for an operation like this.

Admiral Struble was chief of staff to Kirk then. He was an irascible little guy, a nice fellow in many ways.

I remember getting up on the bridge with John Mason Brown very, very early, it must have been about eleven o'clock or midnight, as we steamed in toward the beaches. Then I remember first, I guess, you couldn't see very clearly because there was still a pretty heavy overcast, you could hear what sounded a little bit like thunder, the bombs back of the invasion beaches. Then as we got in closer and as the hour grew later, you could see an occasional flash. Then I remember vividly as we were coming in to our assigned position, (of course the Augusta moved up and down the beaches, but she had an anchorage) one plane that had been over the invasion beaches was obviously hit and it came out flaming toward the Augusta like a shooting star or fireball and it crashed into the sea some distance from us. It was very visible; it was on fire as it fell. You couldn't tell whether it was one of ours or a German, but we were almost sure it was one of ours. There weren't many Germans, if any, around at that time of night. It was still night. As we got in closer to our assigned places, you could see more and more of the fireworks on shore, the antiaircraft, and the great flash of the bombs bursting, and so on.

Then, as we got into the transport anchorages and saw them starting to unload their troops, climb down the cargo nets into these bobbing craft, we saw that in some instances the sea was going to give a good bit of trouble. It was quite rough, and many of these men being unloaded had great difficulty getting into the landing craft. There were quite a few delays from the set hours of departure. We saw quite a few pieces of artillery and other equipment dropped into the drink, of course, by error.

Then, as I recollect it, we opened up a couple of times with antiaircraft and once the entire invasion fleet seemed to open up. They were probably just either firing at their own planes or at a "ghost". They had that trigger-happy feeling, which is understandable. We moved then round the American invasion beaches a little, as I recollect it. I don't know how long we remained anchored, but we did for a while.

Kirk was virtually incommunicado this whole time. He was so busy. He was up on the bridge. I saw Struble occasionally, but not often. I saw Bradley much more often. He had his headquarters on the main deck and an office had been put there for him, a large map room. He would say, "What's going on?" He didn't know what was going on himself, absolute blank. Neither did Kirk really because those first hours information was delayed and there was sort of ordered chaos, if indeed it was ordered.

I remember vividly in the middle of the afternoon that Bradley still hadn't had any word from the beaches at all. He really didn't know anything directly from the beaches. He had reports from the area commanders, still aboard ship, Omaha and the rest, but he didn't have anything direct from the beaches except that he'd heard rumors that it was tough going on Omaha, and he was a little nervous himself at that time. That was in the middle of the afternoon.

During this time was talking chiefly to John Mason Brown who was carrying on his famous descriptions over the loudspeaker system. He'd tell whatever he could see or find out about. There was a Colonel Jeschke, I think his name was, of the Marine Corps, who was assigned to the Augusta and he and I hung around a good bit together. I was taking notes of anything and everything during this whole period.

D-Day passed in this way with a paucity of information. There was very, very little hard news. We just saw what went on around us, the ships unloading and more ships coming in.

Q: Were you curious about some of these ingenious things like the Mulberrys?

Mr. B.: Oh, yes. They hadn't come yet, of course. They didn't come over till later. I saw them later on.

Incidentally, I knew what to expect because complete descriptions of these things were in the plans that I'd read.

At the end of D-Day I got some sleep. I've forgotten what time it was but I remember being waked up by a burst of anti-aircraft fire that night, probably about ten o'clock or something like that. I think I was up most of the rest of that night. Gradually a few pieces of information filtered back and we saw flotsam and jetsam. By that I mean lifejackets, gas masks, one or two sunken small landing craft, the small craft, not the ships; drifting by. We didn't see any bodies actually at that time. This was the kind of atmosphere and it was becoming more tense in some ways because things obviously weren't going according to the preconceived plans, especially on Omaha beach, where there were supposed to be a certain number of troops well inland, and they weren't. The British hadn't taken Caen, which should have been taken very early on in the game and various other things like this. Tempers were a little irascible.

I remember drinking copious quantities of extremely hot tea which helped me to stay awake that way.

I think it was the second day that I got into a slight tiff with Admiral Struble. They were going to send one of the ship's boats to the beach to try to find out, I guess for Bradley and for Kirk, exactly what was going on at Omaha, and I said I wanted to go. Struble said, "You can't. You're accredited to the Navy and you can't go ashore." So I said nonsense, or words to that effect. We had quite an argument. I didn't go ashore that day, and I don't think they got very much information. But on the third day things were piling up on Omaha and elsewhere and the Army was blaming the Navy for failure to get a lot of its supplies ashore. Admiral Hall was the naval commander concerned.

Q: Jimmy Hall, yes.

Mr. B.: So Admiral Kirk decided as how he himself would go and see, so I hooked a ride in with him. Kirk and Bradley and Hall all met on Omaha beach on D plus 3. It was a rather grim scene because there was quite a heated debate between the three of them, standing there on the beach, because Bradley was insistent they had to get more Army supplies, and Hall was sort of angry, and Kirk, you know how decisive he was and almost fiesty in insisting that Hall get to it. There were quite a few heated words. I was trying not to listen, to stand out of earshot, but they were standing right next to a row of bodies of American GIs that had been brought down to the beach and covered with ponchos. I always felt this was most dramatic.

Here they were, arguing about this, and here the dead are.

There was a lot of wreckage on the beach, landing craft destroyed, and so forth. I spent as much time there as I could, talking to all the officers and GIs I could find, getting the picture of the situation, how they'd gotten up the beach, and what they'd done. Then I went back to the Augusta and later - I think it was that day or the next day, went up to another American beach, the one farther up where we had not great opposition . . .

Q: That was a British beach, wasn't it?

Mr. B.: No. The British were Juno and Gold, our other American beach was up on the Cotentin Peninsula, on the other side, Utah beach, and briefly got ashore there. Of course, there was not the same argument there because they were getting supplies ashore much more rapidly. There was less opposition and they had pushed inland rather fast.

Outside of fragments of memory about various episodes, which I think I reported at the time, and various officers leading their men, I really think that about covers it.

Q: Did you have any close calls in the Augusta?

Mr. B.: No, the Augusta was never really under fire directly. One or two of the destroyers that were closer in during the actual bombardment were, but the Augusta was never really under fire.

Q: What about the effectiveness of the shore fire from the Channel, the bombardment squad?

Mr. B.: I don't think it was too effective. It did not knock out most of the coastal defenses, neither did the bombing. The bombing was too far inland. It did disrupt a lot of the German communications and did to a certain extent cut off resupply and damage the roads, but the beach fortifications really had to be taken by assault. In one or two instances where some of the destroyers got in very close like at Pointe du Hoc or at another point near Omaha beach where there was a known commanding fortification, they were firing almost point-blank fire, very close in. I think they were pretty effective against those specific points.

Q: We used some old battleships, didn't we?

Mr. B.: Oh, yes, but they were up at Cherbourg, the _Texas_. She was hit. The _Texas_ was hit, you know.

I was trying to think of the other place. I think it was near Saint Laurent where there's a draw down to the beach and there was a heavy casemate which commanded this draw. The beach rises rather perceptibly. I remember that first day walking up there and climbing over the sort of sandy cliff to get up to the escarpment and the village of Saint Laurent is just behind that, about half a mile or so. In this kind of valley, or draw, which led up from the beach was a really heavy casemate with large guns, I should think around 5- inch, in it and heavy concrete and steel. That was not perceptibly damaged. They neutralized it with infantry fire and with explosive charges and things like that.

So I don't think the naval gunfire support was too effective against the beach fortifications. They didn't do it long enough nor was it precise enough. In the Pacific we did it for a long, long time. And there was another point here that I found one of contention. I've talked about this before and then I talked about it again during and after the invasion.

There was a corps commander from the Army, Major-General Charles H. Corlett of the XIX Corps, who had served in the South Pacific and he came to England very dedicated to the idea of the amtrack, which he had used and liked. He tried desperately to sell this as a kind of vehicle that could get up on the beach and at the same time provide firepower for the attack waves. There were virtually none of them used, or very few of them. The British had their idea of their flotable tank. They had this flotation gear round the tank and they lowered the tank in the water and it waddled ashore. We tried this with a good many of our tanks and I think about eight out of ten sank, didn't get to shore at all.

Corlett tried his best to break through this screen in England before the invasion to get more and more amtracks there but he didn't succeed. He got some, a very few, but he couldn't quite sell the British and Eisenhower's staff on it.

There's one other point about the invasion itself which I should have mentioned before, a rather important one from the point of view of the press.

On those first three or four days of the invasion, (I think I actually stayed aboard the Augusta the fourth or fifth day when our beachheads were secure) I wrote thousands of words. I literally wrote everything I could think of. I knew this was a tremendous story and even though I didn't have direct information about a lot of it, I was with Kirk and Bradley and I could get what they said. We put these dispatches daily each time in a pouch. John Mason Brown would take care of them on the Augusta. I was about the only one who was filing daily on the Augusta. I think the radioman was sending in brief bulletins.

Then, going back to the old days of the British Navy, you know how they arranged to collect these dispatches, they actually had a pinnace come around to each ship in the fleet that carried correspondents and take it back across the English Channel in this little tiny boat to Portsmouth, where it would then be put on the land wire to London, then censored, and then sent out. It was stormy weather, particularly after the first day, you remember, the wind increased and the waves increased. It was pretty rough. There were at least forty ships in this tremendous fleet along the miles of beachhead that carried correspondents and these little ships had to make interminable stops. They'd spend a whole day just visiting the ships that they were supposed to visit before they even started across the Channel. Many of them sank. The copy disappeared. It got all fouled up. The biggest story I guess I ever covered, I think I got about eight paragraphs in the paper or something like that! All was lost, garbled or arrived much too late to be any good. Very disorderly.

Q: Why was this? Because of the antiquated way of . . . ?

Mr. B.: The British Navy was ostensibly in charge of all the naval arrangements including press arrangements. Actually, there was a British admiral in command.

Q: Admiral Ramsay?

Mr. B.: Yes. Unfortunately, British public relations doesn't rate very high. Our people had protested but the Admiralty hadn't devised any modern way of getting this stuff out. This was in strong contrast to what later developed on the beach, where the Army established a Press Wireless radio station for direct communications with the United States, a radio station which was financed by the papers.

So the Navy again was the silent service and it never really did get an awful lot of publicity at the time about its efforts in the invasion. It got very little actually because most of the interest was focused later on the Army and by the time the dispatches got out it was all a land war.

Q: I wonder if you'd say something about the lack of cross fertilization in experiences between the European front and the Pacific? You mentioned the general who'd come from the South Pacific and tried to inculcate some of the ideas learned there.

Mr. B.: I think there was a decided feeling that pappa knows best in Europe, particularly because the British felt that way about these upstart Americans, originally. And originally they had a lot going for them in that belief because we weren't as skilled in staff practices and some other things as they were. So, in part, I would say that this feeling stemmed from the British, and also I think there was a feeling in the Army that they had, after all, developed some very important amphibious techniques of their own in the Mediterranean, in Sicily and Italy, and they didn't need to ask the Navy how it was done in the Pacific. And in any case this was an Army show. There was that feeling.

This general, Corlett, that I speak of did not share this feeling. He felt very strongly, partly because he had served in the Pacific. And that's one reason Marshall assigned him to England. They ought to have, Marshall felt, I believe, an officer who had experienced Pacific amphibious techniques and could give some of his knowledge to Europe. Cross-fertilization was desirable. It only worked up to a point and not completely by any means. I talked to Corlett, I'd known him before and I talked to him several times and he felt his efforts had been partially in vain. He felt he'd made some progress but not enough.

There was some jealousy involved.

Q: Later on, it seemed to work the other way. Any experience gained in the Atlantic area, theatre, was just not carried to the Pacific, and this included officers, did it not? I've heard Alan Kirk on this subject, and Hewitt.

Mr. B.: I think those things are natural, that you feel that. I think that's also true. I can't speak from firsthand knowledge about whether these ideas were carried to the Pacific or not. I doubt if they were specifically.

Q: Hall was about the only major one who went to the Pacific after the Atlantic experience.

Mr. B.: Yes, I guess he was.

I don't want to leave the impression that Corlett's work was in vain, the corps commander who came from the Pacific, because he did make some impression and they did have, to my recollection, a few amtracks. But the objective of getting heavy firepower on the beaches initially, which the amtracks could do — you remember the Marines used amtracks with field artillery pieces with guns in their as they landed, was not achieved. The reason that this wasn't achieved is that he could not break through this British creed which believed that their so-called floating tanks could take on this job. The floating tanks were pretty well demolished by the weather on our beach their flotation gear washing loose, and, as I say, in our section of Omaha beach most of them sank.

Q: They were not used in the Mediterranean, were they?

Mr. B.: No, they were new for the Normandy invasion, I think.

After this period aboard the Augusta I went back to England; I've even forgotten how I got back there, but I'm sure I got back in some small craft. I purposely went back to write and also be accredited to the Army because I couldn't go directly from the Augusta and stay ashore with the Army unless I got accreditation.

I got back to London just in time for the first of the V-1s. They had started bombarding England in the meantime with the V-1s. At that time Min Miller was naval attache in London and I used to have dinner with Min. He was the most intrepid guy I ever saw because I would cower and get under tables when these things came over. The Savoy was right on their path and I had originally a room on the top floor and our chief correspondent arranged to get me moved down to a lower floor. The things sounded like they were flying right in my window and I used to pull the covers over my head at night and try to forget them!

One of the fads in England at that time, while this bitter

battle for the beachhead and in the hedgerows going on and while
these things were coming over and wreaking havoc, really wreaking havoc, was to "play the game", a form of charades where people act out a word and that sort of thing. The *Times* bureau at night, when we were relaxed, all the correspondents would come in and play the game along with their wives and friends to try to forget the war for a little while.

Min used to take me out and he'd hear one of these things coming and say, "Let's get up on the rooftop so I can see this thing," and he'd train his glasses on it. It was the early days and they hadn't quite figured out how these things worked. He was very conscientious and very anxious to find out exactly how many seconds it took before the flying bombs started to dip after the engine went off. That was the terrifying period, you know, because they had an automatic cut-off and you never knew after that just how long it was going to be before the bomb hit or where it would hit, because the thing might glide down for a long distance or it might dive. To my mind, that waiting was an awful period. I've never forgotten Min, always anxious to see these damned things when they came over, and I'd keep saying, "Get out of here, you fool!"

Anyway, after a brief time in England I was accredited to the Army and I went back across the Channel, this time with Buckley in a motor torpedo boat. He was the one who had the PTs in the Philippines and he had some motor torpedo boats off Normandy, which didn't do much really except act as sort of messenger boats and liaison craft. I had taken a seasick pill to make sure I wouldn't get seasick and I didn't, fortunately. It was a relatively calm day.

Ernie Pyle went in the same boat. He was a little tiny runt and he had his Army duffle bag with him. We had to get out with this thing in almost waist-deep water. Buckley got in as far on the beach as he could near Omaha beach and Ernie was almost submerged and I was still above water so I carried his duffle bag.

I went around the beachhead.

Q: Were you interested in Cherbourg, in the operation there?

Mr. B.: I didn't get to Cherbourg at all until just after we'd captured it. I didn't get up there with the Navy. The Navy gunfire support ended very soon, I guess they did come in again at the last crack, the very last crack, but that wasn't going on, while I was there.

I went around the whole beachhead from the American sector to the British sector. The Americans were bogged down in these hedgerows. It was very bitter, very nasty fighting. And there were a lot of German bodies around from the earlier fighting. Our troops were only a mile or a mile and a half inland in most places, in some places not as far as that.

Then I went down to the British sector and stayed at the British hostel in Bayeux. The British were supposed to have captured Caen but hadn't been able to do it. Then we started instituting these series of carpet bombings from these big heavy armadas from England to knock the Germans loose in the British sector and they did nothing except knock down the ruins of Caen and prevent the British tanks from penetrating the town. They couldn't get in there. It was just a mess of rubble and the Germans still hung on.

In our sector, we started it off unfortunately by bombing our own lines the first day. I remember going down to an observation point to see this. I'd been in the British sector and I'd been assigned, as is the customery British procedure for someone they don't know what to do with, a lord, who was a captain in the British army, to be my escort officer. He looked like a Lord Haw Haw or something. He was awful dumb and had a broad accent. It was much more difficult to get in to see the British generals, as I remember, than it was to see our own chaps. I saw one or two British generals, but the Canadians were simpler to talk to.

Then, while I was still on the British part of the front, we were all called to a press conference by "His Most High Majesty" Field Marshal Montgomery, who was then in charge supposedly, much to Bradley's ire, of all the ground forces before Ike had moved his headquarters to the continent. Monty had rigged up his caravan in an apple orchard and spread camouflage nets over it. He actually had a big tent this time, and his caravan was off in the distance. The idea of a British press conference is sort of to pay obeisance. It's like the Queen's honors or something. I mean they don't dare open their mouths, really. Most of the British press were so meek and didn't ask questions to amount to anything, especially with Monty.

After a due interval they had the press all arranged properly and all checked to see if they were all there, for Monty had ordered a command performance. He wanted to see *all* the correspondents from both parts of the front. Of course, the Americans paid no attention. Practically none of them came; I was there because I was with the British. They weren't interested in Monty but he thought they were. In addition to that, he was under fire at the time because our troops weren't making much progress and he was holed up at Caen and we were tied down in the hedgerows, and there was some of this American-British feeling developing again.

Well, after due process in which the stage was set and Monty's bull pups appeared, Rommel and Rundstedt, as he called them, and they pranced around the camouflage net, the great man came out in a black beret, which was his traditional uniform, and his turtle neck sweater and slacks; he had on a gray turtleneck sweater and slacks, he sat down on his camp stool and deigned to say a few words to the assembled press. It was all about "my" campaign again and what he was trying to do, he didn't elucidate really, he gave no information of any value. I didn't write a line on it. It was just a typical appearance of Monty. I don't think there were more than two questions and very respectful questions from British members of the press, and all of them said, "Sir, can you tell us this" or something, and that was about it.

Yet, there were some first-rate correspondents there like

Alan Moorehead, who was a top-notch Australian, and later did any number of very fine books, and Christopher Buckley, who was killed in Korea later, from The Daily Telegraph. They would often make fun of Monty behind his back, but they were respectful to him.

Q: Why the fear of him?

Mr. B.: I don't know. The British press operates in a very different way than we do. They really don't in many ways have as free a press as we do. We have abused that freedom sometimes. They're controlled, of course, by the British Official Secrets Act. There is one and it's pretty rigorous. I think it's wrong. I don't think it's the right way to deal with the problem.

I don't know that I'd call it a fear, but there was this attitude, anyway. There wasn't any real probing. And yet they knew the story pretty well and they knew what was going on. They'd talked to other commanders and had been down with the troops in the field.

Anyway, I was with my lord escort at this time and I knew the first bombing was to come off over near the American lines, near St. Lo, later on, so I got in a jeep with the lord and went over to the American lines. Before going down to this vantage point near the front where we were going to observe, I stopped in to see Bradley and Collins (Major-General J. Lawton Collins). Joe Collins had the VII Corps and he was a very affable

Irishman and a very nice guy. These two generals were standing outside Collins' tent, very informal, they had their helmets on and, as I was walking up, Bradley said, "Hey, Baldwin." and I walked over and introduced my lord and accompanying officer who saluted and bowed respectfully. I talked to Bradley and Collins for quite a long time and they told me what they were hoping to do with the bombing and what this plan meant. Then we went away and got down to this observation point and this lord said:

"I say, your chaps are frightfully informal, aren't they?"

Anyway, we went down to this high point of ground overlooking the front lines. You couldn't really see the front lines because it's all hedgerow country and heavily forested; a lot of trees and a lot of shrubs, but you could see where the bomb path was to be laid, beyond our front line, in the German rear chiefly, and not right on the German front line because that would have been almost too close to us, but to cut off all their communications and leave nothing but a thin crust.

In that gathering there were all sorts of Air Force officers. Generals Bradley and Collins were not there, but General Simpson, who later took command of the Ninth Army, was there, no Navy. General Brereton was there and three or four others including General Ralph Royce. We saw the bombing start out. At first we just heard a rumble and saw some flashes in the distance, and then great clouds of dust and smoke started to come up, and pretty soon the whole scene was absolutely obscured.

They couldn't possibly have bombed on a bomb line if they'd tried. They couldn't see anything.

Gradually, the bombs started to creep back towards where we were. We saw them coming and coming, then they were dropping obviously on our own front lines and our own attack troops. Then I heard one of these Air Force generals - there was still this feeling about air force and ground force and what an air force could do, that was always under the surface throughout part of the war, in fact much of it.

One of these Air Force generals, General Royce, I think, who was there just to see the air power clear the way for the infantry, as they thought they were going to do, I saw him throw himself down on his face and he said, "Jesus Christ." Bombs were dropping very close to us by that time, so I hastily followed his example! They got it called off apparently just in time, before it did any more damage.

I remember getting up and leaving, as they called the whole thing off, including the attack, and walking back we saw some of the wounded on our own side who'd been struck by our own bombs and the completely disorganized front line, our own front line. These people were dazed.

I stayed on at the beachhead. I came back from the British Army to the American Army, stayed there for some time, and went up to the base of the Cotentin Peninsula before we captured Cherbourg and visited General Manton Eddy's Ninth Division which was trying to cut off the peninsula.

General Manton Eddy was quite a character. He was a very

good combat commander and later became a corps commander. I'd know him before the war.

Q: He was from New York State, wasn't he?

Mr. B.: He spent his life later in Georgia, so I don't know whether he was from New York State or not, really.

I went with a couple of other correspondents to his headquarters and we went over to find out what the situation was. He proceeded to start to tell us and there was suddenly a burst of firing in a nearby field and he said:

"Excuse me, gentlemen. Have a martini while I'm gone."

He had his batman bring out the most perfectly chilled martinis in a silver pitcher with little silver glasses. He disappeared and came back shortly and said:

"It's the Germans just counterattacking in a nearby field. We've stopped them now."

He was like that, an imperturbable guy, and he had delicious martinis, too!

I was in France when Teddy Roosevelt, Jr., died of a heart attack. He was an assistant division commander, I guess, of; what was it, the Fourth Division? The one that landed on the other beach, not Omaha, the other one.

Q: Utah?

Mr. B.: Utah. I should have mentioned this. He had had a

career in North Africa with the First Division. I saw the First Division and spent some time with them during the war at one time and another. The First Division was commanded by two glory-hunters. One was Terry de la Mesa Allen and Teddy Roosevelt was assistant division commander. Both of them are the type of men always wanting to be where the action was thickest, so nobody was really back running the division. That was usually left to the chief of staff or somebody like that. They both liked glory. I'm going back to North Africa now and leading up to Teddy Roosevelt at Utah.

When I visited the division command post in, I think it was Gafsa, a little Tunisian town, they were in a sort of bombed-out gendarmerie, up on the second floor, the windows were blown out and blankets over the windows for the blackout, I was directed by the sergeant to what he told me was the general's quarters. I saw Teddy, whom I'd met before, sitting on his bunk in his woolen underwear; in North Africa it's cold in the winter, you know, having a brandy, and Terry Allen was sitting over on the side. Of course, Teddy got up in his ebullient way immediately, slapped me on the shoulders, and said hello. I had not met Allen prior to that, so he introduced me to Allen, then I tried to talk about the situation and Teddy was sort of anxious to talk all about it but Terry was his division commander.

While I was there a French officer came in who commanded the desert wing. He was ostensibly under the First Division's command; he had a group of irregulars who were holding the desert flank. He came in to report. He didn't know who the division commander was. He came in the room and said:

"Mon commandant!"

Teddy stood up and started sprouting French at this man. The colonel thought he was the division commander, so he'd talk in French and Terry didn't speak French so his nose was very out of joint. Finally, they got that straightened out, but the long and short of it was that, as you remember, in Italy, in Sicily, there was a great letdown in morale in the First Division after they'd taken rather severe casualties. Teddy, or somebody in the division, apparently told the men that after Sicily they could come home, which was a fatal mistake. The rumor got around. Who told them, I don't know. So, as a result, Marshall had both Terry Allen and Teddy relieved. Teddy was assigned to another division in England, the Fourth Division, and Terry came home to take over another division and train it. He did and made very good with it. He did a fine job later, in the Battle of the Bulge.

They were both hard-drinking men and they were both glory-hunters. This brings me back to Teddy on the beachhead. He then was assistant division commander of the Fourth Division. He was personally, I think, fearless. He had a lot of his father's traits. I'd known him in New York before the war. He was not terribly bright, I don't think, and I'm not sure his judgment was always good. He walked ashore on Utah with his walking cane in hand and led his troops with that. The Fourth Division was in some pretty heavy fighting around the peninsula later on, and he died of a heart attack in the midst of the beachhead fighting. I wrote his obituary. I'd seen his wife in London, who was working, I think, with the Red Cross there just before the invasion.

I left France, I think, in late June, if I'm not mistaken, or early July. Early July, I guess. We were just about ready to make the breakout. I wanted to get back and write what I'd gotten and also catch up with the war in the Pacific and the rest of the things I was supposed to analyze. So I went back to England and then back to the United States. I've forgotten now how I got back.

Q: By clipper again?

Mr. B.: Possibly. I just don't really remember.

There are two things that I revert back to in talking about points that might have helped the enemy in my writing, and the judgment question would come up as to whether they would help us more than the enemy.

One of the things that was discovered very early on in Normandy and which I think had been known or at least estimated by some of the best-informed Army officers before that was the weakness of our tanks as compared to the Germans'. Their gun power was far inferior and they were no match for the opposing German Tiger tanks. The only way they could defeat them would be by ganging up three or four at a time against one. This had been a subject of debate for some time. I remember in the Army the Ordnance Department had a lot to do with tank design and the using forces at that time had less to do with it. The tankers had been arguing for a long time for bigger guns and more penetrating power. Also a lower silhouette. Our tanks stood up too high on the ground and weren't easily disguised.

Some of the stories I wrote, not only as a result of the invasion but also previously and afterwards were about tanks and their weaknesses and their inferiority to the German tanks. I specifically stated this in these pieces and I said it was a disgrace. I said what some of the GIs called them. They didn't call them "flaming coffins" but they had a name for them almost equivalent to that. I pointed out we had taken one hell of a long time to even get diesel engines into our tanks, we had used some gasoline engines, which were nothing but funeral pyres, at the start of the war, and so forth.

I did this deliberately and I talked to people before I did it. I think it may have given a little comfort to the Germans but it gave a lot more comfort to our own people.

Q: It was a goad, was it?

Mr. B.: Well, not only a goad to the people in Washington in tank design, but also the people that were fighting these tanks were constantly saying the American people don't know what we're putting up with, and they were very sore about it. I got letters from a lot of them afterwards claiming this. On the other hand, I got some letters of criticism from people who hadn't been there.

That was one instance. The Army made no attempt to shut me up on this, although I got some letters of criticism.

The other instance was the replacement depots in Italy. I didn't see the replacement depots, I hadn't been to Italy, didn't get there during the war, but this was a later stage of the war when we had captured Rome and were on our way up the peninsula. The state of affairs in these replacement depots had been an open scandal. I'd gotten a number of letters about them for some time.

In the Army a replacement depot is a lot like a receiving ship in the Navy. They send individual personnel there to act as fillers for a ship's crew; not a ship's crew, but a battalion in the Army or what not, to replace casualties, men on leave, and so on. They're supposed to be, in the Army, a place where the soldier gets all the latest equipment he'll need at the front and is fitted out with boots and anything else he needs, his tickets punched, his records are kept, he's given good food and as much rest and recreation as possible before he's assigned to his unit and sent up. Usually, the stay in these places is supposed to be relatively brief, maybe ten days, it depends on the situation, sometimes longer.

Well, I'd gotten letters from GIs who'd been in them complaining about the state of affairs and I checked this out once or twice in Washington with people I knew. The men in some of the Italian replacement depots were living in seas of mud with inadequate housing. There were no boots; this and that was lacking, the food was lousy, and so forth.

So, sometime in the latter part of the war, after we'd captured Rome, I started to get more letters of this sort about these same replacement depots. They focused on Italy. There wasn't criticism about any other place but right there, north of Naples and north of Rome, those areas. I checked it out in Washington again and found that virtually all these allegations were true, and I had a lot of detail. So I started to write a series of two articles on this. I numbered them I and II, and the first article was pretty strong. It told about how lousy these places were and so forth and said this had been checked.

Well, that afternoon a colonel came in to see Eddie James, who was the managing editor of the Times. I didn't know this till much later. I didn't know it till after the war, I guess. He said he came directly from General Marshall and that General Marshall was very incensed with my article. These replacement depots were the apple of his eye and he had given strict orders a long time ago, after he'd been to Italy, to see that they were cleaned up and made absolutely perfect and he was sure they were.

Eddie James was never very definite one way or the other when you talked to him. He was sort of a gruff old guy. He would listen and make some wisecracks or comments. He listened to this fellow, and the colonel left and went back to Washington, and I was told later that he assured General Marshall that he had stopped the series, there'd be no more. I didn't know anything about that and I duly sent in the second piece and it was published the next day!

I never got many more repercussions from that. General Marshall himself never spoke to me about it. The allegations were true and I think they helped to clean the replacement depots because they were cleaned up. Marshall, I think, hit the ceiling when he found out that his orders hadn't been carried out. I think he chopped off a lot of heads.

Those are two of the instances I can think of in which I believe some information of comfort to the enemy did more good than harm.

Q: Very concretely.

INDEX

to

Series of Interviews with

Hanson Weightman BALDWIN

U. S. Navy (Ret.)

ADLER, General Julius Ochs: Number 2 man on TIMES (1930s) interested in military coverage by the paper, p. 240-1; his attitude towards conscription as U. S. preparedness, p. 298. p. 544-5.

AIRCRAFT CARRIERS: Baldwin on the controversy (early 1930s) in the Navy over BBs and Aircraft Carriers, p. 316 ff.

ALEXANDER, Field Marshall Harold R.L.G.A.: p. 375

ALLEN, Major General Terry de la Mesa: Commander, First Division in North Africa, p. 428.

ALMOND, Lt. Gen. Edward (Ned) Mallory: Acting Chief of Staff to General MacArthur in Tokyo, p. 495-6; Mrs. Almond's dinner party in Tokyo, p. 500-1; the general in Korea, p. 502; p. 513.

ALSOP, Joseph Wright, Jr. (Joe): p. 496-7.

SS AMERICAN LEGION: 1929 Baldwin takes job as Quartermaster p. 211; his account of lack of attention on this Munson Line ship to Safety Rules, p. 212-216.

ANDERSON, Admiral George: Baldwin talks with him about Cuban Missile Crisis, p. 609; Anderson and McNamara, p. 690.

ANDREWS, General Frank: p. 242.

ANNAPOLIS, Maryland: a picture of Annapolis in the early 1920s p. 94 ff.

ARAB NATIONALISM: The boost given this by the British-French intervention at Suez, p. 598-600 ff.

ARGUS: code name for scientific expedition under aegis of Navy in South Atlantic, p. 642 ff.

ARNOLD, General H. H. (Hap): p. 310 ff; p. 355-6; p. 381-2.

ASWAN DAM: p. 569; p.571; p. 605; p. 607; p. 617.

USS AUGUSTA: Baldwin is assigned to the flagship of Admiral Kirk for the Normandy invasion, p. 402 ff; p. 405; she moves around the invasion beaches, p. 408; p. 412-13; p. 415; p. 419.

AUSTIN, Vice Admiral Bernard L.: p. 61

AWATI: Flagship of Admiral Zengo Yoshida, Japanese Imperial Navy - on visit to New Yrok (1936), p. 266.

B-36 Controversy: p. 458 ff; Baldwin reviews the statement of Admiral Denfeld before delivery to Congressional Committee, p. 470-1.

BALDWIN, Hanson Weightman: personal data, p. 1-2; his grandfather in newspaper work, p. 2, 4; his father on the Baltimore SUN, P. 4-5; attendance at Boy's Latin School, p. 7-10; interest in the U. S. Naval Academy, p. 12-16; Severn School, p. 15; U. S. Naval Academy, p. 18 ff; his accident during 2nd class year, p. 86-7; first ship duty after graduation, p. 117 ff; advancement to Lt. j.g., p. 177-8; his resignation from the Navy (1927), p. 181-6; Naval Reserve, p. 187; promotion to Lt. (1934) Reserves, p. 190-1; resigns Reserve Commission, 192; offered commission again in 1942 - refuses, p. 198-9; launches newspaper career with Sun Papers. (Jan. 1928), p. 204; his marriage, p. 232-4; military correspondent for New York TIMES (1937), p. 244-5; speaking engagements that developed as result of his newspaper articles, p. 286; Baldwin's concept of the objectives of the military analyst, p. 291-2; the demands on him in period 1939-41; p. 299-300; Air Force offers him commission in Intelligence, p. 311; his reaction to attack on Pearl Harbor - his article This is a War we Could Lose, p. 313; p. 333; his trip to Pearl Harbor and South Pacific (Aug. 1942), p. 340 ff; Savo Island Battle story, p. 350; censorship in Pearl Harbor, p. 352; Baldwin takes Savo Island story to Washington for clearance, p. 353; talk before Joint Strategic Survey Committee of JCS, p. 355 ff; awarded Pulitzer Prize, p. 367-8; his method of covering various war fronts, p. 367-8; North African trip, p. 367-80; United Kingdom visit, p. 380 ff; problems involved in analyzing war news, p. 391-2; differences with TIMES over outside writing/radio appearances, p. 392-5; his writing on various invasions based on detailed knowledge of ports, logistics, p. 396-8; use of quotations from Baldwin by foreign propagandists, p. 398-400; England and the Normandy operations, p. 400 ff; views on antiquated methods of British for handling dispatches from invasion fleet, p. 415-7; accredited to U. S. Army, p. 419 ff leaves France (July), p. 430; critizes American tanks in France, p. 430-1; criticizes Replacement Depots in Italy - Gen. Marshall reacts, p. 432-3; Baldwin and the A bomb, p. 449 ff; Baldwin on the events of the postwar period, p. 455 ff; his part in the B-36 Unification fight, p. 458 ff; serves on Eberstadt T.F. on National Defense, p. 468-9; his personal view on unification, p. 476-7; his confrontation with CNO Sherman, p. 481-4; Baldwin's reaction to our unpreparedness for Korean War, p. 491-2; Baldwin's visit to the Far East (fall of 1950), p. 492 ff; his picture of the French in Indo-China, p.514 ff; on Quemoy, p. 522 ff; Baldwin and the Congress - seeking their views, p. 529-30; his tour of NATO countries (1952-3), p. 531; Baldwin on security in nation without becoming a garrison state, p. 541-3; Baldwin on use of nuclear weapons in isolated situations, p. 554-5; The Suez Crisis, p. 563-595; Baldwin's assessment of the British-French action at Suez, p. 584-5; p. 592; p. 595;

goes to Moscow for Soviet Air Forces Day (1956), p. 623 ff; the farewell luncheon party, p. 633-4; Baldwin on ultimate loyalty reporter owes to his country, p. 648-9ff; Baldwin's TV program on CBS, p. 660-663; writes about SOSUS and underwater sound detection, p. 664-5; Baldwin and the Board of the National War College, p. 666-7; a series of awards in post-war period, p. 673-5; on the subject of awards in general, p. 675-8; his first meeting with Robert McNamara, p. 691 ff; Baldwin writes about some of Dept. of Defense studies - angers McNamara, p. 695-6; more on relations with McNamara, p. 700-1; Baldwin's article on Vietnam - "Should we Bug out, etc." p. 711; visits Vietnam in fall of 1965, p. 713 ff; his accounts of several units going into action, p. 713-6; his trip (late 1967) to Vietnam, p. 717 ff; his visit with godson (Joe Worthington, Jr.), p. 717-8; Baldwin's review of situation in late 1967, p. 720-1; reports on general attitude of press representatives in Vietnam, p. 721; talks with Westmoreland and Sharp, p. 722; Baldwin's discussion of decline in standards - My Lai and loss of moral values, p. 725-8; OCS and lowered standards - deferrments from draft, p. 728; Baldwin's comments on Westmoreland book, p. 730-1; his discussion of our failings in Vietnam, p. 733-7; his comments on effect of propaganda from North Vietnam, p. 737-40; Baldwin's feelings about the attitude of N.Y. TIMES in his last years with it - the anti-military bias, etc., p. 741-2; Baldwin in retirement, p. 752 ff; his arrangements with READER'S DIGEST, p. 753-58; his book - STRATEGY FOR TOMORROW for Georgetown center for Strategic Studies, p. 753; the Chinese-Russian relationship, p. 754-5; the Mandated Islands, p. 756-7; his trip to Mediterranean for look at results of Zumwalt reforms, p. 758-764; Baldwin on idea of overseas basing for fleet, p. 767-9; Baldwin's articles in retirement for N.Y. TIMES, p. 770-1; his account of his four years on Board of Advisers of Naval War College, p. 772 ff; Russian reactions to Baldwin's writings, p. 785-7; BATTLES LOST AND WON (campaigns in WWII), p. 784; his latest book - CRUCIAL YEARS - 1939-41, p. 788.

BALTIMORE SUN: Baldwin's grandfather on staff, p. 4; his father on staff for almost fifty years, p. 4-5; Hanson Baldwin begins his newspaper career with Sun Papers (Jan. 1928) p. 204 ff;

BARRETT, Colonel David D: U. S. Army Intelligence Officer - Far East, p. 504 ff; p. 511.

BARRETT, George: Chief assistant to Baldwin at the TIMES in WWII, p. 331.

BARTON, BATTEN, DURSTINE and OSBORN: employed by the TIMES (1956) to increase circulation of paper, p. 545-6.

BARUCH, Bernard: his attitude towards industrial mobilization p. 306 ff.

BAY OF PIGS: p. 678 - news story on loss of volunteer American flyers, p. 698-9; FBI investigates Baldwin's contacts in Defense Department, p. 699-700.

BEAKLEY, Vice Admiral Wallace (Wally): p. 42-3.

BERLIN AIRLIFT CRISIS: p. 680-86.

BIRCHALL, Fred: Acting Managing Editor of TIMES under Adolph Ochs, p. 226.

BLAKE, Red: football coach at West Point Military Academy, p. 555.

BLANCHARD, Butch: p. 629-30

BOWEN, Vice Admiral Harold B: head of Bureau of Engineering, U.S.N., p. 252-3. the controversy over high temperature-high pressure steam, p. 320-1.

BOY'S LATIN SCHOOL - Baltimore: p. 7-10.

BRADLEY, General Omar: p. 379.; his headquarters on USS AUGUSTA, p. 403; p. 406, p. 409; p. 411-12; p. 415; - p. 422; p. 424-5. his 'fancy dan' testimony on the B-36 controversy, p. 472-3.

USS BRECK: Baldwin reports for duty (Jan. 1926), p. 157 ff; duties on board - fleet maneuvers off Panama, p. 157-61; duty in the Mediterranean, p. 161; Baldwin as Commissary officer, p. 165; the unusual steward, p. 168 ff ; the BRECK'S seagoing qualities, p. 168-70; athletic encounters with the Royal Navy, p. 173-4.

BROWN, Admiral Charles (Cat) R.: protests Baldwin's remarks before the Joint Strategic Survey Committee of the JCS (1942), p. 357-60.

BROWN, John Mason: aide to Admiral Alan Kirk for the Normandy invasion, p. 402-3; p. 407; p. 409; p. 415.

BULGANIN, Premier Nikolai A.: p. 629-31; p. 634; p. 641.

BUNKER, The Hon. Ellsworth: U. S. Ambassador to Vietnam, p. 734.

BURKE, Admiral Arleigh A: p. 494; p. 498; p. 527; p. 532-3; p. 728-9; Baldwin does his book - STRATEGY FOR TOMORROW at request of Burke, p. 753.

CAEN, France: p. 421-423.

CAIMANERA: p. 135; Baldwin as boat officer for expedition to Caimanera, p. 136-7.

CARTWRIGHT, Labrador, p. 216.

CATLEDGE, Turner: managing editor of the TIMES, p. 545; p. 547.

CHURCHILL, The Hon. Sir Winston S.: attitude of TIMES's London Bureau towards Churchill in 1937, p. 270-1. p. 374; p. 376; p. 381. Baldwin's support for Churchill's concept of post-war Europe, p. 442-3; p. 569.

COLBERT, Admiral Richard Gary: (Dick): p. 759; p. 773; p. 780; p. 782-4.

COLLINS, Maj. Gen. J. Lawton (Joe): Commander of VII Army Corps on Normandy front, p. 424-5; p. 475.

COMINTERN: Information on plans of COMINTERN for South Korea - as outlined by U.S. Intelligence Officer, p. 504-5.

COPPEDGE, Captain John O (Bo): Director of Athletics, p. 559; p. 561.

CORLETT, Major General Charles H: General Marshall assigned him to United Kingdom - has knowledge of Pacific amphibious techniques, p. 417-8.

COURTS-MARTIAL: Ensigns required to act as recorders, p. 143-4.

CRETE: p. 293

CROMMELIN, Captain John: p. 456-8; p. 468.

CRYPTOGRAPHY: p. 446-8.

CUBAN MISSILE CRISIS: p. 686 ff; White House disturbed over Senator Keating's disclosures in Senate, p. 687; Kruschchev's gamble, p. 688.

CURTIS, Charlotte: her opposition to a Baldwin article on Intelligence, p. 770-1.

CYPRUS: Baldwin's visit to Cyprus, p. 563 ff; British Expeditionary Force departs from Cyprus - Baldwin attached as a reporter, p. 557-8; p. 571. p. 617.

DAHLGREN: p. 115-6.

DANANG: p. 718-21.

DANIELS, The Hon. Josephus: p. 249.

DAVIS, Elmer: head of office of War Information - asks help

of Baldwin to get navy's story across, p. 361 ff.

DE GAULLE, General Charles: p. 380-1.

DENFELD, Admiral Louis E.: Chief of Naval Operations - Radford wanted him to take strong stand in the B-36 controversy, p. 470-4.

DENNY, Harold: TIMES correspondent in Moscow, p. 280-1;

deSEVERSKY, Alexander: influence of his ideas about airpower at outset of WWII, p. 311-12.

DOBIE, Gilmour (Gil): head football coach (1919) at U.S. Naval Academy, p. 13-14.

DRAKE, Waldo: Public Affairs officer to Admiral Nimitz - executive of the Los Angeles TIMES - p. 341-2.

DREXLER, Ensign Henry Clay: killed in turret explosion of the USS TRENTON, p. 127-8.

DREYFOOS, Orvil E.: son-in-law of Arthur Hays Sulzberger and Publisher of the TIMES (1961-63), p. 546; p. 548-9.

DRUM, Lt. Gen. Hugh A.: p. 256.

DULLES, Allen: p. 679

DULLES, John Foster: his policy of massive retaliation, p. 453-4; p. 520 ff; p. 553; the Aswan Dam, p. 569; p. 574-5; p. 586-7; p. 592-3.

Du MAURIER, Daphne (Lady Browning): her home near Fowey, Cornwall, p. 403-4.

EBERSTADT, Ferdinand: headed task force on national security for Hoover Commission, p. 468; emphasis placed on danger of garrison state - and a bankrupt state, p. 469-70.

ECCLES, Rear Admiral Henry Effingham: on faculty at Naval War College, p. 778; p. 780.

EDDY, Major General Manton S.: Commander of Ninth Division - Normandy, p. 426.

EDEN, Anthony (Lord Avon): p. 569; p. 586-7.

EDWARDS, Admiral Richard S.: p. 361-2.

EGYPT: Baldwin visits Egypt, the Sinai - and has interview with Nasser, p. 563-4; military readiness, p. 566-7; operation of the canal, p. 568-9; the Russians in Egypt, p. 608-9; Baldwin's view of the Egyptian military, p. 609-13;

EISENHOWER, General Dwight D.: p. 300; p. 422; p. 373 ff; his reaction to Gen. Montgomery, p. 375; under fire because of loss of Kasserine Pass, p. 375-7; his view on the invasion of Southern France, p. 442; p. 454-5; p. 473-474; p. 520-3; his defense department team, p. 524-5; p. 527; his Council of Foreign Relations, p. 538-9; p. 540; p. 561-2; p. 592.

ENTHOVEN, Dr. Alain C.: p. 694; an illustration of the kind of study instituted by Enthoven, p. 694-5; p. 705-7.

EWEN, Vice Admiral Edward C. (Eddie): Captain of the Naval Academy football team (1920), p. 45-6;

FAYMONVILLE, Col: U.S. Military Attache in Russia, (1937) p. 280-2.

FEDERAL BUREAU OF INVESTIGATION (F.B.I.): investigates Baldwin's sources of information in Department of Defense, p. 699-700; p. 749 ff.

FELT, Admiral H.D.: his outspoken remark in Saigon to the press, p. 649; p. 652.

FENTON, Walter: Assistant City Editor of TIMES (1929) p. 229.

FITCH, Admiral Aubrey W.: takes Baldwin with him to the South Pacific, p. 343; p. 346; p. 349; p. 350.

FORRESTAL, The Hon. James: p. 314; p. 333; p. 342; p. 361-3; p. 455; p. 459-61; his final months in office, p. 461-5; p. 467; p. 477-80; takes action on Baldwin's complaint that CNO Sherman was trying to limit Baldwin's visits to naval installations, p. 481-2 ff.

GAMELIN, General (French): attitude on state of the French Army just prior to WWII, p. 271-2.

GHORMLEY, VADM Robert Lee: p. 344: his defeatist attitude in South Pacific, p. 345; p. 349; relieved in Oct. 1942 Baldwin's stories falsely credited, p. 354; p. 364-6;

GILPATRIC, Roswell L.: Deputy Secretary of Defense, p. 693.

GOOD, ADM. R.F.: Sent by Nimitz to New Caledonia to get logistics straightened out, p. 344-5; p. 351; Baldwin's interpretation of the value of his report to Nimitz, p. 365-6.

GREEN BOWLERS: p. 42. p. 456; the Crommelin fight against the society, p. 456 ff.

GREENE, General Wallace (Wally) M.Jr.: p. 710.

GRIFFIN, Admiral C.D.: p. 471.

GUADALCANAL: p. 346-8; Baldwin's view of Admiral King on 'hot seat' for pushing occupation of Guadalcanal, p. 359.

GUANTANAMO: p. 133-7.

GULLION, The Hon. Edmund A.: Counselor, U.S. Legation, Saigon, p. 514.

GUN FACTORY - Washington: Baldwin assigned to Gun Factory after graduation - an ordnance summer, p. 113-4.

GYMKHANA - at the Naval Academy: p. 84

HAIPHONG, North Vietnam: Baldwin writes about need to mine harbor, p. 711.

HALL, Admiral John Lesslie, Jr.: p. 411-412.

HANSELL, Brig. Gen. Haywood S. (Possum): p. 310-11; p. 381.

HAPPY HOURS - at the Naval Academy: p. 84-5.

HAYWARD, Vice Admiral John T.: p. 537; p. 544.

HEATH, The Hon. Donald R.: U.S. Ambassador to Vietnam, p. 514 ff.

HEWITT, Admiral H. Kent: p. 377-8.

HILL, Admiral Harry W: Superintendent of the U.S. Naval Academy, p. 557-8.

HIRSCH, Seymour: New York TIMES journalist, p. 743-4.

HITLER, Adolph: p. 267; p. 274; p. 304.

HORNE, Admiral Frederick Jos.: p. 199; p. 201; p. 338; Baldwin's relationship with him during WWII, p. 361-2; the Navy's debt to him for his role in WWII, p. 362-3; p. 369.

HOULIHAN, Richard: first head of TIMES' Washington Bureau, p.250.

HOWARD, Roy: p. 80

HUNGARIAN REVOLUTION: p. 588

INCHON: p. 493; p. 497; p. 502; p. 511

INDUSTRIAL MOBILIZATION - WWII; p. 306-7.

INGERSOLL, Admiral Royal E.: p. 197.

ISRAEL: position vis-a-vis the Suez Canal, p. 560; p. 570; p. 586; p. 592; p. 603-4.

JACOBS, VADM Randall: p. 189; offers Baldwin a navy commission - 1942, p. 198-9.

JAMES, Edwin Leland: Managing Editor, New York TIMES, hears complaint from General Marshall on a Baldwin article, p. 433-4; his son in Korea, p. 503

JAPAN: Leahy's estimate of Japanese condition in 1945, p. 436-8.

JEAN BART - French BB.: p. 598.

JOHNSON, General Briard Poland: Chief of Staff of U.S. Army, p. 710.

JOHNSON, The Hon. Louis: Secretary of Defense, p. 456-7; p. 460; p. 469-70; p. 487-9.

JOHNSON, The Hon. Lyndon: President of the United States: Baldwin's belief that Johnson had been oversold on use of Air Power in Vietnam, p. 709 ff; his dilemma in 1965, p. 712; cancels plans for calling up Reserves and National Guard, p. 712-3; p. 723; p. 733; p. 735.

JOINT CHIEFS OF STAFF: as organized by F.D.R., p. 355-6; p. 369-70; Bradley as Chairman puts the JCS in politics, p. 473.

JOSEPH, David: City editor of the TIMES (1929), p. 228.

KAPLAN, Captain Leonard: p. 104-5.

KASSERINE PASS: p. 367; p. 370-71; p. 375.

KAUFFMAN, Rear Admiral Draper L.: a dinner party in Washington to which Baldwin is bidden, p. 706 ff.

KEATING, The Hon. Kenneth: U. S. Senator from New York; his role in Cuban Missile Crisis, p. 686-7;

KEITEL, General (German): Baldwin has an interview with him during Europian tour, p. 276.

KENNEDY, The Hon. John F.: President of the United States; p. 687-8; p. 706.

KENNEDY, Robert: Attorney General of the U.S.; on Bay of Pigs, p. 679, p. 698-9.

KENNEDY ADMINISTRATION: attempts at controlling news, p. 749-52.

KING, Fleet Admiral Ernest J.: p. 345; p. 355-6; his orders to keep details of Savo Island losses a secret, p. 357 ff; Baldwin's analysis of his reasons for this secrecy, p. 359; p. 363-4; p. 369; p. 384; p. 475.

KIRK, Admiral Alan G.: U.S. Naval Commander for the Normandy invasion, p. 402 ff; p. 409; p. 411; p. 415; p. 418.

KISSINGER, The Hon. Henry: p. 538

KOREA: p. 487-8; p. 490; p. 498; p. 501; Baldwin's trip to
Korea, p. 501 ff; his information from U.S. Army intelligence officer Barrett on Chinese units invading Korea,
p. 504-5 ff; naval aspects of war, p. 508 ff; mines and
minesweeping, p. 510-11; proposed use of atomic weapons,
p. 512-3; p. 518-20; p. 523.

KROCK, Arthur: head of TIMES' Washington Bureau, p. 250.

KRUEGER, General Walter: p. 243-4; p. 300.

KRUSHCHEV, Nikita: Entertains General Nate Twining in Moscow,
p. 629-30; p. 632; p. 634; p. 638; p. 641; p. 687-8.

KUTER, General Lawrence S.: p. 381.

LAWRENCE, Wm. H.: Science Editor of the New York TIMES - his
reluctance to accept idea of thermo-nuclear bomb, p. 535-8.

LEAHY, Fleet Admiral Wm.: an invaluable source of information
for Baldwin in WWII, p. 285. Presided at sessions of JCS
as Assistant to President, p. 355; p. 369-70; stressed
his role as spokesman for President, p. 435-6; strongly
opposed to an invasion of Japan, p. 436-8; p. 440.

LEAR, General Ben: p. 300.

LEBANON: U.S. Landings, p. 618-22.

LeBOURGEOIS, Vice Admiral Julien Johnson: President of the
U.S. Naval War College, p. 774; p. 778-9.

LEWIS, Anthony (Tony): p. 747.

LINDBERG, Col. Charles Augustus: his flight to Paris (1927)
p.174-5.; p. 294

LODGE, The Hon. Henry Cabot: p. 734.

MacARTHUR, General Douglas and his Staff in Tokyo: p. 493ff;
p. 498-9; his manner of greeting guests, p. 499; concern
for son's welfare, p. 499; proposed use of atomic weapons,
p. 512-3; his misinterpretation of intelligence reports on
Chinese intervention, p. 512-3.

MacCOLL, Rene: reporter for Baltimore SUN (1928) - later with
London DAILY EXPRESS, P. 206.

MALAYSIA: p. 734; p. 736.

MALTA: p. 617.

MANSFIELD, The Hon. Michael Jos.: U.S. Senator from Montana, p. 530.

MARETH LINE: See entries under Eisenhower, Montgomery.

MARKEL, Lester: Sunday Editor of the N.Y. TIMES, p. 547.

MARSHALL, General George C.: his off-the-record press interview on subject of Philippine defenses - 3 weeks before attack on Pearl Harbor, p. 308-310; influence of deSeversky's ideas on him, p. 311-12; p. 355-6. his reaction to Baldwin's articles on Replacement Depots in Italy, p. 432-2; p. 439; his stratgy in Europe, p. 444;

McCARTHYISM: p. 561-2.

McNAMARA, The Hon. Robert S.: Secretary of Defense, p. 691; on the Missile Gap - an issue in political campaign, p. 691-2; p. 694-5; his reaction to Baldwin's report on status of Army-Air Force Units in Germany, p. 696-7; more on relations with Baldwin, p. 700-1; a heated exchange, p. 702; his policy on military supplies, p. 702-3; Baldwin's analysis of the McNamara character, p. 704-6; McNamara and Vietnam policy, p. 708-9; his re-ordering of communications after Tonkin Gulf, p. 711; raises up a generation of 'yes men' in the military, p. 728-9.

USS MEMPHIS: flagship of U.S. units in foreign waters, p. 174-5; conveyed Lindberg and plane back to U.S., p. 175.

MIDDLETON, Drew: p. 652.

MILITARY ANALYST: Baldwin's concept of what such a person should be, p. 291-2.

MILLER, Vice Admiral Gerald (Gerry): Cinc 6th Fleet, p. 759 ff; p. 766.

MILLER, RADM Harold Blaine (Min): takes over from Waldo Drake as PR officer for Admiral Nimitz, p. 342-3. Naval Attache in London at time of V-1 bombardment, p. 419-20.

MOMSEN LUNG: Baldwin covers tests conducted by Momsen in Chesapeake Bay - 1928, p. 207-8.

MONTGOMERY, Field Marshall Bernard Law: in North Africa, p. 373 ff; his press conference in Normandy, p. 422-4.

MORALE - in the Navy (1920s): p. 139

SS MOUNT SHASTA: Baldwin's story about attempt of army fliers to bomb her off Virginia Capes, p. 231; p. 262.

MY LAI (Vietnam): Baldwin's discussion of moral atmosphere out of which My Lai grew, p. 725 ff.

NAPALM: Baldwin's experience on a napalm mission, p. 739-40.

NASSER, Gamal Abdel: p. 597-99; p. 604; p. 608; p. 613.

NATIONAL GUARD - Reserves: Baldwin's comments on p. 681-5.

NATIONAL WAR COLLEGE: Baldwin serves on the Board of Advisers, p. 666-71.

NEW YORK HERALD-TRIBUNE: the mecca of newspaper world in 1920s p. 225; p. 226-7; competitive influence on the New York TIMES, p. 550-1; p. 748-9.

NEW YORK TIMES: Navy objects to some of Baldwin articles, p. 189-90; his newspaper connections a reason for resignation from the Naval Reserve, p. 190-2; his trip to Russia in 1937-, p. 193; p. 197; the role of Carr Van Anda, p. 225; p. 227; Baldwin hired by TIMES (1929) as general assignment reporter, p. 227-8; growing practice of by-lines, p. 230; p. 243; Baldwin asks for Naval Assignments, p. 231-2; p. 235-6; rifle matches at Camp Perry, p. 232; Army and Air Force assignments, p. 234; Baldwin's early difficulties with navy assignemnts, p. 237-9; policy of the TIMES -greater coverage of military affairs - attitude of Arthur Sulzberger, p. 239-40; p. 242-3; problems created by Baldwin's (military reporter)-making trips to Washington, p. 250; Baldwin writes military editorials, p. 250-1 some of his experiences with government departments and military units, p. 252-4; Editorial policy of TIMES in days of Adolph Ochs, p. 260; in time of Arthur Sulzberger, p. 261; in more recent times p. 262; policy on gifts to reporters, p. 264-5; Baldwin's European trip (1937) for TIMES, p. 270 ff; Baldwin's articles on that trip - his book, p. 283; organized criticism of Baldwin's articles, p. 295-7; attempts to neutralize Baldwin's opinions, p. 297; TIME'S system of having regional bureaus, p. 325-6; Baldwin sets up his own chartroom of war theatres, p. 330-2; TIMES sends Baldwin to South Pacific in August, 1942, p. 340 ff; TIMES wants to carry Baldwin's articles on Savo Island, Guadalcanal, etc - approval from Washington - Baldwin gets a Pulitzer Prize, p. 353-4; p. 360-1; p. 387; policy of TIMES on outside writing of staff - radio and TV appearances, p. 392-3; p. 394-5; p. 403; TIMES did not restrain Baldwin when he wrote on Replacement Depots in Italy - p. 433-4; Baldwin defends Secy. Forrestal against Drew Pearson - in print, p. 464; p. 469; TIMES sends Baldwin on trip to various military installations, p. 481-3; articles and book result, p. 484-6; p. 503; TIMES and the coverage of development of thermo-nuclear bomb, p. 534-6; paper's position on military and security considerations, p. 544-5; publicity campaign to increase circulation, p. 545-6; protracted strike brings on heart attack of Dreyfoos p. 548; resultant changes in TIMES management p. 548 ff; policy vis-a-vis reporters and military hazards, p. 594-6; Baldwin tours Middle East after Suez crisis, p. 597 ff; TIMES sends Baldwin (1956) to Moscow for Soviet Air Forces Day, p. 624 ff; p. 644-5;

Baldwin and his policy of secrecy, p. 644-6; p. 652; TIMES and the Pentagon papers, p. 653; Baldwin tells TIMES that he plans to retire when 65, p. 717; p. 718; the anti-military bias of the TIMES - Baldwin's reflections, p. 741-3; TIMES reporters in Vietnam, p. 743-7; the H. Salisburg story from Hanoi - the Baldwin story in refutation, p. 745-6; p. 748-9; Baldwin in retirement - articles for the TIMES, p. 770-1.

NEW YORK TIMES - WASHINGTON BUREAU: p. 250; p. 252.

NILES, David K.: Administrative Assistant to President Truman - opposed to Secretary Forrestal, p. 459, p. 461.

NIMITZ, Fleet Admiral Chester W.: p. 342-3. and the relief of Adm. Ghormley, p. 364-5;

NORMANDY LANDINGS: see entries under: BALDWIN, BRADLEY, KIRK OMAHA BEACH.

USS NORTH CAROLINA: Baldwin as a correspondent on the NORTH CAROLINA for her gun trails in North Atlantic (1941), p. 323-4.

NURI-al-SAID: p. 600; Baldwin has an interview with him, p. 601; p. 603; p. 607.

OAKES, John: in charge of editorial page of the New York TIMES, p. 742-3.

OCHS, Adolph: Publisher of the New York TIMES, p. 225-6; his concept of the paper as a public trust, p. 227; p. 240; editorial policy of the TIMES in his day, p. 260-1.

O'DONNELL, General Emmett, Jr: USAF (Rosie): p. 459; p. 467.

OLMSTEAD, Jerauld Lockwood: ranked number one in class of 1922 - editor of the LUCKY BAG, p. 104-6.

OMAHA BEACH: p. 409-13; p. 419; p. 421.

OPPENHEIMER, Dr. Robert: p. 535; p. 542-3; p. 553.

PALAU: Baldwin visits, p. 756-7.

PALMYRA: p. 602.

PANTELLERIA: p. 376.

PATTON, General George: his concern for his son-in-law, p. 371.; plans for landing his 3rd army in Normandy are changed, p. 406.

PEARL HARBOR: p. 307-8; p. 312-13; Baldwin goes to Washington after Japanese attack to get picture of fleet damage, p. 313-15; p. 328-30; Baldwin's picture of the disorganization in Washington, p. 333-4; Baldwin stresses fact that army had task of defending Navy Bases overseas, p. 336; Baldwin interviewed by the son of RADM Husband Kimmel, p. 336.

PEARSON, Drew: publishes information on Savo Island losses, p. 357-8; p. 360; p. 464.

PHILIPPINE ISLANDS: Fall of the Philippines to Japanese surprise to many Americans - failure of our SSs, p. 334-5.

POLARIS: p. 532-3; program speeded by impact of SPUTNIK, p. 659-60.

PORT SAID: the first objective of the British landings, p. 575; Baldwin's description of D Day and thereafter, p. 575-80; p. 585; incident involving a mob and British MPs, p. 589-90.

PRATT, Admiral Wm. Veazie: his opinion of air power in early 1930s, p. 235; p. 316-7; p. 319.

PRINZ EUGEN: German cruiser - used by U.S. for experimental purposes at Bikini, p. 452.

PUBLIC RELATIONS: Army and Navy Attitude towards, p. 245-7; p. 255-6.

PULITZER PRIZE: p. 367-8;

PYLE, Ernie: p. 421, p. 674-5.

QUEMOY and MATSU: installation of a nuclear cannon, p. 523-3; p. 525; p. 527-9.

QUESADA, Gen. Elwood Richard (Pete): p. 459-60. p. 536; p.544.

RABI, Dr. Isador Isaac: p. 538-9; p. 542; p. 553.

RABORN, Vice Admiral Wm. F. Jr.; p. 532.

RADFORD, Admiral Arthur: his switch from emphasis on conventional weapons to the use of the atomic bomb, p. 454-5; p. 466; p. 471. p. 521-2; p. 527.

REFO, Captain Miles P.: gunnery officer on TEXAS, p. 118-119; p. 136-7; p. 144; p. 148-9.

REINA MERCEDES: p. 106-7.

RICKOVER, Admiral Hyman: p. 103; p. 322-3.

RILEY, Vice Admiral Herbert: p. 465, p. 488.

ROOSEVELT, The Hon. Franklin Delano: p. 251; Baldwin's recollections of him before WWII, p. 289; p. 355; p. 370; p. 384; p. 438; question of his sophistication in dealing with world affairs, p. 443-4.

ROOSEVELT, Major Gen. Theodore (Teddy) Jr.: In North Africa - his death at Utah Beach, p. 427-30.

ROSENTHAL, A.M.: Managing editor of the N.Y. TIMES, p. 550.

ROYCE, Gen. Ralph: p. 425-6.

RUSSIA - in the Middle East: p. 605; p. 607-8; problems with the Palestinian Liberation Organization; p. 608; p. in Egypt, p. 608; p. 615-16; Russian aviation, p. 627-8; behavior of Russian leaders in Moscow, p. 629-30.

RUSSIAN ARMY - in WWII: p. 296.

SAINT ANTHONY, Newfoundland: Grenfell headquarters - site of hospital, p. 218 ff.

SAINT LO (France): Baldwin goes to observe American effort in this sector of front, p. 424-5; the bombing attack that fell on our own lines, p. 425-6.

SALISBURY, Harrison: p. 650; p. 741; his despatch from North Vietnam with propaganda cited as fact - Baldwin asked to write the Pentagon point of view in reply, p. 744-5; p. 746-7.

SATURDAY EVENING POST: p. 492; p. 496; p. 502.

SAVO ISLAND losses: P. 356-8.

SCIENTISTS - and defense policy in the U.S.: p. 552-3.

SEBALD, Captain Wm. J.: p. 119-121; p. 132-3. p. 494; p. 498-9.

SEVERN SCHOOL: Baldwin goes there in 1920 to prep for Naval Academy exams, p. 15.

SHARP, Admiral U.S. Grant: p. 722; p. 733.

SHERMAN, Admiral Forrest: As CNO tried to limit Baldwin's access to various installation, p. 481-3.

SLESSOR, Air Chief Marshal Sir John C. (Jack): head of Coast Command-1943, p. 383.

SMITH, General Bedell: Chief of Staff to General Eisenhower, p. 374.

SMITH, C. Alphonso: Head of English Department at Naval Academy, p. 37-8; p. 51; his deathbead remark to the midshipmen, p. 98-99.

SMITH, General H.H.: USMC: his controversy with the army, p. 395-6.

SMITH, Truman: Military Attache in Berlin, p. 275.

SOCIAL CUSTOMS: Their bearing on the food and amenities supplied soldiers in the field, p. 389-91.

SOUTHERN FRANCE: invasion of, p. 441 ff; Eisenhower's view of this operation, p. 442.

SPUTNIK: p. 658-9.

STANDLEY, Admiral Wm. H.: useful to Baldwin as a source of information, p. 285.

STARK, Admiral Harold: p. 383-4; p. 440-1.

STENNIS, The Hon. John: Chairman of the Senate Committee on Armed Services, p. 687-8, his role in cancelling plans for calling up Reserves, p. 712-3.

STEREOPTICAN RANGE-FINDER: tests made in the U.S. Navy, p. 141ff.

SS STRATHCONA: old yacht used by Sir Wilfred Grenfell, p. 220; Baldwin becomes her skipper for trip with Grenfells to Railhead in Newfoundland, p. 221.

STRAUSS, RADM Louis: p. 543-4.

STRIKEBACK: the NATO operation (1958) and problems of the press, p. 654-5.

STRUBLE, Admiral Arthur Dewey: Chief of Staff to Admiral Alan Kirk, p. 407; 409; p. 411-12.

SUEZ CRISIS (1956): p. 563-595 ff; the convoy from Cyprus and Malta, p. 572-4; U. S. Opposition, p. 574-5; a 'shoe-string' operation, p. 583-4 ff; circumstances that interfered with British-French success at Suez, p. 588-9; the moral issue involved, p. 606; Russian policy and involvement, p. 605; p. 607 ff.

SULLIVAN, Walter: Science Editor of the New York TIMES, p. 644-5; p. 648; p. 654.

SULLIVAN, RADM Wm. A.; p. 378-9.

SULZBERGER, Arthur Hays - Publisher of the New York TIMES (1935-61); wanted Baldwin to specialize on military matters, p. 240; sends Baldwin to Europe - 1937 - to take a look at military forces of powers, p. 244 ff; editorial policy of the TIMES in his day, p. 261-2; p. 545; p. 547.

SULZBERGER, Arthur Ochs (Punch): son of Arthur Hays Sulzberger, who becomes publisher of the TIMES after death of Orville Dreyfoos (1963), p. 549; p. 550; p. 742.

SUN PAPERS of Baltimore: Baldwin becomes a cub reporter, Jan. 1928 - p. 204 ff.

SUTHERLAND, Lt. Gen. R.K.: p. 495.

SWANSON, The Hon. Claude - Secretary of the Navy: p. 248-9.

SYLVESTER, Arthur: McNamara's press representative in Defense Department, p. 698; his relations with Baldwin, p. 701.

SYMINGTON, Stuart: Secretary of the Air Force under President Truman, p. 459-60; p. 467-8.

SYRIA: Baldwin trip to Damascus, p. 601 ff; p. 616.

TAIWAN (Formosa): p. 525 ff.

TALESE, Gay: p. 549.

TARANTO: Italian Naval Base - RAF attack on ships there, p. 337.

TAYLOR, General Maxwell: p. 553; as Superintendent of West Point Military Academy - his view on star football players and need to exempt them from the ordinary rules, p. 556-7; p. 734.

TET OFFENSIVE: (1968) a psychological turning point in Vietnam, p. 722; p. 724.

USS TEXAS: Baldwin's first ship assignment - p. 117 ff; target practice in Narragansett Bay, p. 138-9; tests with stereoptican range-finder, p. 140-1; the mascot, p. 149; p. 150.

THE POWER AND THE GLORY: Gay Talese's book on the New York TIMES, p. 549.

THERMO-NUCLEAR Power: see entry under LAWRENCE, Wm. H.

TORCH OPERATION: p. 367-9.

TRUMAN, President Harry S.: p. 439; p. 459; p. 461; Baldwin's feeling that Truman's ideas were expressed through Secretary Johnson, p. 487-8.

TURNER, Vice Admiral Stansfield: President of the Naval War College, p. 772 ff.

TWINING, General Nathan F.: Chief of Air Staff - invited to Russia for Soviet Air Force Day (1956), p. 623 ff; Krushchev impresses him greatly, p. 640-1.

UNIFICATION: p. 458 ff; p. 465; p. 475; interest in subject

during WWII, p. 475-6.

US ARMY TANKS: Baldwin's articles in criticism, p. 430-432.

U.S. MARINES: p. 490.

U.S. NAVAL ACADEMY: Entrance examinations, p. 18-19; plebe summer, p. 20-21; hazing, p. 23-35; a plebe-year incident involving dismissal of a midshipman, p. 39; lessons of plebe year, p. 40-41; more on plebe year - athletics, p. 43-55; youngster year cruise, p. 56-60; youngster year, p. 79 ff; athletics, p. 82-3; Baldwin's accident in second class year, p. 86-7; lack of an honor system, drinking, etc. p. 99 ff; negroes in the navy, p. 102; anti-semitism at the Academy, p. 103-6; 'The Burial of Math', p. 108; hops and customs surrounding them, p. 108-9; Army-Navy games and traditions, p. 110-1; Baldwin writes series of articles on the honor system, p. 558-9; Baldwin's attitude towards football competition, p. 559-61.

U. S. NAVAL ACADEMY - ALUMNI ASSOCIATION: Baldwin serves as President, p. 771-2.

U.S. NAVAL WAR COLLEGE: p. 668-70. Baldwin appointed to Board of Advisers, p. 772, p. 784.

UTAH BEACH: p. 412; the death of Teddy Roosevelt, Jr. on the beachhead, p. 427-30;

VAN ANDA, Carr: his role on the New York TIMES, p. 225-7.

VANCE, The Hon. Cyrus: Deputy Secretary of Defense, p. 696.

VANDERGRIFT, General Alexander A.: his determination to hold Guadalcanal, p. 349.

SS VESTRIS: Baldwin covers story of her loss, p. 208-210.

VIETMINH: The communist guerrillas in Vietnam who fought the French, p. 514 ff.

VIETNAM: p. 606; p. 613; p. 673-4; p. 686-7; p. 700; the McNamara policy on supplies for Vietnam, p. 702-4; p. 706; policy discussions in Washington during Vietnam era, p. 708-9; p. 709-11; Baldwin writes about need to mine Haiphong Harbor, p. 711; Baldwin's trip to Vietnam in fall of 1965, p. 713 ff.

VON BOTTICHER, Lt. General (German): Military Attache in U.S. prior to WWII, p. 266-8.

von BRAUN, Dr. Wernher: p. 659-60; p. 662.

USS WASHINGTON: sinking of the BB of the Virginia Capes, p. 128; experiments with mines, torpedoes, p. 129-131; Baldwin writes a poem about her demise, p. 143.

USS WASHINGTON - BB: WWII, p. 356.

WATERS, General John (Johnnie): p. 371; p. 555; p. 557.

WEDEMEYER, General Albert C.: serving on a joint strategic survey committee for the JCS - asks Baldwin to appear, p. 354-9.

WEST GERMANY: Baldwin's estimate of quality of their fighting forces, p. 531.

WEST POINT MILITARY ACADEMY: The cheating scandal, p. 555; p. 557; Commandant of Cadets resigns because of priviledged position of football coach and team, p. 557; p. 608.

WESTMORELAND, General Wm. Childs: p. 722-23; his views on Vietnam War as contained in his book (Jan. 1976), p. 730-1; p. 733; p. 735; p. 741.

WETTENGEL, Captain Ivan Cyrus: Captain of Battleship TEXAS, p. 119, p. 122; p. 125; p. 131.

WEYLAND, General Otto P. (Opie); p. 501-2.

WHEELER, General Earle G. (Buzz): p. 709-10.

WHITE, General Thomas D. (Tommy): U.S. Air attache in Rome (1937), p. 278; p. 310; p. 382; p. 544.

WHITE RUSSIAN FLEET Remnants: Bizerte Harbor, 1926, p. 164.

WILLOUGHBY, Major General Charles A.: p. 492-3; p. 495; p. 497-8; p. 501-2; p. 512.

WILSON, Admiral Henry B.: Superintendent of the U.S. Naval Academy - p. 60; letter from him to Baldwin's father, p. 61-2; p. 80-1.

WILSON, The Hon. Charles: Secretary of Defense (Engine Charley): p. 520; p. 523.

WIRTH, RADM Theodore R.: p. 119; p. 148; p. 151.

WONSON, Korea: p. 500-1; p. 510-11.

WORLD WAR II - THOUGHTS AND OPINIONS: Baldwin's conviction that European war was inevitable, p. 287-8; p. 291-2; p. 296-8; Pacific War plans, p. 301 ff; Baldwin's disagreement with supplies for Britain at the expense of our own preparedness, p. 303-5; Baruch and industrial mobilization, p. 306 ff.

WORTH, Cedric: reporter on WORLD-TELEGRAM - employed by Navy to put across its story in the B-36 inquiry, p. 466.

WORTHINGTON, RADM Joseph M.: p. 33; p. 87-8; p. 93; p. 99; p. 112-3; p. 121; p. 149; p. 185; p. 197.

WORTHINGTON, Joseph Jr.: Baldwin's god son, p. 718-20.

YALU RIVER: p. 510-512.

ZHUKOV, Marshal Georgi K.: member of the Presidium of the Central Committee of the Russian government p. 632, p. 636.

ZUMWALT REFORMS: Baldwin visits fleet to learn about results, p. 759-769; p. 781.

www.ingramcontent.com/pod-product-compliance
Lightning Source LLC
Chambersburg PA
CBHW080624170426
43209CB00007B/1510